UNDER THE BRIDGE

A Study Guide for the Film

Vivian Ling

大橋下面

ISBN 0-89264-113-4

Printed in the United States of America

5 4 3 2 1

大橋下面

一. 電影對白及生詞表

Part I: Script and Vocabulary Annotations

CONTENTS OF PART I

SCRIPT AND VOCABULARY ANNOTATIONS

FOREWORD

The set of materials presented here - the videotaped film "大橋下面 Under the Bridge," the filmscript and vocabulary annotations, and the grammatical notes and exercises - is designed to respond to the need for teaching materials for developing aural comprehension and speech skills at the intermediate level. In the West, the teaching of Chinese language beyond the beginning level has traditionally emphasized reading to the neglect of the other three skills: comprehension, speech, and writing. The concept of using films to teach comprehension and speech is not new, but it is only in the last few years that the popularization of videotape technology and the availability of films appropriate for our pedagogical purpose have made it feasible to carry this concept into practice. The film "Under the Bridge" is ideal for our purpose in that it fulfills the following criteria: 1) Its language - in terms of pronunciation, vocabulary, and discourse patterns - conforms with the standard spoken in contemporary China. The vocabulary is rich, containing some common colloquialisms not normally found in traditional language texts. Moreover, it contains many "irregular" discourse structures which are excluded from dictionaries and textbooks, but which occur with high frequency in authentic Chinese. 2) Its subject matter consists of significant and common societal phenomena in the early 1980's, and thereby provides a glimpse of contemporary Chinese society while serving as a vehicle for language development. 3) It has an engaging plot that is neither too simplistic nor too complicated to follow. 4) It embodies considerable cinematic artistry and human interest, and therefore promises to have long-lasting value. Materials based on films are not intended to replace traditional texts, but to supplement them. Through film-based materials, students will be exposed to language use in simulated real life situations, and will thereby develop their proficiency in comprehension and speech. It is also hoped that film-based materials will add variety and fun along the hard road toward mastery of Chinese.

This set of materials is designed for students who have completed two years of Chinese in a typical American college Chinese program. However, it has some built-in flexibility to accommodate students at varying levels of proficiency. The filmscript is divided into twelve segments, each one corresponding to approximately ten minutes of the film.

The vocabulary annotations are pitched at approximately the 800 character level. However, because students using these materials presumably have studied Chinese from a wide variety of elementary texts, the choice of vocabulary items to be annotated is based on a "common denominator," that is, on a "generic" background at a level slightly lower than two years of study. Some students may find many annotations unnecessary, others may need to resort to a dictionary occasionally. Students may find the number of annotated vocabulary items overwhelming. Therefore, as an aid in determining which items one should commit to memory, they are categorized into three levels of importance. The top priority vocabulary items - those that occur most commonly in the language and are therefore most useful - are marked with "*". The vocabulary items of secondary priority are marked with "^". Those which remain unmarked are of least importance. A list of the vocabulary items of top and secondary priority, which can be used as a list of vocabulary for required learning, appears on pp. 147-156 of Part I: Script and Annotations. In the interest of broadening knowledge of vocabulary usage beyond the immediate context, the following principles have been adopted in the vocabulary annotations:

1) Words that occur with erization (兒 -r tagged on) in the script but are not widely erized in putonghua will appear in the glossary with parentheses around the character 兒 and the r. E.g., "飯兜(兒) fàndōu(r) apron."

2) If a word in the English gloss can be either a verb or a noun, the verb is indicated by the infinitive form "to..." E.g., "to quarrel" is a verb, and "quarrel" should be construed as a noun.

3) The grammatical category (noun, verb, adverb, etc.) of a word will be given only if it is not clear from the gloss itself, or if the word belongs to different grammatical categories in English and Chinese.

4) In annotating a verb-object or resultative verb compound that has been split in the given context, or can be split but is not in the given context, a "≠" appears in the romanization separating the two parts of the splittable compound. For example, the compound 出事 appears in the context "自從他們家出了那件事以後, ..." In the annotation for 出事, the romanization is given as "chū≠shì."

5) In the context of the filmscript, many V-O compounds are split and placed in other grammatical structures. These V-O compounds will be glossed in their root form rather than in their contextual form. For example, the V-O compound 還債 in the phrase 把債還了 will appear in the gloss as 還債. Because underlining is used in the script to indicate glossed items, it should not be difficult for students to locate these split compounds in the glossary.

6) In annotating a term that contains a bound form (BF) or an "affix," a "-" is used to separate the BF or affix from the "root." For example, the romanization for 手續費 is given as "shǒuxù-fèi" to indicate that 費 is a BF. Likewise, the romanization for 神秘地 is given as "shénmì-de," to indicate that 地 is an affix. When the root, BF, or affix warrants further explanation, it is given in the glossary. For example, 手續費 is glossed as "processing fee (-費: fee)," and 神秘地 is glossed as "(adv.) mysteriously (神秘: mysterious)."

To promote comprehension of the plot and the "substance" of the film, a set of discussion questions (討論問題) is provided at the end of each segment of the script. The instructor may use the discussion questions as a comprehension and discourse exercise after viewing the segment, either before or after having read through the script. Students may also preview these questions before viewing the segment so as to be prepared to look for certain things in the development of the plot. The discussion questions may even be used as prompts for short essays. Thus, this set of questions may be used variously depending on the relative emphasis the instructor wishes to give to the oral and written aspects of the course.

The discourse patterns included in Part II: Grammatical Notes and Exercises are selected with the intermediate student in mind. As in the selection of vocabulary items to be annotated, a "common denominator" is used. Often, a pattern typically introduced at the beginning level is included for review and reinforcement, in order to help the student advance from the "passive knowledge" to the "active usage" level. Many patterns included in this section occur only in colloquial spoken Chinese. Some are in fact not "sentence patterns" per se, but discourse structures. These colloquial sentence patterns and discourse structures are typically excluded from traditional reading texts even though they are an important component of the spoken language. In this part, each pattern is labeled by a pattern heading, followed by the contextual example, an explanation in English, then a couple of further examples, and exercises to be done either orally or in writing. The clarity of the explanations is sometimes limited by the nature of these discourse patterns. Often they convey nuances which cannot be translated or explained easily, and therefore can be "brought to life" only through examples given by a skilled teacher.

In Part II: Grammatical Notes and Exercises, aside from the exercises under each discourse pattern, each segment ends with a set of inclusive translation exercises in which the patterns are represented in random order to foster their active use. In these inclusive exercises as well as those under each pattern, an attempt has been made to reinforce the student's newly-acquired key vocabulary and to place the patterns and vocabulary in a larger linguistic context beyond that of the film.

I wish to express special thanks to my late colleague Ming-huei Feng and to Prof. Kai Li, both of whom have given me valuable comments and suggestions based on their test-use of this set of materials, and to Prof. James E. Dew, who has perused the filmscript and annotations with a fine-toothed comb and made excellent editorial suggestions. Any remaining errors and infelicities are of course my own responsibility.

大橋下面

人物　CAST OF CHARACTERS

Codes:
- * Primary characters
- ˆ Secondary characters

In order of appearance:

Traditional	Simplified	Pinyin	Description
*秦楠	*秦楠	Qín Nán	female protagonist, seamstress
周大媽	周大妈	Zhōu Dàmā	"Big Mother" Zhou, friendly neighborhood woman
毛毛	毛毛	Máomao	周大媽的兒子
*秦父	*秦父	Qín Fù	秦楠的父親
管理員	管理员	guǎnlǐyuán	monitor (in charge of checking licenses for private stalls)
*高志華	*高志华	Gāo Zhìhuá	male protagonist, bicycle repairman
郵遞員	邮递员	yóudìyuán	mailman
*高母	*高母	Gāo Mǔ	高志華的母親
ˆ蕭健	ˆ肖健	Xiāo Jiàn	高志華的朋友, had been in the same unit with 秦楠 "down under" in the countryside
顧客	顾客	gùkè	customer
尤奶奶	尤奶奶	Yóu Nǎinai	Granny You, gossipy self-righteous neighborhood woman
鄰居	邻居	línjū	neighbor
男男	男男	Nánnan	尤奶奶的孫子 a spoiled brat and bully
某人	某人	mǒurén	a "certain person," 蕭健's accomplice in the bicycle scam
*高英華	*高英华	Gāo Yīnghuá	高志華的妹妹, a track star
*冬冬	*冬冬	Dōngdong	秦楠's illegitimate son
舅媽	舅妈	Jiùmā	秦楠's aunt (wife of 秦楠's mother's brother)
舅舅	舅舅	Jiùjiu	秦楠's uncle (秦楠's mother's brother), lives in Suzhou with his wife
ˆ蕭雲	ˆ肖云	Xiāo Yún	蕭健's invalid sister, artist and seal carver
郭奶奶	郭奶奶	Guō Nǎinai	Granny Guo, Party secretary of 蕭雲's Neighborhood Committee
老師	老师	lǎoshī	在蕭雲家教繪畫的
眾	众	zhòng	group (of art students)
警察	警察	jǐngchá	policeman
醫生	医生	yīshēng	physician
病友	病友	bìngyǒu	"sick friend," 冬冬's fellow patient in the hospital
ˆ孟彬	ˆ孟彬	Mèng Bīn	秦楠's former faithless boyfriend, 冬冬's natural father

SEGMENT I

Scene 1

One day Qin Nan has bought her father's breakfast at the market and is on her way back home. She meets a neighbor, Zhou Dama, at the doorway and chats with her.

秦楠： 喲！周大媽早。
周大媽：早點都買好了？小楠，你看你幫我做的飯兜兒多合身哪！
秦楠： 以後要作什麼，儘管找我好了。
周大媽：喲，你連工錢都不肯收，我怎麼好意思呀？
秦楠： 那有什麼。
周大媽：毛毛，走！
毛毛： 啊，來了！

Scene 2

Qin Nan enters the room.

秦楠： 爸，吃吧。
毛毛： (through the doorway) 喲，早！

---

^1.	喲	哟	yō	ah! oh!
2.	大媽	大妈	dàmā	familiar term of address for middle-aged women
^3.	早點	早点	zǎodiǎn	breakfast "snack," light breakfast
4.	飯兜(兒)	饭兜(儿)	fàndōu(r)	(Shanghai dialect) apron; (Northern Chinese) meal bag (for carrying a lunch box and utensils)
^5.	合身	合身	héshēn	to fit (the body)
*6.	哪	哪	na	sentence final particle, same as third usage of 啊 (cf. note 12 below), but used after words ending in "n" due to sandhi
*7.	儘管... (好了)	尽管... (好了)	jǐnguǎn... (hǎole)	feel free to..., don't hesitate to...(cf. Grammatical Note I.2.)
*8.	工錢	工钱	gōngqián	wages, fee
*9.	肯	肯	kěn	willing to

SEGMENT I

Scene 1 ——————————

One day Qin Nan has bought her father's breakfast at the market and is on her way back home. She meets a neighbor, Zhou Dama, at the doorway and chats with her.

秦楠： 哟！周大妈早。
周大妈：早点都买好了？小楠，你看你帮我做的饭兜儿多合身哪！
秦楠： 以后要作什么，尽管找我好了。
周大妈：哟，你连工钱都不肯收，我怎么好意思呀？
秦楠： 那有什么。
周大妈：毛毛，走！
毛毛： 啊，来了！

Scene 2 ——————————

Qin Nan enters the room.

秦楠： 爸，吃吧。
毛毛： (through the doorway) 哟，早！

---

*10.	怎麼好意思	怎么好意思	zěnme hǎo yìsi	how can (I) feel at ease (not be embarrassed)?
*11.	呀	呀	ya	sentence final particle, same as third usage of 啊 (cf. note 12 below), but used after words ending in "a, e, i, o, ü" due to sandhi; (at beginning of a sentence Ah! Oh!
*12.	啊	啊	a	a particle used in the following ways (each carrying a different intonation): a) used alone or at the beginning of an utterance as an expletive or to convey surprise; b) tagged on after a sentence, meaning "OK?" c) sentence final particle used optionally to round off the tone of the sentence

秦楠：　早。(back to 秦父) 爸，我都替你弄好了。晚飯你自己燒着吃吧！我下午走，最遲大後天就回來。

秦父：　好。

秦楠：　爸，把縫紉機的錢還了吧。

秦父：　你到鄉下去，不是還給你舅舅生活費嗎？

秦楠：　我算過了。這個月縫紉攤擺下來，還了債，還有餘錢。

秦父：　噢，好！

秦楠：　爸，代課的事兒，下學期別再幹了。

秦父：　再說吧！

秦楠：　你老是再說再說的。爸，快點兒吧！錢放好了，出門別忘了帶鑰匙。

秦父：　小楠，你要理解我昨天晚上跟你說的話。都這麼些年啦，還是找個對像，結婚吧。

秦楠：　你還要擠車呢，快走吧。

Qin Nan's father helps her take the sewing machine from their apartment to the entrance of the alley where Qin Nan usually sets up her stall.

秦楠：　上下車要當心。

秦父：　你早點兒回來。

Scene 3 ——————————

Because the alleyway is narrow, Qin Nan's stall is in a vehicle's way. She pulls her things up against the wall and the vehicle goes by. She has just set up her stall again when a monitor comes by and asks to see her license.

---

*13. 弄	弄	nòng	to manage, to handle
*14. 燒	烧	shāo	to cook, to burn
*15. 遲	迟	chí	late, tardy
16. 縫紉機	缝纫机	féngrèn-jī	sewing machine
^17. 舅舅	舅舅	jiùjiu	uncle (mother's brother)
^18. 生活費	生活费	shēnghuó-fèi	living allowance (in this case, for Qin Nan's child)
19. 擺攤	摆摊	bǎi≠tān	(攤: stall) to set up a stall; (here the V-O 擺攤 is split and rearranged with the object of verb functioning as the topic of clause)
^20. ...下來	...下来	V-xialai	as a result or attainment of having done V
^21. 還債	还债	huán≠zhài	to repay a debt

秦楠： 早。（back to 秦父）爸，我都替你弄好了。晚饭你自己烧着吃吧！我下午走，最迟大后天就回来。
秦父： 好。
秦楠： 爸，把缝纫机的钱还了吧。
秦父： 你到乡下去，不是还给你舅舅生活费吗？
秦楠： 我算过了。这个月缝纫摊摆下来，还了债，还有余钱。
秦父： 噢，好！
秦楠： 爸，代课的事儿，下学期别再干了。
秦父： 再说吧！
秦楠： 你老是再说再说的。爸，快点儿吧！钱放好了，出门别忘了带钥匙。
秦父： 小楠，你要理解我昨天晚上跟你说的话。都这么些年啦，还是找个对象，结婚吧。
秦楠： 你还要挤车呢，快走吧。

Qin Nan's father helps her take the sewing machine from their apartment to the entrance of the alley where Qin Nan usually sets up her stall.

秦楠： 上下车要当心。
秦父： 你早点儿回来。

Scene 3 ——————————

Because the alleyway is narrow, Qin Nan's stall is in a vehicle's way. She pulls her things up against the wall and the vehicle goes by. She has just set up her stall again when a monitor comes by and asks to see her license.

22.	餘	余	yú	surplus, left over
^23.	噢	噢	o	oh!
^24.	代課	代课	dài≠kè	substitute teaching
*25.	幹	干	gàn	(colloquial) 做
^26.	鑰匙	钥匙	yàoshi	key
*27.	理解	理解	lǐjiě	to comprehend
*28.	都	都	dōu	already, after all
^29.	啦	啦	la	sentence final particle (can also be used in a rhetorical question)
*30.	對像	对象	duìxiàng	potential spouse, an "intended"; target, object
*31.	擠	挤	jǐ	to squeeze (onto, into, etc.); crowded
^32.	當心	当心	dāngxīn	小心

管理員：你的執照呢？
秦楠：　在。
管理員：給我看看。這樣吧。你先把攤子收了，跟我到小組辦公室來一趟，啊？
秦楠：　哎，老師傅！請你先把執照還給我吧。
管理員：要不先收掉你的執照...哎呀，你們這些個體戶哇！真是...*
高志華：欸，個體戶怎麼啦？
管理員：你是幹什麼的？
高志華：我也是個體戶，對面修腳踏車的。
管理員：修你的腳踏車吧。這裡沒你的事。(to Qin Nan) 請你到小組辦公室來。啊？
高志華：他爲什麼沒收你的執照？你還愣着幹什麼？還不快把執照要回來。縫紉機我幫你看着，沒事！你不認識我，可我知道你姓秦。你爸爸是我小學的老師，我叫高志華。
秦楠：　那麻煩你了。

Scene 4 ——————

郵遞員：高志華，信！
高志華：謝謝！

---

*In the early years after the Cultural Revolution, private enterprises - considered capitalistic and therefore criminal during the Cultural Revolution - were again permitted. At this time, this form of employment was taken up by many otherwise unemployed youths recently returned from the countryside. It lacked the status, security, and benefits (such as housing and medical care) of state-assigned jobs. Society generally disdained this form of employment and those engaged in it typically had low self esteem. This situation changed toward the end of the 1980s, when non-state enterprises proved to be highly lucrative and posed a serious challenge to state enterprises.

^33. 執照	执照	zhízhào	license, permit
*34. 收	收	shōu	to pack up, to put away, to collect, to confiscate
35. 小組	小组	xiǎozǔ	committee, a government unit
*36. 趟	趟	tàng	number of times (said of trips)
^37. 哎	哎	ā; ài	an expletive, sometimes conveying a sigh or a plea
^38. 師傅	师傅	shīfu	polite address for a worker (driver, cook, street monitor, etc.); (formerly) master of a craft
*39. 要不	要不	yàobu	if not (if you don't come with me right now); otherwise, as an alternative (cf. Grammatical Note I.6.)

管理员：你的执照呢？

秦楠：　在。

管理员：给我看看。这样吧。你先把摊子收了，跟我到小组办公室来一趟，啊？

秦楠：　哎，老师傅！请你先把执照还给我吧。

管理员：要不先收掉你的执照...哎呀，你们这些个体户哇！真是...*

高志华：欸，个体户怎么啦？

管理员：你是干什么的？

高志华：我也是个体户，对面修脚踏车的。

管理员：修你的脚踏车吧。这里沒你的事。（to Qin Nan）请你到小组办公室来。啊？

高志华：他为什么沒收你的执照？你还愣着干什么？还不快把执照要回来。缝纫机我帮你看着，沒事！你不认识我，可我知道你姓秦。你爸爸是我小学的老师，我叫高志华。

秦楠：　那麻烦你了。

Scene 4 ————————————

邮递员：高志华，信！

高志华：谢谢！

---

^40.	哎呀	哎呀	āiyā	an expletive
^41.	個體戶	个体户	gètǐ-hù	(戶: household) self-employed individuals who operate businesses, either singly or in small groups
^42.	哇	哇	wa	sentence final particle, same as third usage of 啊 (cf. Note I.12), but used after words ending in "u, ao" due to sandhi
43.	欸	欸	ēi, éi, ěi, èi	an interjection conveying greeting, surprise, disenchantment, disagreement, or assent (said with different intonations)
*44.	對面	对面	duìmiàn	across the way, on the opposite side
^45.	腳踏車	脚踏车	jiǎotà-chē	自行車(bicycles are called自行車in the North, 腳踏車 in the Yangtze River area, and 單車 in the South.)
*46.	沒…的事	沒…的事	méi...de shì	It's none of ...'s business
^47.	沒收	沒收	mòshōu	to confiscate
^48.	愣	愣	lèng	stupefied, dazed
*49.	要回來	要回来	yào≠huílai	to ask (for something) back
*50.	沒事	沒事	méishì	沒關係, it's not a big deal, no problem

高母：　志華，誰的信？

高志華：小妹的。

高母：　這鬼丫頭。出去一個多月，今天才來信。瞧這死丫頭神的！信上怎麼說？哎，問你信上怎麼說！

高志華：她說，她們現在在廣西集訓，下個月才能回來。 她說訓練緊張得很，沒有時間給家裡寫信。請媽媽不要罵她。

高母：　罵她 ？我還打她呢。好，我上班去了，泡飯在爐子上，快吃去吧。

高志華：媽，這鹹肉您帶到廠裡去吧！

高母：　你吃吧！

高志華：哎呀！您幹嘛什麼都留給我呢？快走吧。快走吧。

Scene 5 ——————————

Xiao Jian, a friend, comes to see Zhihua and plays a trick on him.

蕭健：　哎，師傅，借個火！

高志華：呵，蕭健，兩三個月沒見，你小子鑽哪兒去了？

蕭健：　我還不是天天送貨，今天特地彎過來看你的。

高志華：噢，看什麼？

蕭健：　想你呀！

51.	鬼丫頭	鬼丫头	guǐ yātou	(丫頭: (formerly) "slave" girls sold or given to other families in childhood) here 鬼丫頭 "devilish slave girl" is a joking, affectionate, deprecatory way of referring to a daughter, especially in exasperation.
*52.	來信	来信	lái≠xìn	to have a letter come from...
^53.	瞧	瞧	qiáo	(colloquial) 看
54.	死丫頭	死丫头	sǐ yātou	(cf. 51 above) "dead slave girl," same as 鬼丫頭
^55.	神	神	shén	cocky, arrogant; spirited, vigorous
56.	廣西	广西	Guǎngxī	中國南部的一個省
57.	集訓	集训	jíxùn	(short for 集合訓練) collective training
*58.	緊張	紧张	jǐnzhāng	intense, keyed up, nervous
*59.	上班	上班	shàng≠bān	to go to work (most often white-collar work)
60.	泡飯	泡饭	pàofàn	cooked rice reheated in hot water
^61.	爐子	炉子	lúzi	stove

高母：　志华，谁的信？

高志华：小妹的。

高母：　这鬼丫头。出去一个多月，今天才来信。瞧这死丫头神的！信上怎么说？哎，问你信上怎么说！

高志华：她说，她们现在在广西集训，下个月才能回来。她说训练紧张得很，沒有时间给家里写信。请妈妈不要骂她。

高母：　骂她？我还打她呢。好，我上班去了，泡饭在炉子上，快吃去吧。

高志华：妈，这咸肉您带到厂里去吧！

高母：　你吃吧！

高志华：哎呀！您干嘛什么都留给我呢？快走吧。快走吧。

Scene 5 ——————————

Xiao Jian, a friend, comes to see Zhihua and plays a trick on him.

肖健：　哎，师傅，借個火！

高志华：呵，肖健，两三个月沒见，你小子钻哪儿去了？

肖健：　我还不是天天送货，今天特地弯过来看你的。

高志华：噢，看什么？

肖健：　想你呀！

---

62. 鹹肉	咸肉	xiánròu	salted preserved meat
*63. 廠	厂	chăng	工廠, factory
ˆ64. 幹嘛	干嘛	gànmá	(colloquial)作什麼，爲什麼 (cf. Grammatical Note I.8.)
65. 借火	借火	jiè≠huǒ	borrow a "fire" (borrow a light, to light a cigarette)
ˆ66. 呵	呵	hē	ah! oh!
67. 小子	小子	xiǎozi	chap, rascal, young fellow (often affectionate)
68. 鑽	钻	zuān	to sneak into, to hide out
*69. 還不是	还不是	háibushì	after all, it's just...(none other than..., nothing more than...)
70. 送貨	送货	sòng≠huò	deliver goods (merchandise, etc.)
ˆ71. 特地	特地	tèdì	especially, with deliberate intention
72. 彎過來	弯过来	wān≠guòlái	to take a detour
*73. ...什麼	...什么	V-shénme	(rhetorical) what's there to V?

高志華：你別來這套。你呀，是無事不登三寶殿的。
蕭健：　哎，你最近忙不忙？
高志華：怎麼説呢，也忙也不忙。
蕭健：　行，就要你這句話。
高志華：幹什麼？
蕭健：　反正讓你幫個忙。哎，三天以後，我來找你。
高志華：三天後，好吧。(Zhihua stops their conversation as he sees Qin Nan coming back from the office, looking very dejected.) (to 蕭健)你等等。

As Xiao Jian recognizes Qin Nan, he gets very excited and runs over.

蕭健：　哎，秦楠！嘿，這不是秦楠嗎？怎麼，不認識啦！
秦楠：　噢，是蕭健。沒想到在這兒碰到你。
高志華：怎麼？你們都認識啊？
蕭健：　豈只認識，我們是在廣闊天地裡修地球的老戰友啦！* 你哪年上來的？
秦楠：　七九年。
蕭健：　現在幹什麼工作？ (Qin Nan motions to the sign which indicates her profession as a seamstress.) 噢，擺縫紉攤，也是個體戶哇！
高志華：哎，你執照要回來了沒有？
秦楠：　執照是要回來了，可.....
高志華：怎麼？
秦楠：　限我今天就把攤子收了。

---

*This kind of euphemistic and militant language was typical of Cultural Revolutionary rhetoric. It is used here sarcastically. Youths sent down to the countryside during the Cultural Revolution were often assigned to work the land, sometimes engaging in the drastic modification of natural terrain that proved ecologically disastrous.

74. 來這套	来这套	lái zhèi tào	to pull this "routine"
75. 無事不登三寶殿	无事不登三宝殿	wú shì bu dēng Sānbǎodiàn	"never go to the Triratna Temple (Buddhist) for nothing," would not go see someone unless for some business or favor
*76. 反正	反正	fǎnzhèng	in any case (cf. Grammatical Note I.10.)
^77. 嘿	嘿	hēi	hey!
*78. 碰到	碰到	pèng≠dào	to encounter, to run into someone unexpectedly

高志华：你别来这套。你呀，是无事不登三宝殿的。
肖健：　哎，你最近忙不忙？
高志华：怎么说呢，也忙也不忙。
肖健：　行，就要你这句话。
高志华：干什么？
肖健：　反正让你帮个忙。哎，三天以后，我来找你。
高志华：三天后，好吧。(Zhihua stops their conversation as he sees Qin Nan coming back from the office, looking very dejected.) (to 肖健)你等等。

As Xiao Jian recognizes Qin Nan, he gets very excited and runs over.

肖健：　哎，秦楠！嘿，这不是秦楠吗？怎么，不认识啦！
秦楠：　噢，是肖健。沒想到在这儿碰到你。
高志华：怎么？你们都认识啊？
肖健：　岂只认识，我们是在广阔天地里修地球的老战友啦！* 你哪年上来的？
秦楠：　七九年。
肖健：　现在干什么工作？ (Qin Nan motions to the sign which indicates her profession as a seamstress.) 噢，摆缝纫摊，也是个体户哇！
高志华：哎，你执照要回来了沒有？
秦楠：　执照是要回来了，可.....
高志华：怎么？
秦楠：　限我今天就把摊子收了。

---

79. 豈只	岂只	qǐzhǐ	not only...(implying that there's much more to it than...) (豈: a rhetorical adverb meaning "how/why...?")
^80. 廣闊天地	广阔天地	guǎngkuò tiāndì	"wide world," euphemism for the countryside (used sarcastically here)
81. 修地球	修地球	xiū dìqiú	to refashion the globe, to change terrain in a major way (also used sarcastically here)
^82. 戰友	战友	zhànyǒu	comrade in arms
83. 上來	上来	shàng≠lái	to come up (from "down under" in the countryside)
*84. 限	限	xiàn	to set a limit or deadline

蕭健： 爲什麼？

秦楠： 說擱這兒妨礙交通。

高志華：這倒也是啊。弄堂太窄了，擺個攤子是礙事。

秦楠： 可除了這兒.....沒地方。

高志華：這樣吧，搬到對過去，擺在我們家門口，沒事兒，我把攤兒往邊兒上挪挪就是了。

蕭健： 不要不好意思，乾脆，說搬就搬，志華，拿這個。來，拿着。哎，把牌兒摘下來。走吧！

秦楠： 你現在幹什麼？

蕭健： 同一命運。你踩縫紉機，我踏黄魚車送貨。

秦楠： 過得怎麼樣？

蕭健： 風裡來，雨裡去，賺倆錢，夠嗆！還.....

秦楠： 是啊，都不容易呀！

蕭健： 秦楠，你結婚了吧？

Qin Nan replies by shaking her head with embarrassment. Xiao Jian looks dismayed and puzzled.

^85.	擱	搁	gē	(colloquial) 放
*86.	妨礙	妨碍	fáng'ài	to block, to obstruct, to hamper
*87.	交通	交通	jiāotōng	traffic
88.	弄堂	弄堂	lòngtáng	(regional) lane, alley
*89.	窄	窄	zhǎi	narrow
^90.	礙事	碍事	ài≠shì	to be in the way, to be a hindrance
^91.	對過	对过	duìguò	對面
*92.	挪	挪	nuó	to move over (a little bit)
*93.	...就是了	...就是了	...jiùshìle	...and that will do, ...and that's all there is to it

討論問題：

1) 秦楠是一個什麼樣的人？ 你看她在生活和工作上可能會有什麼問題？

2) 高志華對他母親、他的朋友蕭健、跟他還不認識的秦楠怎麼樣？ 從這些你能不能看出他是一個什麼樣的人？

3) 蕭健是誰？ 你猜 (cāi: to guess) 他要高志華幫他什麼忙？

4) 蕭健怎麼會認識秦楠的？ 那天他碰到秦楠就怎麼樣？ 秦楠呢？ 爲什麼？ 爲什麼他最後問秦楠她結婚了沒有？

5) 秦楠那天下午要去哪兒？ 她爲什麼要給她舅舅生活費？

肖健：　为什么？

秦楠：　说搁这儿妨碍交通。

高志华：这倒也是啊。弄堂太窄了，摆个摊子是碍事。

秦楠：　可除了这儿.....沒地方。

高志华：这样吧，搬到对过去，摆在我们家门口，沒事儿，我把摊儿往边儿上挪挪就是了。

肖健：　不要不好意思，干脆，说搬就搬，志华，拿这个。来，拿着。哎，把牌儿摘下来。走吧！

秦楠：　你现在干什么？

肖健：　同一命运。你踩缝纫机，我踏黄鱼车送货。

秦楠：　过得怎么样？

肖健：　风里来，雨里去，赚俩钱，够呛！还.....

秦楠：　是啊，都不容易呀！

肖健：　秦楠，你结婚了吧？

Qin Nan replies by shaking her head with embarrassment. Xiao Jian looks dismayed and puzzled.

*94.	乾脆	干脆	gāncuì	lit., "dry and crisp": straight forward, clear-cut, in a decisive snappy way, might as well (cf. Grammatical Note X.1.)
*95.	牌(兒)	牌(儿)	pái (pár)	sign
^96.	摘	摘	zhāi	to pluck, to pick off, to take down
^97.	命運	命运	mìngyùn	fate
^98.	踩	踩	cǎi	to pedal, to step on, to trample
^99.	踏	踏	tà	to pedal, to step on
100.	黄魚車	黄鱼车	huángyú-chē	large tricycle for hauling goods
*101.	賺	赚	zhuàn	to earn (money, work points, etc.)
^102.	倆	俩	liǎ	(colloquial)兩個; some, several
103.	夠嗆	够呛	gòuqiàng	(colloquial) "it's tough enough!"

讨论问题：

1) 秦楠是一个什么样的人？ 你看她在生活和工作上可能会有什么问题？

2) 高志华对他母亲、他的朋友肖健、跟他还不认识的秦楠怎么样？ 从这些你能不能看出他是一个什么样的人？

3) 肖健是谁？ 你猜 (cāi: to guess) 他要高志华帮他什么忙？

4) 肖健怎么会认识秦楠的？ 那天他碰到秦楠就怎么样？ 秦楠呢？ 为什么？ 为什么他最后问秦楠她结婚了沒有？

5) 秦楠那天下午要去哪儿？ 她为什么要给她舅舅生活费？

SEGMENT II

Scene 6 ——————————

That afternoon, Qin Nan looks at her watch and discovers that it has stopped. She asks Zhihua for the time because she has a train to catch.

秦楠：　哎。
高志華：叫我嗎？叫我小高好了，有什麼事？
秦楠：　你的表幾點了？
高志華：快四點半了。
秦楠：　哎呀！
高志華：怎麼這麼早收攤了？
秦楠：　我要去趕五點半的火車。
高志華：哎，這裁衣板就不用搬回家了。
秦楠：　也好。小高，還有件事想麻煩你。這兩天我有事不來了，這些衣服顧客要來拿的，請你交給他們。
高志華：噢，好！
秦楠：　錢你也代我收一下，謝謝你了。再見。
高志華：再見。

Qin Nan takes a train to go on a trip.

Scene 7 ——————————

One morning, Zhihua is fixing an electric fan for Zhou Dama. Later on, they begin discussing Qin Nan. She reveals something about Qin Nan's past.

---

*1.	趕	赶	gǎn	to rush (to catch a train, bus, etc.)
2.	裁衣板	裁衣板	cáiyī-bǎn	cutting board for making clothes
*3.	顧客	顾客	gùkè	customer, client
*4.	交給	交给	jiāogěi	to hand over/in to

SEGMENT II

Scene 6 ——————————

That afternoon, Qin Nan looks at her watch and discovers that it has stopped. She asks Zhihua for the time because she has a train to catch.

秦楠： 哎。
高志华：叫我吗？叫我小高好了，有什么事？
秦楠： 你的表几点了？
高志华：快四点半了。
秦楠： 哎呀！
高志华：怎么这么早收摊了？
秦楠： 我要去赶五点半的火车。
高志华：哎，这裁衣板就不用搬回家了。
秦楠： 也好。小高，还有件事想麻烦你。这两天我有事不来了，这些衣服顾客要来拿的，请你交给他们。
高志华：噢，好！
秦楠： 钱你也代我收一下，谢谢你了。再见。
高志华：再见。

Qin Nan takes a train to go on a trip.

Scene 7 ——————————

One morning, Zhihua is fixing an electric fan for Zhou Dama. Later on, they begin discussing Qin Nan. She reveals something about Qin Nan's past.

---

*5. 代 代 dài... 替, for...(someone), in ...'s stead (cf. 代課, Note I.24, and Grammatical Note XII.5.)

高志華：周大媽！
周大媽：哎！
高志華：開！
周大媽：噢！
高志華：行了，關！
周大媽：好，快洗洗吧！
高志華：哎。線圈有點鬆了，還能用。
周大媽：謝謝你啊。
高志華：周大媽，這一大清早可夠您忙的啊。
周大媽：可不是嘛！

A customer comes in and interrupts their conversation.

顧客：　請問一下，弄堂口那邊的縫紉攤擺哪兒去了？
高志華：有什麼事嗎？
顧客：　人家介紹她衣服做得又好又快，想找她做幾件衣服。
周大媽：噢，她到蘇州去了，改天再來吧。
顧客：　啊，麻煩你們了。
周大媽：沒什麼。
顧客：　走吧。

Scene 8 ———————

高志華：周大媽，你們家毛毛和小陳的事兒差不多了吧？

---

*6.	開	开	kāi	to turn on (a light, a machine, etc.)
*7.	關	关	guān	to turn off (a light, a machine, etc.)
8.	線圈	线圈	xiànquān	coil
^9.	鬆	松	sōng	loose
^10.	一大清早	一大清早	yí dà qīngzǎo	early in the morning, crack of dawn
^11.	夠…的	够…的	gòu...SV de	SV enough for...(cf. Grammatical Note II.1.)
^12.	嘛	嘛	ma	sentence final particle used to lend weight to an opinion or advice

高志华：周大妈！
周大妈：哎！
高志华：开！
周大妈：噢！
高志华：行了，关！
周大妈：好，快洗洗吧！
高志华：哎。线圈有点松了，还能用。
周大妈：谢谢你啊。
高志华：周大妈，这一大清早可够您忙的啊。
周大妈：可不是嘛！

A customer comes in and interrupts their conversation.

顾客： 请问一下，弄堂口那边的缝纫摊摆哪儿去了？
高志华：有什么事吗？
顾客： 人家介绍她衣服做得又好又快，想找她做几件衣服。
周大妈：噢，她到苏州去了，改天再来吧。
顾客： 啊，麻烦你们了。
周大妈：沒什么。
顾客： 走吧。

Scene 8 ————————

高志华：周大妈，你们家毛毛和小陈的事儿差不多了吧？

13.	弄堂口	弄堂口	lòngtáng-kǒu	(-口: opening, junction) the front of a lane where it meets the street
*14.	人家	人家	rénjia	someone, other people
15.	蘇州	苏州	Sūzhōu	離上海不遠的一個城
^16.	改天	改天	gǎitiān	another day
^17.	差不多了	差不多了	chàbuduōle	"just about there" (here, ready to finalize the match) (cf. Grammatical Note II.2.)

周大媽：咳，他們哪，一會兒颳風，一會兒下雨，一會兒又打雷，誰搞得清他們的事兒！志華，忙合了半天，快把這碗餛飩吃了。

高志華：周大媽，我剛吃完早飯，我……

周大媽：哎，你坐下，吃！不吃我生氣了啊！坐下！

高志華：好，好，我吃。

周大媽：志華，你讓她把縫紉攤擺在你們家門口，可解決她大問題了。

高志華：這有什麼呢！

周大媽：咳，說起來，小秦這孩子也是命苦哇。我是看着她長大的。以前是有說有笑，自從她們家出了那件事以後，她心裡的疙瘩一直解不開，簡直就像換了一個人。

高志華：她們家出什麼事了？

周大媽：噢，當時她爸爸隔離審查，小秦呢，又去插隊落戶，家裡就剩她媽媽孤老太婆一個人。造反派又逼着她揭發她老伴，她說什麼也抹不開，那天天剛亮……(makes a gesture indicating suicide)*

高志華：啊？她媽媽是自殺的？

---

*The tragedies that befell Qin Nan's family were typical of the Cultural Revolution, during which intellectuals were especially denigrated.

18.	咳	咳	hài	an audible sigh
ˆ19.	颳風	刮风	guā≠fēng	to have a wind storm
ˆ20.	打雷	打雷	dǎ≠léi	to thunder
ˆ21.	搞清	搞清	gǎo≠qīng	to clarify
22.	忙合	忙合	mánghe	(colloquial) to bustle about, to be busy
*23.	碗	碗	wǎn	bowl
24.	餛飩	馄饨	húntun	wonton
*25.	解決	解决	jiějué	to solve or resolve (a problem)
26.	命苦	命苦	mìngkǔ	to have a "bitter fate," to have a hard life
ˆ27.	有說有笑	有说有笑	yǒushuō yǒuxiào	gregarious and jolly
*28.	出事	出事	chū≠shì	to have an accident or unfortunate incident
ˆ29.	疙瘩	疙瘩	gēda	lump (here, in the heart), knot; hang-up
ˆ30.	解開	解开	jiě≠kāi	to untie (a knot), to resolve or dissolve

周大妈：咳，他们哪，一会儿刮风，一会儿下雨，一会儿又打雷，谁搞得清他们的事儿！志华，忙合了半天，快把这碗馄饨吃了。

高志华：周大妈，我刚吃完早饭，我……

周大妈：哎，你坐下，吃！不吃我生气了啊！坐下！

高志华：好，好，我吃。

周大妈：志华，你让她把缝纫摊摆在你们家门口，可解决她大问题了。

高志华：这有什么呢！

周大妈：咳，说起来，小秦这孩子也是命苦哇。我是看着她长大的。以前是有说有笑，自从她们家出了那件事以后，她心里的疙瘩一直解不开，简直就象换了一个人。

高志华：她们家出什么事了？

周大妈：噢，当时她爸爸隔离审查，小秦呢，又去插队落户，家里就剩她妈妈孤老太婆一个人。造反派又逼着她揭发她老伴，她说什么也抹不开，那天天刚亮……(makes a gesture indicating suicide)*

高志华：啊？她妈妈是自杀的？

---

*31.	換	换	huàn	to change (clothing, etc.); to transform
*32.	當時	当时	dāngshí	在那個時候
^33.	隔離	隔离	gélí	to separate, to be isolated
^34.	審查	审查	shěnchá	to investigate, to undergo investigation
^35.	插隊	插队	chā≠duì	to join ("insert into") a rural production team
^36.	落戶	落户	luò≠hù	(often in combination with 插隊) to settle one's residence (in the countryside)
*37.	剩	剩	shèng	to be left, to remain
38.	孤	孤	gū	solitary, alone
*39.	老太婆	老太婆	lǎotàipó	old woman
40.	造反派	造反派	zàofǎn-pài	(-派: faction) rebel faction
*41.	逼	逼	bī	to force, to coerce
^42.	揭發	揭发	jiēfā	to expose, to uncover (wrong-doings)
^43.	老伴	老伴	lǎobàn	"old companion," a spouse of long standing
44.	抹不開	抹不开	mòbukāi	unable to act impartially (due to conflict of loyalty, fear of embarrassing or offending someone, etc.); to be in a difficult personal dilemma

周大媽：嗯。噢，志華，以後她在你身邊幹活，你要多開導開導她，一個人活在世上幹嘛要那麼苦呢？總該樂樂呵呵的才對嘛。

高志華：是啊。

Xiao Jian comes to see Zhihua and calls him from beneath his window.

蕭健：　小高！

高志華：噢，有人叫我，您忙吧。

周大媽：噢。

Scene 9 ——————————

蕭健：　小高！小高！

高志華：來了，喊什麼？

蕭健：　咳，我以爲你在屋里睡懶覺呢。

高志華：怎麼着？

蕭健：　秦楠呢？她怎麼不在？

高志華：兩天沒來了，説是上蘇州去了。

蕭健：　交給你也一樣。(hands Zhihua a bundle.)

高志華：什麼？

蕭健：　請她幫我妹妹做件襯絨夾襖，尺寸、裡、面都在裡面。

高志華：嘿，蕭健，咱們倆可是打小學到現在了，你打什麼時候又蹦出來個妹妹呀？你小子別跟我玩兒噱頭了。

---

^45.	嗯	嗯	ǹg	mm...(a quiet assent); uh-huh (assuring the other party that one is listening or has heard what was said)
*46.	身邊	身边	shēnbiān	close by (a person) (lit., "next to one's body")
^47.	幹活	干活	gàn≠huó	(colloquial) 工作
^48.	開導	开导	kāidǎo	to enlighten and guide, to help someone see what is right and sensible
49.	樂樂呵呵	乐乐呵呵	lèlè hēhē	cheerful and gay
*50.	…才對	…才对	...cái duì	it is only right that...(cf. Grammatical Note II.5.)
51.	喊	喊	hǎn	叫
^52.	睡懶覺	睡懒觉	shuì lǎn jiào	to have a "lazy sleep," to sleep in late

周大妈：嗯。噢，志华，以后她在你身边干活，你要多开导开导她，一个人活在世上干嘛要那么苦呢？总该乐乐呵呵的才对嘛。

高志华：是啊。

Xiao Jian comes to see Zhihua and calls him from beneath his window.

肖健：　小高！

高志华：噢，有人叫我，您忙吧。

周大妈：噢。

Scene 9 ————————

肖健：　小高！小高！

高志华：来了，喊什么？

肖健：　咳，我以为你在屋里睡懒觉呢。

高志华：怎么着？

肖健：　秦楠呢？她怎么不在？

高志华：两天沒来了，说是上苏州去了。

肖健：　交给你也一样。(hands Zhihua a bundle.)

高志华：什么？

肖健：　请她帮我妹妹做件衬绒夹袄，尺寸、里、面都在里面。

高志华：嘿，肖健，咱们俩可是打小学到现在了，你打什么时候又蹦出来个妹妹呀？你小子别跟我玩儿噱头了。

53.	襯絨夾襖	衬绒夹袄	chènróng jiá'ǎo	jacket with flannel lining
*54.	尺寸	尺寸	chǐcùn	"feet and inches," i.e., measurements
55.	裡	里	lǐ	lining material
56.	面	面	miàn	material for the outer face of a garment
*57.	咱們	咱们	zánmen	inclusive "we" (including the person or persons being spoken to, but no third party)
^58.	可是	可是	kěshì	indeed
^59.	打	打	dǎ	(colloquial) 從 (cf. Grammatical Note II.7.)
60.	蹦	蹦	bèng	to crop up, to bounce or jump
61.	噱頭	噱头	xuétou	(Shanghai dialect) a trick meant to deceive or amuse

蕭健： 千萬可別誤會，真是我妹妹，騙你呀，這個！(He forms the turtle sign with his hand.*) 不過是同父不同母的。她一直住在上海鄉下。

高志華：我說呢。

蕭健： 告訴秦楠，衣裳過兩天我來取。哎，五點半，我在金星碼頭三號倉庫等你。

高志華：幹什麼？

蕭健： 哎，不是說好了嗎？三天後找你幫忙啊？五點半，金星碼頭，不見不散。來，推我一把。

高志華：好嘞！

Scene 10

Coming back from Suzhou, Qin Nan walks through the alley and meets a couple of neighbors. Her frequent trips to Suzhou have aroused their suspicion.

尤奶奶：小秦啊，兩天不見了，又到蘇州去啦？

秦楠： 是啊。

鄰居： 楊梅剛上市，從蘇州買來的？

男男： 奶奶，我要吃楊梅，我要吃楊梅嘛！

尤奶奶：別死不要臉，快放手吧！

秦楠： 來，自己拿吧。

---

*"Turtle" and "turtle's egg" (王八 and 王八蛋 in Chinese), mean "cuckold" and "bastard" respectively. Both are curse words in Chinese. There are several explanations for the origin of the derogatory meanings. Since 王八 and 忘八 "forgetting the eight" are homophonous, 王八 can be taken to mean "forgetting the eight characters that describe the traditional Chinese virtues." In one version, the eighth character is 恥 chǐ "sense of shame," so 王八 can be taken to mean "forgetting the eighth character," which in turn can be interpreted as "無恥 wúchǐ shameless." As another explanation goes, the turtle mates with the snake (i.e., mates indiscriminately, and is therefore worthy of scorn) and produces "turtle's eggs" or "bastards."

*62.	千萬	千万	qiānwàn	by all means, be sure (usually used with a negative to mean "you must not...")
*63.	誤會	误会	wùhuì	to misconstrue, to misinterpret, to misunderstand; misunderstanding
*64.	騙	骗	piàn	to deceive
65.	我說呢	我说呢	wǒ shuō ne	(colloquial) "I see!"

肖健： 千万可别误会，真是我妹妹，骗你呀，这个！(He forms the turtle sign with his hand.*) 不过是同父不同母的。她一直住在上海乡下。

高志华：我说呢。

肖健： 告诉秦楠，衣裳过两天我来取。哎，五点半，我在金星码头三号仓库等你。

高志华：干什么？

肖健： 哎，不是说好了吗？三天后找你帮忙啊？五点半，金星码头，不见不散。来，推我一把。

高志华：好嘞！

Scene 10 ——————————

Coming back from Suzhou, Qin Nan walks through the alley and meets a couple of neighbors. Her frequent trips to Suzhou have aroused their suspicion.

尤奶奶：小秦啊，两天不见了，又到苏州去啦？

秦楠： 是啊。

邻居： 杨梅刚上市，从苏州买来的？

男男： 奶奶，我要吃杨梅，我要吃杨梅嘛！

尤奶奶：别死不要脸，快放手吧！

秦楠： 来，自己拿吧。

---

*66.	衣裳	衣裳	yīshang	衣服
*67.	取	取	qǔ	拿, to pick up
68.	碼頭	码头	mǎtóu	dock
69.	倉庫	仓库	cāngkù	warehouse
70.	不見不散	不见不散	bújiàn búsàn	(散: to disperse, to go separate ways) don't leave if we don't see each other, i.e., wait around until we meet
71.	推…一把	推…一把	tuī...yibǎ	to give...a push
^72.	好嘞!	好嘞!	hǎo lei!	okay!
73.	楊梅	杨梅	yángméi	red bayberry
^74.	上市	上市	shàng≠shì	to come on the market
^75.	奶奶	奶奶	nǎinai	grandma, granny
^76.	死…	死…	sǐ...	to persist or insist relentlessly (cf. Grammatical Note II.9.)
^77.	不要臉	不要脸	búyào liǎn	"not want face," to be shameless
*78.	放手	放手	fàng≠shǒu	to let go (lit., "to release the hands")

尤奶奶：還不快謝謝小秦阿姨。
秦楠：　不客氣。
鄰居：　尤大媽，你注意到沒有，小秦怎麼淨往蘇州跑哇？
尤奶奶：我早就注意了，一個月至少去兩趟。
鄰居：　就是！你説，這裡頭有沒有花頭？一個大姑娘家！

Scene 11 ————————

One day while Qin Nan is working, Zhihua's mother comes out looking for Zhihua and starts talking with Qin Nan.

高母：　志華，志華，志華！
秦楠：　小高開會去了。
高母：　這孩子，身上穿條破褲子，也不想着脱下來。
秦楠：　您今天休息？
高母：　啊，説休息，家務活比廠裡還忙。

Qin Nan tries to take over Zhihua's mother's mending.

秦楠：　高媽媽，交給我吧。
高母：　不要，不要，不要！
秦楠：　縫紉機踩一下，很快。
高母：　怎麼好意思啊，那扣子我來釘。

Zhihua's mother has a difficult time threading a needle. Qin Nan offers to help.

79.	阿姨	阿姨	Āyí	"auntie," familiar address used by children for young women
80.	淨	净	jìng	(colloquial) 總是，老是 (cf. Grammatical Note II.10.)
81.	花頭	花头	huātou	(Shanghai dialect) something shady or fishy
82.	大姑娘家	大姑娘家	dà gūniang jiā	(姑娘: a young unmarried girl) a woman slightly past the usual age of marriage

尤奶奶：还不快谢谢小秦阿姨。
秦楠： 不客气。
邻居： 尤大妈，你注意到沒有，小秦怎么净往苏州跑哇？
尤奶奶：我早就注意了，一个月至少去两趟。
邻居： 就是！你说，这里头有沒有花头？一个大姑娘家！

Scene 11 ———————————

One day while Qin Nan is working, Zhihua's mother comes out looking for Zhihua and starts talking with Qin Nan.

高母： 志华，志华，志华！
秦楠： 小高开会去了。
高母： 这孩子，身上穿条破裤子，也不想着脱下来。
秦楠： 您今天休息？
高母： 啊，说休息，家务活比厂里还忙。

Qin Nan tries to take over Zhihua's mother's mending.

秦楠： 高妈妈，交给我吧。
高母： 不要，不要，不要！
秦楠： 缝纫机踩一下，很快。
高母： 怎么好意思啊，那扣子我来钉。

Zhihua's mother has a difficult time threading a needle. Qin Nan offers to help.

---

*83.	條	条	tiáo	M for trousers
*84.	褲子	裤子	kùzi	trousers, pants
^85.	脫下來	脱下来	tuō≠xialai	to take off (clothing)
86.	家務活	家务活	jiāwù-huó	(活: (colloquial) work) housework, domestic chores
^87.	扣子	扣子	kòuzi	button
88.	釘	钉	dīng	to sew on (buttons); nail; to nail, to fasten

秦楠： 我來吧。

高母： 啊，老了，眼睛不行了。

秦楠： 看您精神還挺好。

高母： 不行，不行了，年底就該退休啦。大女兒還在崇明農場等着頂替我呢！啊，瞧，(shows Qin Nan a photo.) 這是我小女兒，叫英華，前兩天剛寄來的。

秦楠： 挺神氣的。

高母： 這孩子，從小就喜歡蹦蹦跳跳的。現在在上海田徑隊，說下個月才能回來呢。(scrutinizes Qin Nan with interest.) 小秦，你今年多大啦？

秦楠： 二十八。

高母： 聽志華說，你爸爸以前是他老師。

秦楠： 大概是吧。

高母： 他怎麼還沒退休哇？他一退休你不就可以頂替了嗎？

秦楠： 我沒上來的時候，他就退休了。現在是代代課，一個月可以多拿十幾塊錢。

高母： 噢，小秦，你現在是一個人吧？

秦楠： 嗯，我和爸爸兩個人。

高母： 不，我問你家裡還有誰？

秦楠： 就我和爸爸。

高母： 那你媽媽呢？

秦楠： 死了。

A customer comes to pick up her garment.

顧客： 我的衣服好了嗎？

秦楠： 好了，你回去試試，不合適拿來改。

顧客： 噢，謝謝。

^89.	挺	挺	tǐng	(colloquial) 相當
*90.	-底	-底	-dǐ	the end of...
*91.	退休	退休	tuì≠xiū	to retire
92.	崇明農場	崇明农场	Chóngmíng Nóngchǎng	(農場: farm) name of a farm on an island not far from Shanghai
^93.	頂替	顶替	dǐngtì	to take over a job (a post-Cultural Revolution system by which grown children "inherit" their parents' jobs when the latter retire. The children may not be assigned the same jobs as their parents', but they are allocated jobs in the same units.)

秦楠： 我来吧。
高母： 啊，老了，眼睛不行了。
秦楠： 看您精神还挺好。
高母： 不行，不行了，年底就该退休啦。大女儿还在崇明农场等着顶替我呢！啊，瞧，(shows Qin Nan a photo.) 这是我小女儿，叫英华，前两天刚寄来的。
秦楠： 挺神气的。
高母： 这孩子，从小就喜欢蹦蹦跳跳的。现在在上海田径队，说下个月才能回来呢。(scrutinizes Qin Nan with interest.) 小秦，你今年多大啦？
秦楠： 二十八。
高母： 听志华说，你爸爸以前是他老师。
秦楠： 大概是吧。
高母： 他怎么还没退休哇？他一退休你不就可以顶替了吗？
秦楠： 我没上来的时候，他就退休了。现在是代代课，一个月可以多拿十几块钱。
高母： 噢，小秦，你现在是一个人吧？
秦楠： 嗯，我和爸爸两个人。
高母： 不，我问你家里还有谁？
秦楠： 就我和爸爸。
高母： 那你妈妈呢？
秦楠： 死了。

A customer comes to pick up her garment.

顾客： 我的衣服好了吗？
秦楠： 好了，你回去试试，不合适拿来改。
顾客： 噢，谢谢。

94.	蹦蹦跳跳	蹦蹦跳跳	bèngbeng tiàotiao	to bounce and jump around (said of a vivacious active person)
95.	田徑隊	田径队	tiánjìng-duì	track and field team
*96.	試試	试试	shìshi	to try (here, to try on a garment)
*97.	合適	合适	héshì	suitable, to fit

討論問題：

1） 秦楠爲什麼不愛説也不愛笑？
2） 你猜 (cāi: to guess) 爲什麼周大媽告訴了高志華秦楠從前家裡的事呢？ 她是個多事 (duōshì: meddlesome) 的人嗎？
3） 蕭健好像是高志華的好朋友，可是爲什麼有些事情不告訴志華呢？
4） 秦楠爲什麼常去蘇州？ 鄰居們 (línjūmen: neighbors) 怎麼想？ 這以後會不會給秦楠帶來困難 (kùnnán: difficulty)？
5） 高母爲什麼那麼關心秦楠的事？ 你對高母有什麼看法？

讨论问题：

1） 秦楠为什么不爱说也不爱笑？

2） 你猜 (cāi: to guess) 为什么周大妈告诉了高志华秦楠从前家里的事呢？ 她是个多事 (duōshì: meddlesome) 的人吗？

3） 肖健好象是高志华的好朋友，可是为什么有些事情不告诉志华呢？

4） 秦楠为什么常去苏州？ 邻居们 (línjūmen: neighbors) 怎么想？ 这以后会不会给秦楠带来困难 (kùnnán: difficulty)？

5） 高母为什么那么关心秦楠的事？ 你对高母有什么看法？

SEGMENT III

Scene 12 ——————————

On the way to the dock for his rendezvous with Xiao Jian, Zhihua passes a park and sees Maomao alone there moping. He goes up and tries to find out what's wrong.

高志華：嗯？毛毛，毛毛，你一個人在這兒幹什麼？
毛毛：　……

Scene 13——————————

When Zhihua arrives at the dock, he asks for Xiao Jian.

某人：　你找誰呀？
高志華：找蕭健。
某人：　你……
高志華：是他約我來的。
某人：　那你等一下兒。
　　　　(aside to Xiao Jian) 你朋友來了，你去跟他談吧。
蕭健：　哎，不是説好咱們一起談嗎？
某人：　還是你去談，要講死，十天完事，我們要早脱手，那點零件也別讓他看見，你快出去談。

Scene 14 ——————————

After talking with Xiao Jian, Zhihua realizes that the business Xiao Jian proposes is illegal. He advises Xiao Jian to get out of the deal.

---

*1. 約	约	yuē	to make an appointment or date with
*2. 一起	一起	yìqǐ	一塊兒
*3. 還是	还是	háishì	after all (implying that after all it would be best if...)

SEGMENT III

Scene 12 ————————————

On the way to the dock for his rendezvous with Xiao Jian, Zhihua passes a park and sees Maomao alone there moping. He goes up and tries to find out what's wrong.

高志华：嗯？毛毛，毛毛，你一个人在这儿干什么？
毛毛：　……

Scene 13————————————

When Zhihua arrives at the dock, he asks for Xiao Jian.

某人：　你找谁呀？
高志华：找肖健。
某人：　你……
高志华：是他约我来的。
某人：　那你等一下儿。
(aside to Xiao Jian) 你朋友来了，你去跟他谈吧。
肖健：　哎，不是说好咱们一起谈吗？
某人：　还是你去谈，要讲死，十天完事，我们要早脱手，那点零件也别让他看见，你快出去谈。

Scene 14 ————————————

After talking with Xiao Jian, Zhihua realizes that the business Xiao Jian proposes is illegal. He advises Xiao Jian to get out of the deal.

4.	講死	讲死	jiǎng≠sǐ	to talk things out and come to a firm agreement
5.	脱手	脱手	tuō≠shǒu	to get (something) off one's hands, to dispose of
6.	零件	零件	língjiàn	spare parts

高志華：那麼多錢？
蕭健： 這還多啊！他們說一輛車能賣兩百三到兩百五呢！
高志華：什麼？雜牌車能賣這麼大價錢？
蕭健： 我也搞不清楚，不過，他們說有辦法搞成名牌車賣出去。小高，明天開始裝怎麼樣？
高志華：咱們倆是好朋友，我覺得這裡面恐怕有鬼，我勸你別幹。
蕭健： 到手的錢不要？
高志華：這錢不能要。聽我的話，別幹！我走了。

Scene 15 ——————————

On his way home, Zhihua sees Maomao still standing in the park alone. Maomao tells him that his girlfriend wants to break up with him because he does not have a state-assigned job.

高志華：嗯？毛毛？毛毛！小陳呢？
毛毛： 這次她下決心跟我一刀兩斷了。
高志華：爲什麼？
毛毛： 她說她很矛盾，心裡是喜歡我的。可在朋友面前覺得我是個個體戶，丟人。
高志華：丟人？我們一不偷，二不搶，靠勞動吃飯，丟什麼人？ (Maomao starts to cry.) 哎呀，你哭什麼？毛毛，別人越是看不起你，你越是要看得起自己。一個人活着得有點兒志氣。走，送你回去。

---

^7.	還…啊	还…啊	hái...a	(rhetorical) "you mean to say...?" (implying disagreement)
^8.	輛	辆	liàng	M for vehicles
9.	雜牌	杂牌	zá-pái	miscellaneous brand (as opposed to 名牌 "name brand")
*10.	搞	搞	gǎo	(colloquial) 弄, to do, to make, to figure out
^11.	名牌	名牌	míng-pái	name brand
*12.	裝	装	zhuāng	to assemble (parts of a machine, bike, etc.), to pack
13.	有鬼	有鬼	yǒu guǐ	"there is a ghost," there is something fishy
14.	到手	到手	dào≠shǒu	to reach one's hands, to arrive, to drop into one's hands

高志华：那么多钱？

肖健： 这还多啊！他们说一辆车能卖两百三到两百五呢！

高志华：什么？杂牌车能卖这么大价钱？

肖健： 我也搞不清楚，不过，他们说有办法搞成名牌车卖出去。小高，明天开始装怎么样？

高志华：咱们俩是好朋友，我觉得这里面恐怕有鬼，我劝你别干。

肖健： 到手的钱不要？

高志华：这钱不能要。听我的话，别干！我走了。

Scene 15 ——————————

On his way home, Zhihua sees Maomao still standing in the park alone. Maomao tells him that his girlfriend wants to break up with him because he does not have a state-assigned job.

高志华：嗯？毛毛？毛毛！小陈呢？

毛毛： 这次她下决心跟我一刀两断了。

高志华：为什么？

毛毛： 她说她很矛盾，心里是喜欢我的。可在朋友面前觉得我是个个体户，丢人。

高志华：丢人？我们一不偷，二不抢，靠劳动吃饭，丢什么人？ (Maomao starts to cry.) 哎呀，你哭什么？毛毛，别人越是看不起你，你越是要看得起自己。一个人活着得有点儿志气。走，送你回去。

---

^15. 下決心	下决心	xià juéxīn	to resolve to..., to make up one's mind
^16. 一刀兩斷	一刀两断	yìdāo liǎngduàn	to make a clean break (with someone)
*17. 矛盾	矛盾	máodùn	to be in conflict (internal or external), contradictory; conflict, contradiction
*18. 面前	面前	miànqián	in front of
*19. 偷	偷	tōu	to steal
*20. 一…，二…	一…，二…	yī..., èr...	for one thing..., for another thing... (this may go on to "three..., four...," etc.) (cf. Grammatical Note III.3.)
^21. 搶	抢	qiǎng	to rob, to grab, to snatch
*22. 勞動	劳动	láodòng	labor (usually manual labor)
^23. 志氣	志气	zhìqì	aspiration, ambition, self-pride, guts
*24. 送	送	sòng	to see or send (someone) off; to escort

Scene 16

After Zhihua comes home, his mother wants to know where he has been. She also tries to match him up with Qin Nan.

高母： 是志華嗎？
高志華：是我。媽，您還沒睡呀？
高母： 你到哪兒去了？
高志華：哎呀，毛毛。
高母： 毛毛怎麼了？
高志華：跟他對像鬧別扭。我勸勸他。
高母： 我看，勸勸你自己吧！
高志華：媽，您又來了。(chuckles)
高母： 笑，一跟你提這事，你就會跟我笑！
志華！
高志華：媽，您明早上還早上班呢，快睡吧！
高母： 你過來。
高志華：哎呀，我知道您要跟我說什麼。又想抱孫子，想抱大頭兒孫子。
高母： 叫你過來！
高志華：哎呀！媽，您到底要跟我說什麼？
高母： 拿去，身上這條破褲子該換下來了。這是小秦替你補的。這姑娘真懂事，又能幹，替我省了不少事。

Zhihua goes to bed, but rather than going right to sleep, he ponders what his mother has just said.

---

25. 鬧別扭	闹别扭	nào bièniu	to be at odds with (someone), to have a tiff
^26. 又來了	又来了	yòu lái le	(colloquial) to be up to the same old stuff again (cf. Grammatical Note III.5.)
*27. 提	提	tí	to bring up (a matter), to mention
*28. 抱	抱	bào	to embrace, to hold or carry in the arms

Scene 16 ——————————

After Zhihua comes home, his mother wants to know where he has been. She also tries to match him up with Qin Nan.

高母：　是志华吗？
高志华：是我。妈，您还没睡呀？
高母：　你到哪儿去了？
高志华：哎呀，毛毛。
高母：　毛毛怎么了？
高志华：跟他对象闹别扭。我劝劝他。
高母：　我看，劝劝你自己吧！
高志华：妈，您又来了。(chuckles)
高母：　笑，一跟你提这事，你就会跟我笑！
　　　　志华！
高志华：妈，您明早上还早上班呢，快睡吧！
高母：　你过来。
高志华：哎呀，我知道您要跟我说什么。又想抱孙子，想抱大头儿孙子。
高母：　叫你过来！
高志华：哎呀！妈，您到底要跟我说什么？
高母：　拿去，身上这条破裤子该换下来了。这是小秦替你补的。这姑娘真懂事，又能干，
　　　　替我省了不少事。

Zhihua goes to bed, but rather than going right to sleep, he ponders what his mother has just said.

---

*29. 孫子	孙子	sūnzi	grandson
*30. 補	补	bǔ	to mend
*31. 懂事	懂事	dǒng≠shì	"to understand matters," sensible
*32. 能幹	能干	nénggàn	capable
^33. 省事	省事	shěng≠shì	to save trouble

Scene 17 ——————————

It is a hot day. Qin Nan and Zhihua are both working on the sidewalk. Zhihua invites Qin Nan to move her sewing machine into his home, but she politely turns him down.

秦楠： 好了，後天來拿。
顧客： 走吧。

Brief dialogue between Gao Zhihua and customer, irrelevant to plot.

高志華：(Offering Qin Nan his hat.) 中午太陽挺厲害的，戴上吧。
秦楠： 謝謝，我不熱。
高志華：(Offering Qin Nan a wash cloth.) 來，擦擦汗。
秦楠： 謝謝，我自己有。
高志華：真的，我看你還是搬到屋裡去做吧。
秦楠： 不，不，我已經夠麻煩你們了。
高志華：我得給你提個意見，我們相處已經不少日子了，你張口謝謝，閉口麻煩的，真讓人受不了。
秦楠： 那以後我不說了，嗯，不過……好，我不說了。
高志華：秦楠，我覺得你……
秦楠： 我怎麼？
高志華：我覺得一個人應該樂觀。聽周大媽講你母親……咳，那些事都過去好多年了，不要總放在心上。
秦楠： 最近你見到蕭健沒有？
高志華：沒有，我找過他幾次也沒見着。怎麼？
秦楠： 他妹妹的衣服我早做好了，怎麼一直不來拿？
高志華：咳，他這個人哪，反正到時候他會來拿的。

---

*34. 厲害	厉害	lìhai	severe, fierce
^35. 戴上	戴上	dài≠shang	to put on (hat)
^36. 擦汗	擦汗	cā hàn	to wipe off sweat
*37. 提意見	提意见	tí yìjian	to make a suggestion, to raise an objection
*38. 相處	相处	xiāngchǔ	to be together, to get along together

Scene 17 ——————————

It is a hot day. Qin Nan and Zhihua are both working on the sidewalk. Zhihua invites Qin Nan to move her sewing machine into his home, but she politely turns him down.

秦楠： 好了，后天来拿。
顾客： 走吧。

Brief dialogue between Gao Zhihua and customer, irrelevant to plot.

高志华：(Offering Qin Nan his hat.) 中午太阳挺厉害的，戴上吧。
秦楠： 谢谢，我不热。
高志华：(Offering Qin Nan a wash cloth.) 来，擦擦汗。
秦楠： 谢谢，我自己有。
高志华：真的，我看你还是搬到屋里去做吧。
秦楠： 不，不，我已经够麻烦你们了。
高志华：我得给你提个意见，我们相处已经不少日子了，你张口谢谢，闭口麻烦的，真让人受不了。
秦楠： 那以后我不说了，嗯，不过……好，我不说了。
高志华：秦楠，我觉得你……
秦楠： 我怎么？
高志华：我觉得一个人应该乐观。听周大妈讲你母亲……咳，那些事都过去好多年了，不要总放在心上。
秦楠： 最近你见到肖健沒有？
高志华：沒有，我找过他几次也沒见着。怎么？
秦楠： 他妹妹的衣服我早做好了，怎么一直不来拿？
高志华：咳，他这个人哪，反正到时候他会来拿的。

39.	張口…，閉口…	张口…，闭口…	zhāngkǒu... bìkǒu...	"to open one's mouth with..., to close one's mouth with...," to keep on saying such things as...and...every time one opens and closes one's mouth
*40.	樂觀	乐观	lè-guān	(-觀: view, outlook) optimistic, to have a cheerful outlook

Qin Nan takes out her cold lunch. Zhihua wants to heat it up for her, but once again, she politely turns him down.

高志華：哎，拿到爐子上去熱熱再吃吧！
秦楠： 不用了。
高志華：很方便嘛！給我吧。
秦楠： 不麻煩了。噢，那給我點兒開水吧！
高志華：好吧。
顧客： 請問，做件襯衫幾天？
秦楠： 明天可以拿。
顧客： 噢，那太好了！

Scene 18 ——————————

Zhihua is upstairs writing to his sister when his mother calls him to dinner.

高母： 志華，吃飯啦！
高志華：來了！
高母： 哎呀，叫了半天，在幹嘛呢？
高志華：給小妹寫信呢。
高母： 小秦在我們門口擺攤的事你告訴英華了嗎？
高志華：跟她說了。
高母： 我猜你就會告訴她的。
高志華：你這是什麼意思？
高母： 媽的意思還不懂？小秦這姑娘文文靜靜，不言不語的，多賢惠。志華，我看……
高志華：好，吃飯，吃飯！吃飯！(His mother chuckles.)
高志華：笑什麼？

---

*41. 熱	热	rè	(used as verb here) to heat up
*42. 開水	开水	kāishuǐ	boiled water, hot water
*43. 襯衫	衬衫	chènshān	shirt, blouse
*44. 猜	猜	cāi	to guess

Qin Nan takes out her cold lunch. Zhihua wants to heat it up for her, but once again, she politely turns him down.

高志华：哎，拿到炉子上去热热再吃吧！
秦楠：　不用了。
高志华：很方便嘛！给我吧。
秦楠：　不麻烦了。噢，那给我点儿开水吧！
高志华：好吧。
顾客：　请问，做件衬衫几天？
秦楠：　明天可以拿。
顾客：　噢，那太好了！

Scene 18 ——————————

Zhihua is upstairs writing to his sister when his mother calls him to dinner.

高母：　志华，吃饭啦！
高志华：来了！
高母：　哎呀，叫了半天，在干嘛呢？
高志华：给小妹写信呢。
高母：　小秦在我们门口摆摊的事你告诉英华了吗？
高志华：跟她说了。
高母：　我猜你就会告诉她的。
高志华：你这是什么意思？
高母：　妈的意思还不懂？小秦这姑娘文文静静，不言不语的，多贤惠。志华，我看……
高志华：好，吃饭，吃饭！吃饭！(His mother chuckles.)
高志华：笑什么？

45.	文静	文静	wénjìng	refined and quiet
46.	不言不語	不言不语	bùyán bùyǔ	unchatty, taciturn
47.	賢惠	贤惠	xiánhuì	virtuous (said of a woman)

高母：　我記得有個歌怎麼唱的了？“白白活了三十五，褲子破了沒人補。”志華，你也三十一了……

高志華：媽媽，又來了，想抱孫子了？

高母：　不，媽這回不是想抱孫子了，媽是要你找個補褲子的。

---

*48. 白-	白-	bái	(adv.) ...for nothing, (to do something) in vain

---

討論問題：

1) 蕭健爲什麼不早就告訴高志華他要志華幫他幹什麼呢？ 他怎麼會去做那種鬼 (guǐ: devilish) 事情的？那怎麼高志華不會呢？
2) 人們對個體戶有什麼看法？ 爲什麼他們會有那種看法呢？ 你覺得他們的看法有沒有道理 (dàolǐ: rationale, reason)？
3) 爲什麼秦楠對高志華那麼“客氣”？ 爲什麼秦楠的“客氣”讓高志華受不了 (shòubuliǎo: cannot bear)？
4) 你能不能從短短的幾句話中看出高志華和他妹妹的關係是怎麼樣的？
5) 你看在第十六幕 (mù: scene) 跟第十八幕表現出 (biǎoxiànchū: to manifest) 的情況 (qíngkuàng: situation, circumstance)，在中國是不是很普遍 (pǔbiàn: widespread)的？
6) 高母爲什麼那麼想要志華結婚呢？ 結婚對她來説意味 (yìwèi: to imply) 着什麼？

高母：　我记得有个歌怎么唱的了？“白白活了三十五，裤子破了沒人补。”志华，你也三十一了……

高志华：妈妈，又来了，想抱孙子了？

高母：　不，妈这回不是想抱孙子了，妈是要你找个补裤子的。

讨论问题：

1) 肖健为什么不早就告诉高志华他要志华帮他干什么呢？ 他怎么会去做那种鬼 (guǐ: devilish) 事情的？那怎么高志华不会呢？
2) 人们对个体户有什么看法？ 为什么他们会有那种看法呢？ 你觉得他们的看法有沒有道理 (dàolǐ: rationale, reason)？
3) 为什么秦楠对高志华那么“客气”？ 为什么秦楠的“客气”让高志华受不了 (shòubuliǎo: cannot bear)？
4) 你能不能从短短的几句话中看出高志华和他妹妹的关系是怎么样的？
5) 你看在第十六幕 (mù: scene) 跟第十八幕表现出 (biǎoxiànchū: to manifest) 的情况 (qíngkuàng: situation, circumstance)，在中国是不是很普遍 (pǔbiàn: widespread)的？
6) 高母为什么那么想要志华结婚呢？ 结婚对她来说意味 (yìwèi: to imply) 着什么？

SEGMENT IV

Scene 19 ——————————

In Qin Nan's home, her father tries to persuade her to put all her painful memories behind and to consider marrying.

秦楠：　爸，你睡去吧。
秦父：　我不明白，你幹嘛總是迴避這個問題呢？
秦楠：　你要我說什麼呀？
秦父：　你總不能折磨自己一輩子嘛。
秦楠：　事情已經過去了，還提它幹什麼？
秦父：　事情是過去了，可痛苦還留在你心裡。
秦楠：　我現在不是活得很好嗎？
秦父：　你在騙我，你長年累月把苦悶在心裡，爸爸不是不知道。我知道你是個有主見的人，可你心裡究竟是怎麼想的？為什麼就不肯跟我說說呢？
秦楠：　爸，你這麼大年紀，我真不忍心你再為我的事情操心了。
秦父：　可你還有個大半輩子的日子要過，你總不能就這樣下去吧？
秦楠：　靠自己勞動，這樣獨立生活下去，有什麼不好？
秦父：　那你就一輩子不結婚了？
秦楠：　哼，還結什麼婚？我把我的心，把我的一切都給了他，可結果呢？他呢？
秦父：　爸理解你，你太善良，太天真，這件事錯不在你。
秦楠：　爸，你說，我的處境要是讓人家知道了，他們會公平地對待我嗎？

---

^1. 迴避	回避	huíbì	to evade
^2. 折磨	折磨	zhémó	to torment continuously (physically or mentally), to suffer (on a long term basis)
*3. 一輩子	一辈子	yíbèizi	one's whole life
*4. 痛苦	痛苦	tòngkǔ	pain, grief, agony; painful; to suffer
5. 長年累月	长年累月	chángnián lěiyuè	for years and months on end
6. 悶在心裡	闷在心里	mēn zài xīnlǐ	to bottle up emotions (悶: to cover tightly, to smother)
*7. 主見	主见	zhǔjiàn	own's own ideas
*8. 究竟	究竟	jiūjìng	after all, actually, in the final analysis (cf. Grammatical Note IV.2.)

SEGMENT IV

Scene 19 ——————————

In Qin Nan's home, her father tries to persuade her to put all her painful memories behind and to consider marrying.

秦楠： 爸，你睡去吧。
秦父： 我不明白，你干嘛总是回避这个问题呢？
秦楠： 你要我说什么呀？
秦父： 你总不能折磨自己一辈子嘛。
秦楠： 事情已经过去了，还提它干什么？
秦父： 事情是过去了，可痛苦还留在你心里。
秦楠： 我现在不是活得很好吗？
秦父： 你在骗我，你长年累月把苦闷在心里，爸爸不是不知道。我知道你是个有主见的人，可你心里究竟是怎么想的？为什么就不肯跟我说说呢？
秦楠： 爸，你这么大年纪，我真不忍心你再为我的事情操心了。
秦父： 可你还有个大半辈子的日子要过，你总不能就这样下去吧？
秦楠： 靠自己劳动，这样独立生活下去，有什么不好？
秦父： 那你就一辈子不结婚了？
秦楠： 哼，还结什么婚？我把我的心，把我的一切都给了他，可结果呢？他呢？
秦父： 爸理解你，你太善良，太天真，这件事错不在你。
秦楠： 爸，你说，我的处境要是让人家知道了，他们会公平地对待我吗？

---

^9.	忍心	忍心	rěn≠xīn	to have the heart to...
^10.	操心	操心	cāo≠xīn	to trouble one's mind, to worry
^11.	哼	哼	hng	humph
*12.	V 什麼 (O)	V 什么 (O)	V shénme (O)	how can one possibly..., what's the point of V(-O) (cf. Grammatical Note IV.4.)
^13.	善良	善良	shànliáng	kind-hearted
*14.	天真	天真	tiānzhēn	naive, innocent, unaffected, guileless
*15.	處境	处境	chǔjìng	situation (usually unfavorable), plight
*16.	公平	公平	gōngpíng	fair, just, impartial, equitable
*17.	對待	对待	duìdài	to treat

秦父： 當然，社會上還有舊的習慣勢力，不過你要相信，舊的習慣勢力並沒有統治所有的人。小楠，對生活你必須要有勇氣。我老了，你不為自己將來好好打算，我的心是不安的。

秦楠： 爸，不早了，睡去吧。

Scene 20 ——————————

One day Zhihua's sister Yinghua comes home from training and meets Qin Nan in front of the house. She introduces herself to Qin Nan.

高英華：哥！哥！

秦楠： 他買零件去了，鑰匙在我這兒，給。

高英華：你是秦楠吧？

秦楠： 是的。

高英華：我哥早就寫信告訴我了。我叫英華，英雄的英，中華的華。哎，我哥跟我媽沒跟你説起過我？

秦楠： 説過。

高英華：我哥哥兩封信都提到過你，還説我媽媽好喜歡你。怎麼説呢？反正我有三天假，找時間咱們好好聊聊，好吧？

秦楠： 嗯。

Scene 21 ——————————

Later Yinghua talks with Zhihua. She asks him about his feelings for Qin Nan.

高英華：這是我特地給媽泡的蛤蚧酒，治氣管炎有特效。

---

*18.	勢力	势力	shìlì	power, force, influence
*19.	統治	统治	tǒngzhì	to govern, to rule, to dominate
*20.	勇氣	勇气	yǒngqì	courage
*21.	英雄	英雄	yīngxióng	hero
*22.	中華	中华	Zhōnghuá	another word for China
*23.	聊	聊	liáo	(colloquial) to chat
^24.	泡	泡	pào	to soak, to steep (in liquid) (cf. 泡飯, Note I.60)

秦父： 当然，社会上还有旧的习惯势力，不过你要相信，旧的习惯势力并沒有统治所有的人。小楠，对生活你必须要有勇气。我老了，你不为自己将来好好打算，我的心是不安的。

秦楠： 爸，不早了，睡去吧。

Scene 20 ——————————

One day Zhihua's sister Yinghua comes home from training and meets Qin Nan in front of the house. She introduces herself to Qin Nan.

高英华：哥！哥！

秦楠： 他买零件去了，钥匙在我这儿，给。

高英华：你是秦楠吧？

秦楠： 是的。

高英华：我哥早就写信告诉我了。我叫英华，英雄的英，中华的华。哎，我哥跟我妈沒跟你说起过我？

秦楠： 说过。

高英华：我哥哥两封信都提到过你，还说我妈妈好喜欢你。怎么说呢？反正我有三天假，找时间咱们好好聊聊，好吧？

秦楠： 嗯。

Scene 21 ——————————

Later Yinghua talks with Zhihua. She asks him about his feelings for Qin Nan.

高英华：这是我特地给妈泡的蛤蚧酒，治气管炎有特效。

---

25. 蛤蚧酒	蛤蚧酒	géjiè-jiǔ	(in the film, 蛤蚧 is pronounced hāgài, as in Shanghainese) a medicinal wine with a kind of lizard soaking in it
*26. 治	治	zhì	to cure, to treat (an illness)
27. 氣管炎	气管炎	qìguǎn-yán	(-炎: inflammation) tracheitis
^28. 特效	特效	tè-xiào	(-效: efficacy) special efficacy

高志華：呵，像四脚蛇嘛！

高英華：哎，你別看它樣子難看，這是廣西特產，名貴的補藥呢。(She tosses him a piece of fruit.) 媽怎麼還不回來呀？

高志華：噢，這兩天廠裡搞體制改革，回來得晚。哎，你這次回來能住幾天？

高英華：放我們三天假，在上海再集訓一個半月，完了就去北京參加全國錦標賽。

高志華：怎麼樣，有希望嗎？

高英華：爲什麼沒有希望？同志們和教練都在給我鼓勁兒。我這次非把冠軍拿下來不可。

高志華：嘿，口氣不小，有把握？

高英華：拼搏嘛。

高志華：哈哈，又是拼搏。

高英華：當然啦。一個人想幹成一件事不拼搏還行？哎，咱們中國女排怎麼獲得世界冠軍的？不就是拼搏出來的嗎？那場電視你看了沒有？

高志華：當然看了。

高英華：嘿，真他媽過癮！

Scene 22 ——————————

Their conversation is interrupted by Qin Nan, who calls from the sidewalk that she is going home.

秦楠： 小高，我回去了。

高英華：秦楠，再見啊！

秦楠： 再見！

29.	四脚蛇	四脚蛇	sìjiǎo-shé	"four-legged snake," lizard
^30.	特產	特产	tè-chǎn	special product (of a region)
*31.	名貴	名贵	míngguì	famous and precious
32.	補藥	补药	bǔ-yào	tonic
^33.	體制	体制	tǐzhì	organization, system
*34.	改革	改革	gǎigé	reform
*35.	參加	参加	cānjiā	to join, to participate in
36.	錦標賽	锦标赛	jǐnbiāo-sài	championship competition
*37.	同志們	同志们	tóngzhì-men	comrades
^38.	教練	教练	jiàoliàn	coach (of a sport)
39.	鼓勁(兒)	鼓劲(儿)	gǔjìn(r)	to encourage, to pep up
40.	冠軍	冠军	guànjūn	champion, championship

高志华：呵，象四脚蛇嘛！

高英华：哎，你别看它样子难看，这是广西特产，名贵的补药呢。(She tosses him a piece of fruit.) 妈怎么还不回来呀？

高志华：噢，这两天厂里搞体制改革，回来得晚。哎，你这次回来能住几天？

高英华：放我们三天假，在上海再集训一个半月，完了就去北京参加全国锦标赛。

高志华：怎么样，有希望吗？

高英华：为什么沒有希望？同志们和教练都在给我鼓劲儿。我这次非把冠军拿下来不可。

高志华：嘿，口气不小，有把握？

高英华：拼搏嘛。

高志华：哈哈，又是拼搏。

高英华：当然啦。一个人想干成一件事不拼搏还行？哎，咱们中国女排怎么获得世界冠军的？不就是拼搏出来的吗？那场电视你看了沒有？

高志华：当然看了。

高英华：嘿，真他妈过瘾！

Scene 22 ——————————

Their conversation is interrupted by Qin Nan, who calls from the sidewalk that she is going home.

秦楠：　小高，我回去了。

高英华：秦楠，再见啊！

秦楠：　再见！

---

*41. 口氣	口气	kǒu-qì	tone of voice
*42. 把握	把握	bǎwò	confidence, self-confidence, assurance
43. 拼搏	拼搏	pīnbó	to go all out, to exert one's utmost, to put one's life on the line
^44. 哈哈	哈哈	hāhā	(onomatopoeia) laughter
45. 女排	女排	nǚ-pái	women's volleyball
^46. 獲得	获得	huòdé	to attain
^47. 他媽	他妈	tā mā	"damn" (usually not used by women, so its occurrence here helps to characterize Yinghua)
^48. 過癮	过瘾	guò≠yǐn	to enjoy oneself to the full, to totally satisfy a craving

Scene 23

高英華：哥，你說秦楠怎麼樣？
高志華：什麼怎麼樣？
高英華：從信上看，你對她印象不錯嘛。
高志華：我信上寫什麼了？我就是說媽喜歡她。
高英華：那你呢？
高志華：我什麼？
高英華：你喜不喜歡她？你別笑眯眯不吭聲，我知道你心裡很喜歡她。
高志華：你別胡說啊！
高英華：哥，咱們說正經的。我跟秦楠雖說第一次見面，可她給我的印象真是好極了。哥，你也三十一了，這個老大難也該解決了。幹嘛老叫媽媽急得團團轉呢？
高志華：我看你也快變成了小老太婆了！
高英華：哎呀，哥，要是你心裡真喜歡她，幹嘛不主動點兒？我覺得你在這方面也得有點兒拼搏精神。(Zhihua gets up to run away, Yinghua grabs him from behind.) 哎，你別走啊，你別走！這樣好不好，明天我找秦楠談談。
高志華：哎呀，你別胡鬧啊！
高英華：這有什麼？先探探她的口氣，有什麼不好？對，明天一早我就到她家去找她談。

Scene 24

Yinghua goes to see Qin Nan the next morning. Her knock is answered by Qin Nan's father.

秦父： 你？
高英華：我是高志華的妹妹。
秦父： 啊，有什麼事嗎？

---

*49.	印象	印象	yìnxiàng	impression
^50.	笑咪咪	笑咪咪	xiàomīmī	to grin, to smile
51.	吭聲	吭声	kēng≠shēng	to utter a sound
^52.	胡說	胡说	húshuō	to talk nonsense, to speak recklessly
*53.	正經	正经	zhèngjing	serious (not frivolous)
^54.	老大難	老大难	lǎo dà nán	an old (i.e. long-standing), big, and difficult problem

Scene 23

高英华：哥，你说秦楠怎么样？
高志华：什么怎么样？
高英华：从信上看，你对她印象不错嘛。
高志华：我信上写什么了？我就是说妈喜欢她。
高英华：那你呢？
高志华：我什么？
高英华：你喜不喜欢她？你别笑眯眯不吭声，我知道你心里很喜欢她。
高志华：你别胡说啊！
高英华：哥，咱们说正经的。我跟秦楠虽说第一次见面，可她给我的印象真是好极了。哥，你也三十一了，这个老大难也该解决了。干嘛老叫妈妈急得团团转呢？
高志华：我看你也快变成了小老太婆了！
高英华：哎呀，哥，要是你心里真喜欢她，干嘛不主动点儿？我觉得你在这方面也得有点儿拚搏精神。(Zhihua gets up to run away, Yinghua grabs him from behind.) 哎，你别走啊，你别走！这样好不好，明天我找秦楠谈谈。
高志华：哎呀，你别胡闹啊！
高英华：这有什么？先探探她的口气，有什么不好？对，明天一早我就到她家去找她谈。

Scene 24

Yinghua goes to see Qin Nan the next morning. Her knock is answered by Qin Nan's father.

秦父：　你？
高英华：我是高志华的妹妹。
秦父：　啊，有什么事吗？

55.	團團轉	团团转	tuántuánzhuàn	to run around in circles; in a tizzy
*56.	主動	主动	zhǔdòng	to take initiative
^57.	胡鬧	胡闹	húnào	mischievous, to make a ruckus
58.	探探	探探	tàntan	to make secret inquiries, to sniff out (same as 探聽)

高英華：秦楠呢？
秦父： 她早班車到蘇州去了。
高英華：啊？噢……

---

*59. 班　　班　　bān　　(M) "run" of a bus, train, or plane (as per schedule)

討論問題：

1) 從第十九幕 (mù: scene) 的對白 (duìbái: dialogue)，你能不能看出秦楠的父親對她的希望？ 他爲什麼有那樣的希望呢？
2) 在那段 (duàn: segment) 對話中，秦楠說“還結什麼婚？我把我的心…都給了他，可結果呢？他呢？”你想秦楠講的“他”是誰？ 爲什麼爲了“他”秦楠覺得她不能結婚了？
3) 高志華妹妹的脾氣 (píqi: temperament) 跟他一樣不一樣？ 跟秦楠呢？
4) 高英華對她哥哥的婚事有什麼看法？ 在這方面，她爲什麼要“幫”她的哥哥呢？

高英华：秦楠呢？
秦父： 她早班车到苏州去了。
高英华：啊？噢……

讨论问题：

1) 从第十九幕 (mù: scene) 的对白 (duìbái: dialogue)，你能不能看出秦楠的父亲对她的希望？ 他为什么有那样的希望呢？
2) 在那段 (duàn: segment) 对话中，秦楠说"还结什么婚？我把我的心…都给了他，可结果呢？他呢？"你想秦楠讲的"他"是谁？ 为什么为了"他"秦楠觉得她不能结婚了？
3) 高志华妹妹的脾气 (píqi: temperament) 跟他一样不一样？ 跟秦楠呢？
4) 高英华对她哥哥的婚事有什么看法？ 在这方面，她为什么要"帮"她的哥哥呢？

SEGMENT V

Scene 25 ———————————

It turns out that Qin Nan has a son, Dongdong, who lives with Qin Nan's uncle and aunt in Suzhou. She goes there to see him often. Arriving at their place...

秦楠： 冬冬！
冬冬： 媽媽！
秦楠： 冬冬！
舅媽： 怎麼樣，冬冬？我說你媽媽今天會來的吧？
秦楠： 舅舅呢？
舅媽： 在屋裡，進去吧。

Scene 26 ———————————

Qin Nan and Dongdong are on an outing in Suzhou. Dongdong is very happy to be with his mother. But seeing another family - a young couple with their child, Qin Nan is saddened to be reminded of her plight. Dongdong asks Qin Nan not to leave anymore, causing her great pain.

秦楠： 冬冬，回家去吧？
冬冬： 媽媽，你以後不要再走啦，冬冬要跟媽媽在一起。
秦楠： 冬冬乖，要聽話！媽媽這回不是給你買了小手槍了嗎？
冬冬： 我不要小手槍！我要媽媽！我要媽媽！
秦楠： 冬冬！

Scene 27 ———————————

When Qin Nan leaves Suzhou after visiting Dongdong, she sneaks away at the crack of dawn before Dongdong is awake in order to avoid a painful parting. Early one morning...

---

*1. 聽話	听话	tīng≠huà	to obey, to listen
2. 手槍	手枪	shǒu-qiāng	pistol (here, a toy)

SEGMENT V

Scene 25

It turns out that Qin Nan has a son, Dongdong, who lives with Qin Nan's uncle and aunt in Suzhou. She goes there to see him often. Arriving at their place...

秦楠： 冬冬！
冬冬： 妈妈！
秦楠： 冬冬！
舅妈： 怎么样，冬冬？我说你妈妈今天会来的吧？
秦楠： 舅舅呢？
舅妈： 在屋里，进去吧。

Scene 26

Qin Nan and Dongdong are on an outing in Suzhou. Dongdong is very happy to be with his mother. But seeing another family - a young couple with their child, Qin Nan is saddened to be reminded of her plight. Dongdong asks Qin Nan not to leave anymore, causing her great pain.

秦楠： 冬冬，回家去吧？
冬冬： 妈妈，你以后不要再走啦，冬冬要跟妈妈在一起。
秦楠： 冬冬乖，要听话！妈妈这回不是给你买了小手枪了吗？
冬冬： 我不要小手枪！我要妈妈！我要妈妈！
秦楠： 冬冬！

Scene 27

When Qin Nan leaves Suzhou after visiting Dongdong, she sneaks away at the crack of dawn before Dongdong is awake in order to avoid a painful parting. Early one morning...

秦楠：　舅舅。
舅舅：　吃了早飯再走吧！
秦楠：　不，趁冬冬沒醒，我得趕緊走，這是冬冬的生活費。
舅舅：　你留着吧。現在鄉下日子好過啦！
秦楠：　您拿着。我走了。

As she leaves, she seems to hear Dongdong's voice crying for her.

Scene 28 ——————————

One day it suddenly starts to rain while Qin Nan and Zhihua are working outside. They quickly move their things inside. Once inside, Zhihua helps Qin Nan set up her sewing machine again.

高志華：真湊巧，接電話的工夫就下起雨來。
秦楠：　我自己來。
高志華：你頭髮濕了，就在屋裡做吧！
秦楠：　好。
高志華：嗯，反正下雨天沒事，我幫你修修縫紉機。
秦楠：　不用了，買來就是舊的。
高志華：踏板松了，看你蹬起來好吃力。
　　　　哎，我妹妹剛才在電話裡問你好。她那天還專門去找過你呢！
秦楠：　我爸爸告訴我了。哎，她找我有事嗎？
高志華：啊？啊！她說她對你印象很好。你怎麼經常到蘇州去？
秦楠：　(Hesitates for a moment) 我舅舅在蘇州。
高志華：噢。

---

*3. 趁	趁	chèn	(coverb) while (the opportunity or opportune moment is at hand), to take advantage of (an opportunity or moment)(cf. Grammatical Note V.I.)
^4. 趕緊	赶紧	gǎnjǐn	quickly, in a hurry
5. 日子好過	日子好过	rìzi hǎoguò	"the days are easy to pass," life is easy (i.e., we don't need the money anymore)

秦楠： 舅舅。
舅舅： 吃了早饭再走吧！
秦楠： 不，趁冬冬沒醒，我得赶紧走，这是冬冬的生活费。
舅舅： 你留着吧。现在乡下日子好过啦！
秦楠： 您拿着。我走了。

As she leaves, she seems to hear Dongdong's voice crying for her.

Scene 28 ——————————

One day it suddenly starts to rain while Qin Nan and Zhihua are working outside. They quickly move their things inside. Once inside, Zhihua helps Qin Nan set up her sewing machine again.

高志华：真凑巧，接电话的工夫就下起雨来。
秦楠： 我自己来。
高志华：你头发湿了，就在屋里做吧！
秦楠： 好。
高志华：嗯，反正下雨天沒事，我帮你修修缝纫机。
秦楠： 不用了，买来就是旧的。
高志华：踏板松了，看你蹬起来好吃力。
哎，我妹妹刚才在电话里问你好。她那天还专门去找过你呢！
秦楠： 我爸爸告诉我了。哎，她找我有事吗？
高志华：啊？啊！她说她对你印象很好。你怎么经常到苏州去？
秦楠： (Hesitates for a moment) 我舅舅在苏州。
高志华：噢。

---

^6. 湊巧	凑巧	còuqiǎo	fortuitous
*7. 頭髮	头发	tóufa	hair
*8. 濕	湿	shī	wet
9. 踏板	踏板	tà-bǎn	(-板: board) treadle
10. 蹬	蹬	dèng	to pedal, to pump with the feet
*11. 吃力	吃力	chīlì	strenuous
*12. 專門…	专门…	zhuānmén...	especially, to make a special effort to...
^13. 經常	经常	jīngcháng	常常

Scene 29 ——————————

高母：　志華，誰來電話？

(Here, a couple of lines seem to have been deleted from the film by mistake.)

高志華：她說訓練緊張，這一段都不回來了。

高母：　就這麼忙？星期天都不放假！那我給她織的毛衣她什麼時候來拿？

高志華：您把毛衣包好，我一會兒給她送去。

高母：　(catching sight of Qin Nan) 哎，小秦，這就對了，我早就說過，就在屋裡做，免得在外面風吹日曬的。

秦楠：　不了。

高母：　這架縫紉機，也別天天搬來搬去的，多麻煩！乾脆！就擱在我這兒。

秦楠：　晚上在這兒幹活，不方便。

高母：　你家離這兒這麼近，有什麼不方便的？

秦楠：　要吵您睡覺的。

高母：　我睡着了，你在我床邊放炮仗也炸不醒的。

高志華：(to his mom) 您把毛衣包好了，我馬上就給她送去。

高母：　好，好。(shifts to Qin Nan) 小秦，就這麼說定了，啊？

Having fixed the sewing machine, Zhihua turns and speaks to Qin Nan.

高志華：行了，平時多上點兒油。

秦楠：　謝謝你。

高志華：我看媽說的也對，縫紉機放在這兒。搬來搬去快散架了，就這樣吧。

秦楠：　嗯。

高志華：秦楠，我買了兩張今天晚上的電影票，想請你去……

秦楠：　不不，今天晚上我有事，我不去。

---

^14.	段	段	duàn	section, segment, period (of time)
*15.	放假	放假	fàng≠jià	to have a holiday or day off, vacation
16.	織	织	zhī	to knit, to weave
^17.	毛衣	毛衣	máo-yī	sweater
*18.	包	包	bāo	to wrap; M for bags or bundles
*19.	免得	免得	miǎnde	so as to be spared, so as to avoid (cf. Grammatical Note V.4.)
20.	風吹日曬	风吹日晒	fēngchuī rìshài	blown by the wind and scorched by the sun

Scene 29 ——————————

高母： 志华，谁来电话？

(Here, a couple of lines seem to have been deleted from the film by mistake.)

高志华：她说训练紧张，这一段都不回来了。

高母： 就这么忙？星期天都不放假！那我给她织的毛衣她什么时候来拿？

高志华：您把毛衣包好，我一会儿给她送去。

高母： (catching sight of Qin Nan) 哎，小秦，这就对了，我早就说过，就在屋里做，免得在外面风吹日晒的。

秦楠： 不了。

高母： 这架缝纫机，也别天天搬来搬去的，多麻烦！干脆！就搁在我这儿。

秦楠： 晚上在这儿干活，不方便。

高母： 你家离这儿这么近，有什么不方便的？

秦楠： 要吵您睡觉的。

高母： 我睡着了，你在我床边放炮仗也炸不醒的。

高志华：(to his mom) 您把毛衣包好了，我马上就给她送去。

高母： 好，好。(shifts to Qin Nan) 小秦，就这么说定了，啊？

Having fixed the sewing machine, Zhihua turns and speaks to Qin Nan.

高志华：行了，平时多上点儿油。

秦楠： 谢谢你。

高志华：我看妈说的也对，缝纫机放在这儿。搬来搬去快散架了，就这样吧。

秦楠： 嗯。

高志华：秦楠，我买了两张今天晚上的电影票，想请你去……

秦楠： 不不，今天晚上我有事，我不去。

---

^21.	架	架	jià	M for machines, airplanes, etc.
*22.	吵	吵	chǎo	noisy; to disturb with noise
23.	炮仗	炮仗	pàozhàng	firecrackers
24.	炸	炸	zhà	to explode, to burst
*25.	說定	说定	shuō≠dìng	to talk out and settle (an agreement), to agree
^26.	平時	平时	píngshí	平常
27.	上油	上油	shàng≠yóu	to oil (a machine, etc.)
28.	散架	散架	sàn≠jià	to have the frame fall apart

The postman comes, which relieves Zhihua's embarrassment.

郵遞員：高志華，信！
高志華：謝謝！(Gao opens the letter and begins to read it.) 啊？我早料到會出這種事。
秦楠： 誰出事了？
高志華：蕭健。不聽我的勸，活該！

Zhihua crumples up the letter and tosses it away in disgust.

高母： 志華。
高志華：來了。

Scene 30 ——————————

Qin Nan picks up the letter and reads it. The letter is from Xiao Jian, who has been sentenced to a labor reformatory for selling bicycles under fake brandnames.

信： 小高，我很後悔，不聽你的勸告，走上了犯罪的道路。政府看我是初犯，給我勞動教養兩年的寬大處理，我現在在安徽農場接受改造。我唯一不放心的是我妹妹蕭雲。她住在大廠西小弄九號樓上。望你經常去關心她。託秦楠做的衣服請您給她送去。我的事不要告訴她。人要臉，樹要皮。我不希望其他朋友知道我的醜事，包括秦楠在內。蕭健。

29.	料到	料到	liào≠dào	to expect, to anticipate
^30.	活該	活该	huógāi	to serve...right, to get one's just deserts
*31.	後悔	后悔	hòuhuǐ	to regret
*32.	勸告	劝告	quàngào	advice, exhortation; to advise, to urge
*33.	犯罪	犯罪	fàn≠zuì	to commit a crime
34.	初犯	初犯	chū-fàn	first offense
^35.	教養	教养	jiàoyǎng	to cultivate, to educate, to nurture
^36.	寬大	宽大	kuāndà	lenient, generous, magnanimous
*37.	處理	处理	chǔlǐ	to deal with; treatment
38.	安徽	安徽	Ānhuī	a province not far from Shanghai
*39.	接受	接受	jiēshòu	to receive, to accept, to undergo
*40.	改造	改造	gǎizào	reform

The postman comes, which relieves Zhihua's embarrassment.

邮递员：高志华，信！
高志华：谢谢！(Gao opens the letter and begins to read it.) 啊？我早料到会出这种事。
秦楠：　谁出事了？
高志华：肖健。不听我的劝，活该！

Zhihua crumples up the letter and tosses it away in disgust.

高母：　志华。
高志华：来了。

Scene 30 ——————————

Qin Nan picks up the letter and reads it. The letter is from Xiao Jian, who has been sentenced to a labor reformatory for selling bicycles under fake brandnames.

信：　小高，我很后悔，不听你的劝告，走上了犯罪的道路。政府看我是初犯，给我劳动教养两年的宽大处理，我现在在安徽农场接受改造。我唯一不放心的是我妹妹肖云。她住在大厂西小弄九号楼上。望你经常去关心她。托秦楠做的衣服请您给她送去。我的事不要告诉她。人要脸，树要皮。我不希望其他朋友知道我的丑事，包括秦楠在内。肖健。

---

*41.	唯一	唯一	wéiyī	sole, one and only (cf. Grammatical Note V.5.)
42.	大廠西小弄	大厂西小弄	Dàchǎng Xī Xiǎolòng	"Big Factory West Little Lane," name of a lane
43.	望	望	wàng	希望
*44.	關心	关心	guān≠xīn	to care for, to feel concern for
*45.	託	托	tuō	to entrust (a task to someone)
*46.	其他	其他	qítā	别的
^47.	醜	丑	chǒu	ugly
*48.	包括…在內	包括…在内	bāokuò... zàinèi	including... (cf. Grammatical Note V.6.)

Scene 31 ————————————

Qin Nan goes to see Xiao Jian's sister Xiao Yun and discovers that she is handicapped.

蕭雲： 請進來吧。是要刻圖章嗎？
秦楠： 不，我是來找蕭雲的。

Qin Nan is startled to see Xiao Yun on crutches.

蕭雲： 我就是蕭雲。幹嘛這麼驚奇地看着我？因爲我是殘廢？
秦楠： 不，不。是高志華叫我來的。
蕭雲： 高志華？
秦楠： 是的。
蕭雲： 我哥哥的好朋友！
秦楠： 他叫我把你哥哥給你做的衣服送來。他還要我告訴你，你哥哥出遠門去了，要……
蕭雲： 不要再說下去了！我哥哥的事，居委會已經通知我了。我恨我哥哥，我萬萬想不到他會……我不能原諒他！
秦楠： 你不要太難過。
蕭雲： 我是很難過，以前我們非常困難的時候，他都能咬着牙挺住。可今天，我們的情況比過去好了，他反倒不珍惜自己了。我只有這一個哥哥，雖然我們不是一個母親生的，可他從小就關心我這個殘廢的妹妹。他本來不是這樣的，他變了。

Qin Nan looks at a portrait of Xiao Jian.

秦楠： 這張畫是你畫的？
蕭雲： 嗯，我要等他回來，我相信他會重新做人的。一個人不怕摔跤，只要有勇氣站起來，他就會過得更好。好了，我們不談這些了。謝謝你，冒這麼大雨來看我。

49.	刻圖章	刻图章	kē túzhāng	to carve a chop
ˆ50.	驚奇	惊奇	jīngqí	surprised, startled
*51.	殘廢	残废	cánfèi	crippled; a handicapped person
*52.	出門	出门	chū≠mén	"to go out the gate," to go out of town
53.	居委會	居委会	jūwěi-huì	short for 居民委員會, "residents' committee"
*54.	通知	通知	tōngzhī	to notify
*55.	恨	恨	hèn	to hate
*56.	原諒	原谅	yuánliàng	to forgive

Scene 31

Qin Nan goes to see Xiao Jian's sister Xiao Yun and discovers that she is handicapped.

肖云： 请进来吧。是要刻图章吗？
秦楠： 不，我是来找肖云的。

Qin Nan is startled to see Xiao Yun on crutches.

肖云： 我就是肖云。干嘛这么惊奇地看着我？因为我是残废？
秦楠： 不，不。是高志华叫我来的。
肖云： 高志华？
秦楠： 是的。
肖云： 我哥哥的好朋友！
秦楠： 他叫我把你哥哥给你做的衣服送来。他还要我告诉你，你哥哥出远门去了，要……
肖云： 不要再说下去了！我哥哥的事，居委会已经通知我了。我恨我哥哥，我万万想不到他会……我不能原谅他！
秦楠： 你不要太难过。
肖云： 我是很难过，以前我们非常困难的时候，他都能咬着牙挺住。可今天，我们的情况比过去好了，他反倒不珍惜自己了。我只有这一个哥哥，虽然我们不是一个母亲生的，可他从小就关心我这个残废的妹妹。他本来不是这样的，他变了。

Qin Nan looks at a portrait of Xiao Jian.

秦楠： 这张画是你画的？
肖云： 嗯，我要等他回来，我相信他会重新做人的。一个人不怕摔跤，只要有勇气站起来，他就会过得更好。好了，我们不谈这些了。谢谢你，冒这么大雨来看我。

57.	咬牙	咬牙	yǎo≠yá	to grit one's teeth
58.	挺住	挺住	tǐng≠zhù	to bear up, to stand firm
*59.	情况	情况	qíngkuàng	circumstances
60.	珍惜	珍惜	zhēnxī	to cherish
*61.	重新	重新	chóngxīn...	(adv.) ...anew, to do something again with a fresh start
^62.	摔跤	摔跤	shuāi≠jiāo	to stumble or trip and fall
63.	冒	冒	mào	to brave (bad weather, danger, etc.)

秦楠： 不要謝我，是高志華叫我來的。他最近很忙，以後他會來看你的。 (Here, Qin Nan tells a fib to give credit to Zhihua instead of herself.)

A neighbor comes in, carrying a basket of groceries for Xiao Yun.

郭奶奶：蕭雲！
蕭雲： 哎！郭奶奶，真謝謝您了！
郭奶奶：吃了晚飯，我來給你套被子。下午我叫小田把煤球給你送來。啊，你們談，你們談。
蕭雲： 郭奶奶，真謝謝您了。
郭奶奶：別送，別送了。 (leaves, closing the door behind her.)
蕭雲： 你當心啊！
秦楠： 她是誰呀？
蕭雲： 我們居委會的黨支部書記，哥哥的事就是她告訴我的。
秦楠： (Handing the jacket to Xiao Yun.) 穿上試試。

Scene 32 ——————————

Meanwhile, Qin Nan's uncle comes to see her about an emergency. His knock at the Gaos' home is answered by Zhihua.

舅舅： 請問，秦楠在這兒嗎？
高志華：她今天沒來，可能去蘇州了。
舅舅： 不，我就是從蘇州來的。我是她舅舅，她家我去過，門鎖着，鄰居告訴我她在這兒。
高志華：那您請進來吧。她一會兒會回來的。
舅舅： 不啦，我得趕回去。麻煩你了，等她回來，叫她馬上到我家來。有要緊的事。好了，我走了。
高志華：您慢走啊。

---

64. 套被子	套被子	tào bèizi	to slip a quilt into a cover
65. 小田	小田	Xiǎo Tián	"Little Tian," 人名
66. 煤球	煤球	méi-qiú	charcoal briquets
ˆ67. 黨支部	党支部	dǎng-zhībù	Party branch (a grassroots unit of the Communist Party)

秦楠： 不要谢我，是高志华叫我来的。他最近很忙，以后他会来看你的。 (Here, Qin Nan tells a fib to give credit to Zhihua instead of herself.)

A neighbor comes in, carrying a basket of groceries for Xiao Yun.

郭奶奶：肖云！
肖云： 哎！郭奶奶，真谢谢您了！
郭奶奶：吃了晚饭，我来给你套被子。下午我叫小田把煤球给你送来。啊，你们谈，你们谈。
肖云： 郭奶奶，真谢谢您了。
郭奶奶：别送，别送了。 (leaves, closing the door behind her.)
肖云： 你当心啊！
秦楠： 她是谁呀？
肖云： 我们居委会的党支部书记，哥哥的事就是她告诉我的。
秦楠： (Handing the jacket to Xiao Yun.) 穿上试试。

Scene 32 ——————————

Meanwhile, Qin Nan's uncle comes to see her about an emergency. His knock at the Gaos' home is answered by Zhihua.

舅舅： 请问，秦楠在这儿吗？
高志华：她今天没来，可能去苏州了。
舅舅： 不，我就是从苏州来的。我是她舅舅，她家我去过，门锁着，邻居告诉我她在这儿。
高志华：那您请进来吧。她一会儿会回来的。
舅舅： 不啦，我得赶回去。麻烦你了，等她回来，叫她马上到我家来。有要紧的事。好了，我走了。
高志华：您慢走啊。

---

^68. 書記	书记	shūjì	secretary
^69. 鎖	锁	suǒ	to lock, a lock
*70. 鄰居	邻居	línjū	neighbor
^71. 慢走	慢走	mànzǒu	"go slowly," "stay a while" (said to a departing friend), goodbye, take care

討論問題：

1) 為什麼這個電影到現在才讓我們知道秦楠有個孩子呢？
2) 為什麼秦楠不跟冬冬一起生活呢？ 你想她在蘇州跟冬冬一起的時候會有什麼感受 (gǎnshòu: feelings)？
3) 為什麼秦楠要趁冬冬沒醒的時候趕緊走？ 她這樣做結果對她自己和冬冬會怎麼樣？
4) 志華為什麼問秦楠"你怎麼經常到蘇州去？" 聽了秦楠的回答以後，他會怎麼想？
5) 為什麼高母和志華那麼願意讓秦楠在他們的家裡工作呢？ 為什麼秦楠答應 (dāying: to agree, consent) 了在他們的家裡工作可是不願意和高志華去看電影呢？
6) 蕭健怎麼了？ 看了蕭健的信，志華有什麼反應 (fǎnyìng: reaction)？ 這跟他平常一樣不一樣？
7) 蕭健的妹妹是什麼樣的人？ 她和她哥哥的關係怎麼樣？
8) 秦楠為什麼去看蕭雲去了？ 她為什麼告訴蕭雲是志華叫她來的呢？
9) 你猜秦楠的舅舅為了什麼急事來上海找秦楠？ 他跟志華說的短短幾句話會讓志華有什麼感覺？

讨论问题：

1） 为什么这个电影到现在才让我们知道秦楠有个孩子呢？
2） 为什么秦楠不跟冬冬一起生活呢？ 你想她在苏州跟冬冬一起的时候会有什么感受 (gǎnshòu: feelings)？
3） 为什么秦楠要趁冬冬没醒的时候赶紧走？ 她这样做结果对她自己和冬冬会怎么样？
4） 志华为什么问秦楠“你怎么经常到苏州去？” 听了秦楠的回答以后，他会怎么想？
5） 为什么高母和志华那么愿意让秦楠在他们的家里工作呢？ 为什么秦楠答应 (dāying: to agree, consent) 了在他们的家里工作可是不愿意和高志华去看电影呢？
6） 肖健怎么了？ 看了肖健的信，志华有什么反应 (fǎnyìng: reaction)？ 这跟他平常一样不一样？
7） 肖健的妹妹是什么样的人？ 她和她哥哥的关系怎么样？
8） 秦楠为什么去看肖云去了？ 她为什么告诉肖云是志华叫她来的呢？
9） 你猜秦楠的舅舅为了什么急事来上海找秦楠？ 他跟志华说的短短几句话会让志华有什么感觉？

SEGMENT VI

Scene 33 ——————————

Meanwhile, back in Xiao Yun's room, Qin Nan and Xiao Yun continue to get acquainted. Qin Nan is very impressed with Xiao Yun's strength and independence.

蕭雲： 我哥哥的母親很早就病死了。
秦楠： 那你的母親呢？
蕭雲： 我媽本來是浙江美院的高才生，和我父親結婚不到三年就離婚了。
秦楠： 爲了什麼？
蕭雲： 因爲我媽是右派。所以她就帶着我搬這兒來了。當時的處境你是可以想像得到的。
秦楠： 那現在呢？
蕭雲： 啊，現在當然不同了。我媽的問題已經徹底改正了。
秦楠： 你爸爸呢？
蕭雲： 他瘋了。
秦楠： 瘋了？
蕭雲： 嗯，他覺得對不起我媽，就到處找啊，鬧啊，要向我媽懺悔。
秦楠： 怎麼，你媽媽不肯諒解他？
蕭雲： 不，在改正前幾年，我媽就死了。(Brief pause. A pet canary chirps.) 啊！你聽，我的小鳥叫得多好聽啊！
秦楠： 那你一個人怎麼生活呢？
蕭雲： 瞧，這是工商行政管理局和公安局批準我篆刻私章的執照，使我的生活有了保障。
(Xiao Yun's courage in facing her difficulties inspires Qin Nan.)

1.	浙江美院	浙江美院	Zhèjiāng Měi-yuàn	short for 浙江美術學院 Zhejiang Art Institute
^2.	高才生	高才生	gāocái-shēng	"highly talented student," outstanding student
*3.	離婚	离婚	lí≠hūn	to divorce
^4.	右派	右派	yòu-pài	Rightist
*5.	搬	搬	bān	to move (large items or one's home)
*6.	想像	想象	xiǎngxiàng	to imagine; imagination
*7.	徹底	彻底	chèdǐ	thorough, thoroughly
*8.	改正	改正	gǎi≠zhèng	to rectify, to correct
^9.	瘋	疯	fēng	insane, to go insane
*10.	到處	到处	dàochù	everywhere

SEGMENT VI

Scene 33 ____________________

Meanwhile, back in Xiao Yun's room, Qin Nan and Xiao Yun continue to get acquainted. Qin Nan is very impressed with Xiao Yun's strength and independence.

肖云： 我哥哥的母亲很早就病死了。
秦楠： 那你的母亲呢？
肖云： 我妈本来是浙江美院的高才生，和我父亲结婚不到三年就离婚了。
秦楠： 为了什么？
肖云： 因为我妈是右派。所以她就带着我搬这儿来了。当时的处境你是可以想象得到的。
秦楠： 那现在呢？
肖云： 啊，现在当然不同了。我妈的问题已经彻底改正了。
秦楠： 你爸爸呢？
肖云： 他疯了。
秦楠： 疯了？
肖云： 嗯，他觉得对不起我妈，就到处找啊，闹啊，要向我妈忏悔。
秦楠： 怎么，你妈妈不肯谅解他？
肖云： 不，在改正前几年，我妈就死了。(Brief pause. A pet canary chirps.) 啊！你听，我的小鸟叫得多好听啊！
秦楠： 那你一个人怎么生活呢？
肖云： 瞧，这是工商行政管理局和公安局批准我篆刻私章的执照，使我的生活有了保障。(Xiao Yun's courage in facing her difficulties inspires Qin Nan.)

---

*11. 鬧	闹	nào	to make a ruckus
12. 懺悔	忏悔	chànhuǐ	to repent, to beg for pardon
^13. 諒解	谅解	liàngjiě	to understand and forgive
14. 工商行政管理局	工商行政管理局	Gōngshāng Xíngzhèng Guǎnlǐ-jú	Bureau of Industrial and Commercial Administration
*15. 公安局	公安局	Gōngān-jú	Public Security Bureau (the police)
*16. 批準	批准	pī≠zhǔn	to approve, to sanction, to permit
17. 篆刻	篆刻	zhuànkē	to carve (seals)
18. 私章	私章	sī-zhāng	私人的圖章, personal chops
*19. 保障	保障	bǎozhèng	guarantee, security

蕭雲： 你説什麼？我怎麼覺得你好像有什麼心事？
秦楠： 啊，不，我是在想你剛才説的話。啊，時間不早了，我走了。以後我會常來看你的。
蕭雲： 嗯。

Scene 34 ————————

Qin Nan goes to Suzhou to find out what the emergency is. Her aunt tells her that Dongdong has pneumonia and has been sent to the hospital.

秦楠： 舅媽，出什麼事了？
舅媽： 冬冬……
秦楠： 冬冬怎麼了？
舅媽： 説是肺炎。昨天夜裡送到公社醫院去了。
秦楠： 啊？

Scene 35 ————————

In the hospital. Dongdong is asleep, with an I.V. bottle hanging by his bed.

冬冬： 媽媽。
秦楠： 媽媽在。媽媽在這兒。

Later, on their way home:

冬冬： 媽媽。

Scene 36 ————————

As Qin Nan rocks Dongdong to sleep, her aunt starts to tell her how miserable Dongdong is whenever Qin Nan leaves.

20.	肺炎	肺炎	fèi-yán	pneumonia
*21.	公社	公社	gōngshè	commune
*22.	醫院	医院	yīyuàn	clinic, hospital

肖云：　你说什么？我怎么觉得你好象有什么心事？
秦楠：　啊，不，我是在想你刚才说的话。啊，时间不早了，我走了。以后我会常来看你的。
肖云：　嗯。

Scene 34 ____________

Qin Nan goes to Suzhou to find out what the emergency is. Her aunt tells her that Dongdong has pneumonia and has been sent to the hospital.

秦楠：　舅妈，出什么事了？
舅妈：　冬冬……
秦楠：　冬冬怎么了？
舅妈：　说是肺炎。昨天夜里送到公社医院去了。
秦楠：　啊？

Scene 35 ____________

In the hospital. Dongdong is asleep, with an I.V. bottle hanging by his bed.

冬冬：　妈妈。
秦楠：　妈妈在。妈妈在这儿。

Later, on their way home:

冬冬：　妈妈。

Scene 36 ____________

As Qin Nan rocks Dongdong to sleep, her aunt starts to tell her how miserable Dongdong is whenever Qin Nan leaves.

舅媽： 每一回，你趁冬冬沒有醒，就偷偷走了。孩子一睜眼見不着娘，就大哭大鬧。至少要有三、四天都不肯好好吃飯。有時候，他一個人站在大門口望着你來的路，哭哭啼啼地要媽媽。

秦楠： 舅媽，別說了。

舅媽： 哎，睡吧。

Scene 37 ——————————

This time, while in Suzhou, Qin Nan resolves to take Dongdong back to Shanghai with her.

舅舅： 小楠這兩天怎麼了？

舅媽： 她打算這次把孩子帶回去。

舅舅： 能帶回去不早就帶回去了！帶回去怎麼辦？ (to Qin Nan) 我可不忍心讓人家把烏七八糟的髒水往你和孩子頭上倒。小楠，不要以爲冬冬生了一場大病，就只顧孩子不顧自己了。

秦楠： 不，舅舅，我不是爲了這個，我應該爲今後想想了。

舅舅： 你怎麼想？

秦楠： 最近我認識了一個女孩兒，她是個殘廢……我不能再這樣下去了，不能！

Scene 38 ——————————

Having been told that Qin Nan will bring Dongdong with her to Shanghai, Qin Nan's father buys a ball and some children's books for Dongdong. Qin Nan and Dongdong are already home by the time her father returns.

秦楠： 爸。

秦父： 你們已經到家了。

---

*23.	偷偷	偷偷	tōutōu	stealthily, on the sly
^24.	睜眼	睜眼	zhēng≠yǎn	to open the eyes
25.	娘	娘	niáng	(regional) 母親
*26.	至少	至少	zhìshǎo	at least
^27.	望	望	wàng	從很遠的地方看, to gaze
^28.	哭哭啼啼	哭哭啼啼	kūkūtítí	to weep and wail endlessly

舅妈： 每一回，你趁冬冬沒有醒，就偷偷走了。孩子一睁眼见不着娘，就大哭大闹。至少要有三、四天都不肯好好吃饭。有时候，他一个人站在大门口望着你来的路，哭哭啼啼地要妈妈。
秦楠： 舅妈，别说了。
舅妈： 哎，睡吧。

Scene 37

This time, while in Suzhou, Qin Nan resolves to take Dongdong back to Shanghai with her.

舅舅： 小楠这两天怎么了？
舅妈： 她打算这次把孩子带回去。
舅舅： 能带回去不早就带回去了！带回去怎么办？ (to Qin Nan) 我可不忍心让人家把乌七八糟的脏水往你和孩子头上倒。小楠，不要以为冬冬生了一场大病，就只顾孩子不顾自己了。
秦楠： 不，舅舅，我不是为了这个，我应该为今后想想了。
舅舅： 你怎么想？
秦楠： 最近我认识了一个女孩儿，她是个残废……我不能再这样下去了，不能！

Scene 38

Having been told that Qin Nan will bring Dongdong with her to Shanghai, Qin Nan's father buys a ball and some children's books for Dongdong. Qin Nan and Dongdong are already home by the time her father returns.

秦楠： 爸。
秦父： 你们已经到家了。

---

^29.	烏七八糟	乌七八糟	wūqī bāzāo	filthy, in a horrible mess
30.	髒水	脏水	zāng-shuǐ	dirty water (used metaphorically here)
*31.	倒	倒	dào	to pour, to dump
*32.	顧	顾	gù	to attend to, to pay attention to, to take care of
^33.	今後	今后	jīnhòu	從今天以後

秦楠：　我們也剛到。
秦父：　今天上午收到你的信，本來想到火車站去接你們的，偏偏下午有課。哎，冬冬呢？
秦楠：　冬冬。
冬冬：　欸。
秦楠：　乖孩子，媽媽怎麼跟你説的？快叫哇！
冬冬：　外公。
秦父：　冬冬，還記得外公嗎？
冬冬：　記得。
秦父：　跟外公親親。來，來！看外公給你買什麼？這是給冬冬買的小皮球，小人書，還有，還有巧克力糖，喜歡不喜歡？
冬冬：　喜歡。
秦楠：　快謝謝外公啊！
冬冬：　謝謝外公。

Scene 39 ————————————

The next day, Qin Nan takes Dongdong with her to work because her father has to go teach and therefore cannot look after him. As soon as the neighbors discover that Qin Nan has a child, they start talking behind her back. Qin Nan, however, has resolved to brave their gossip. Qin Nan and Dongdong meet a neighbor as they walk down the lane.

尤奶奶：小秦呀，這次到蘇州去了不少日子，什麼時候回來的？
秦楠：　昨天回來的。
尤奶奶：喲，這是誰的孩子？
秦楠：　是我的。

---

*34. 偏偏	偏偏	piānpiān	"it just so happens," "it had to be," "as fate would have it" (contrary to what one wished or hoped); (with human subjects) with obstinate contrariness (cf. Grammatical Note VI.3.)
*35. 乖	乖	guāi	(said of children) well-behaved
^36. 叫	叫	jiào	to greet someone by calling his title or

秦楠： 我们也刚到。
秦父： 今天上午收到你的信，本来想到火车站去接你们的，偏偏下午有课。哎，冬冬呢？
秦楠： 冬冬。
冬冬： 欸。
秦楠： 乖孩子，妈妈怎么跟你说的？快叫哇！
冬冬： 外公。
秦父： 冬冬，还记得外公吗？
冬冬： 记得。
秦父： 跟外公亲亲。来，来！看外公给你买什么？这是给冬冬买的小皮球，小人书，还有，还有巧克力糖，喜欢不喜欢？
冬冬： 喜欢。
秦楠： 快谢谢外公啊！
冬冬： 谢谢外公。

Scene 39 ————————————

The next day, Qin Nan takes Dongdong with her to work because her father has to go teach and therefore cannot look after him. As soon as the neighbors discover that Qin Nan has a child, they start talking behind her back. Qin Nan, however, has resolved to brave their gossip. Qin Nan and Dongdong meet a neighbor as they walk down the lane.

尤奶奶：小秦呀，这次到苏州去了不少日子，什么时候回来的？
秦楠： 昨天回来的。
尤奶奶：哟，这是谁的孩子？
秦楠： 是我的。

---

				kinship term (considered by the Chinese to be a respectful thing for a child to do when meeting a more senior relative or teacher, etc.)
^37.	外公	外公	wài-gōng	grandpa (maternal)
^38.	親親	亲亲	qīnqin	to give a little kiss (on the cheek)
39.	皮球	皮球	píqiú	ball (toy, usually made of rubber)
40.	小人書	小人书	xiǎorén-shū	picture-story book
^41.	巧克力糖	巧克力糖	qiǎokèlì-táng	chocolate candy

尤奶奶：你，你的孩子啊？！
秦楠： 嗯。冬冬，叫尤奶奶。
冬冬： 尤—奶—奶—。
尤奶奶：哎。
秦楠： (to Dongdong) 走。

Granny You motions to a neighbor to come over.

尤奶奶：哎，丁大媽！

Two neighbor women come over to Granny You. The three whisper in a huddle.

尤奶奶：真怪！從來沒聽說她嫁過人，怎麼一下子會有這麼大孩子啦？
鄰居： 野種，肯定是野種！
尤奶奶：對，是野種！

*42. 嫁	嫁	jià	to marry (said of a woman, who usually marries "out")
*43. 一下子	一下子	yíxiàzi	suddenly, in an instant, in a short time (cf. Grammatical Note VI.5.)

討論問題：

1) 請談談蕭雲父母的遭遇 (zāoyù: bitter experience)，並談談這個對蕭雲的影響。為什麼蕭雲的父親為了他母親是個“右派”就跟她離婚了呢？
2) 蕭雲父母親的離婚對她和她哥哥蕭健有什麼影響 (yǐngxiǎng: influence, effect) 呢？ 她父親瘋了以後就沒有再和他們來往了嗎？
3) 在第三十七幕，秦楠說“我應該為今後想想了……我不能再這樣下去了。” 她的“意思”是什麼呢？ 她想過了些什麼？
4) 冬冬見到他的外公很高興嗎？ 他願意不願意叫外公？ 為什麼？ 他願意叫尤奶奶嗎？為什麼？
5) 你想秦楠的鄰居們對一個沒有結過婚而有孩子的女人的看法在中國是不是很典型 (diǎnxíng: typical) 的？ 在美國呢？

尤奶奶：你，你的孩子啊？！
秦楠：　嗯。冬冬，叫尤奶奶。
冬冬：　尤—奶—奶—。
尤奶奶：哎。
秦楠：　(to Dongdong) 走。

Granny You motions to a neighbor to come over.

尤奶奶：哎，丁大妈！

Two neighbor women come over to Granny You. The three whisper in a huddle.

尤奶奶：真怪！从来没听说她嫁过人，怎么一下子会有这么大孩子啦？
邻居：　野种，肯定是野种！
尤奶奶：对，是野种！

44.	野種	野种	yězhǒng	bastard (lit. "wild seed")
*45.	肯定	肯定	kěndìng	for sure

讨论问题：

1) 请谈谈肖云父母的遭遇 (zāoyù: bitter experience)，并谈谈这个对肖云的影响。为什么肖云的父亲为了他母亲是个“右派”就跟她离婚了呢？
2) 肖云父母亲的离婚对她和她哥哥肖健有什么影响 (yǐngxiǎng: influence, effect) 呢？ 她父亲疯了以后就没有再和他们来往了吗？
3) 在第三十七幕，秦楠说“我应该为今后想想了……我不能再这样下去了。” 她的“意思”是什么呢？ 她想过了些什么？
4) 冬冬见到他的外公很高兴吗？ 他愿意不愿意叫外公？ 为什么？ 他愿意叫尤奶奶吗？为什么？
5) 你想秦楠的邻居们对一个没有结过婚而有孩子的女人的看法在中国是不是很典型 (diǎnxíng: typical) 的？ 在美国呢？

SEGMENT VII

Scene 40 ——————————

Zhihua reads a letter written by Maomao's girlfriend which Maomao has presumably shown him. Then Zhihua gives Maomao some advice.

高志華：這信寫得不錯嘛，你幹嘛不去？你不要把人看死了，一個月不見，你就不想？
毛毛：　想當然也想了，不過，你説的也對，一個人活着要有志氣。這回呀，我要好好考驗考驗她啦。

Qin Nan brings Dongdong to Zhihua's house to work. Zhihua is happy to see Qin Nan, but he is also shocked to see Qin Nan with a child.

高志華：喲，秦楠回來啦？
秦楠：　你們好！
高志華：你去了這麼多天。差不多天天有顧客來找你。
秦楠：　我也急死了。
高志華：這孩子……
秦楠：　叫叔叔。
冬冬：　叔叔。
高志華：這是誰家的孩子？
冬冬：　媽媽，我要看小人書。
秦楠：　到屋裡媽媽拿給你看。
高志華：這是你的孩子？
秦楠：　對，是我的孩子。上午爸爸有課，我就把他帶來了。走，乖乖地看書，別鬧啊！

Qin Nan begins to sew. Zhihua is obviously unsettled. He comes into the house and talks to Dongdong.

---

^1. V-死	V-死	V-sǐ	to be inflexible or rigid in V-ing (cf. Grammatical Note VII.1.)
*2. 考驗	考验	kǎoyàn	to test (by trial); test, trial

SEGMENT VII

Scene 40 ——————————

Zhihua reads a letter written by Maomao's girlfriend which Maomao has presumably shown him. Then Zhihua gives Maomao some advice.

高志华：这信写得不错嘛，你干嘛不去？你不要把人看死了，一个月不见，你就不想？
毛毛：　想当然也想了，不过，你说的也对，一个人活着要有志气。这回呀，我要好好考验考验她啦。

Qin Nan brings Dongdong to Zhihua's house to work. Zhihua is happy to see Qin Nan, but he is also shocked to see Qin Nan with a child.

高志华：哟，秦楠回来啦？
秦楠：　你们好！
高志华：你去了这么多天。差不多天天有顾客来找你。
秦楠：　我也急死了。
高志华：这孩子……
秦楠：　叫叔叔。
冬冬：　叔叔。
高志华：这是谁家的孩子？
冬冬：　妈妈，我要看小人书。
秦楠：　到屋里妈妈拿给你看。
高志华：这是你的孩子？
秦楠：　对，是我的孩子。上午爸爸有课，我就把他带来了。走，乖乖地看书，别闹啊！

Qin Nan begins to sew. Zhihua is obviously unsettled. He comes into the house and talks to Dongdong.

---

*3. SV-死了	SV-死了	SV-sǐle	"...to death," extremely... (cf. Grammatical Note VII.1.)
^4. 叔叔	叔叔	shūshu	"uncle," familiar address used by children for youngish men

高志華：你叫什麼名字？
冬冬： 冬冬。
高志華：你爸爸呢？
冬冬： 我沒有爸爸。我爸爸死了。

Presently, Zhihua's mother walks in. At first she is very happy to see Qin Nan, but she too is shocked when she finds out about Dongdong.

高母： 哎，小秦，回來啦？
秦楠： 高媽媽！
高母： 真想你呀！
秦楠： 您今天休息？
高母： 啊，這是誰家的孩子，這麼乖，一個人在這兒看小人書啊？
秦楠： 我的孩子。
高母： 什麼？你的？你的孩子？
秦楠： 是的，是我的孩子。冬冬，叫奶奶。
冬冬： 奶奶。

Zhihua's mother is so flustered that she becomes absent-minded.

高母： 乖，乖，他叫什麼名字？
秦楠： 叫冬冬。
高母： 冬冬？挺好聽的，幾歲了？
秦楠： 五歲了。
高母： 你已經有這麼大的孩子啦？你忙，你忙。

Zhihua is so agitated that he becomes absent-minded and cannot find his matches, which are right in his hand.

秦楠： 找什麼？
高志華：我的火柴呢？
秦楠： 不是在你手上嗎？

---

5. 你忙	你忙	nǐ máng	"go ahead with your busyness" (don't let me keep you from your work)
^6. 火柴	火柴	huǒchái	matches

高志华：你叫什么名字？
冬冬：　冬冬。
高志华：你爸爸呢？
冬冬：　我沒有爸爸。我爸爸死了。

Presently, Zhihua's mother walks in. At first she is very happy to see Qin Nan, but she too is shocked when she finds out about Dongdong.

高母：　哎，小秦，回来啦？
秦楠：　高妈妈！
高母：　真想你呀！
秦楠：　您今天休息？
高母：　啊，这是谁家的孩子，这么乖，一个人在这儿看小人书啊？
秦楠：　我的孩子。
高母：　什么？你的？你的孩子？
秦楠：　是的，是我的孩子。冬冬，叫奶奶。
冬冬：　奶奶。

Zhihua's mother is so flustered that she becomes absent-minded.

高母：　乖，乖，他叫什么名字？
秦楠：　叫冬冬。
高母：　冬冬？挺好听的，几岁了？
秦楠：　五岁了。
高母：　你已经有这么大的孩子啦？你忙，你忙。

Zhihua is so agitated that he becomes absent-minded and cannot find his matches, which are right in his hand.

秦楠：　找什么？
高志华：我的火柴呢？
秦楠：　不是在你手上吗？

Scene 41 ————————

The fact that Qin Nan has a child puts Zhihua in a dilemma. Not knowing what to do, he writes to Yinghua for advice. Later, as Yinghua is training at a gymnasium, she is called over to get a letter, which turns out to be from her brother.

運動員：高英華…… (hands a letter to Yinghua) 喏。
高英華：謝謝！
高志華的信：小妹，我要告訴你一件意想不到的事：秦楠是個沒有丈夫而有個五歲孩子的母親！今天我才明白秦楠平時爲什麼那麼沈默和憂鬱。現在外面對她有些流言。媽媽也好多天不講話了。小妹，真心愛一個人，碰上這種情況，究竟應該怎樣做？

Scene 42 ————————

Qin Nan is leaving the Gaos' homes with Dongdong after a day's work.

秦楠： 高媽媽，我們回去了。
高母： 啊，吃了晚飯再走吧。
秦楠： 不啦，冬冬，跟奶奶再見。
冬冬： 奶奶再見。
高母： 再見。再見。
....
志華，吃飯了。
....

After a long silence at the dinner table, Zhihua's mother impatiently puts a piece of meat in his bowl. Since Dongdong's appearance, Zhihua's mother's attitude toward Qin Nan has changed. Although earlier she tried to make a match between Zhihua and Qin Nan, she now warns him not to get involved with Qin Nan.

---

7. 喏	喏	nuò	"here/there you are" (accompanied by eye or hand gesture); (expletive in front of a phrase pointing out something that is right there or is obvious), "there," "look"
^8. 意想不到	意想不到	yìxiǎng búdào	想不到, unexpected, surprising

Scene 41 ————————

The fact that Qin Nan has a child puts Zhihua in a dilemma. Not knowing what to do, he writes to Yinghua for advice. Later, as Yinghua is training at a gymnasium, she is called over to get a letter, which turns out to be from her brother.

运动员：高英华…… (hands a letter to Yinghua) 喏。
高英华：谢谢！
高志华的信：小妹，我要告诉你一件意想不到的事：秦楠是个没有丈夫而有个五岁孩子的母亲！今天我才明白秦楠平时为什么那么沈默和忧郁。现在外面对她有些流言。妈妈也好多天不讲话了。小妹，真心爱一个人，碰上这种情况，究竟应该怎样做？

Scene 42 ————————

Qin Nan is leaving the Gaos' homes with Dongdong after a day's work.

秦楠： 高妈妈，我们回去了。
高母： 啊，吃了晚饭再走吧。
秦楠： 不啦，冬冬，跟奶奶再见。
冬冬： 奶奶再见。
高母： 再见。再见。
....
志华，吃饭了。
....

After a long silence at the dinner table, Zhihua's mother impatiently puts a piece of meat in his bowl. Since Dongdong's appearance, Zhihua's mother's attitude toward Qin Nan has changed. Although earlier she tried to make a match between Zhihua and Qin Nan, she now warns him not to get involved with Qin Nan.

---

*9.	丈夫	丈夫	zhàngfu	husband
*10.	沈默	沈默	chénmò	reticent, dejectedly silent
^11.	憂鬱	忧郁	yōuyù	melancholy, heavy-hearted
^12.	流言	流言	liú-yán	rumors, gossip
*13.	碰上	碰上	pèng≠shang	to encounter

高母：　媽不能不提醒你一聲兒。
高志華：什麼？
高母：　你是沒結過婚的人，千萬不能糊塗哇！
高志華：我的事，您別管。
高母：　我怎麼能不管呢？你搞得清那孩子是怎麼回事嗎？聽人家外邊說……
高志華：那些人是吃飽了飯沒事幹！
高母：　哎呀，吃飯，小祖宗！

Scene 43 ——————————

The scene shifts to the dinner table at the Qins' home. Qin Nan's father is troubled by the neighbors' gossip about Qin Nan.

秦父：　你怎麼吃這麼少哇？
秦楠：　我不餓。
秦父：　這兩天你怎麼了？
秦楠：　沒什麼！

Mr. Qin goes to a back room and calls Qin Nan over so he can speak to her privately.

秦父：　小楠，你來。
秦楠：　(to Dongdong) 乖，自己吃。

Qin Nan leaves the dinner table and goes to her father.

秦父：　自從冬冬回來以後，這兩天外面有些流言蜚語吧？你怎麼想？

---

*14.	提醒	提醒	tíxǐng	to remind, to warn, to alert
^15.	V... 一聲(兒)	V... 一声(儿)	V... yì shēng(r)	to briefly or succinctly voice something (without belaboring the point)
*16.	糊塗	糊涂	hútu	muddle-headed, confused
^17.	吃飽了飯沒事幹	吃饱了饭沒事干	chī≠bǎole fàn méi shì gàn	"to have filled the belly and have nothing to do," to have nothing better to do (than to engage in something frivolous or meaningless)

高母：　妈不能不提醒你一声儿。
高志华：什么？
高母：　你是沒结过婚的人，千万不能糊涂哇！
高志华：我的事，您别管。
高母：　我怎么能不管呢？你搞得清那孩子是怎么回事吗？听人家外边说……
高志华：那些人是吃饱了饭沒事干！
高母：　哎呀，吃饭，小祖宗！

Scene 43 ——————————

The scene shifts to the dinner table at the Qins' home. Qin Nan's father is troubled by the neighbors' gossip about Qin Nan.

秦父：　你怎么吃这么少哇？
秦楠：　我不饿。
秦父：　这两天你怎么了？
秦楠：　沒什么！

Mr. Qin goes to a back room and calls Qin Nan over so he can speak to her privately.

秦父：　小楠，你来。
秦楠：　(to Dongdong) 乖，自己吃。

Qin Nan leaves the dinner table and goes to her father.

秦父：　自从冬冬回来以后，这两天外面有些流言蜚语吧？你怎么想？

---

18. 小祖宗　小祖宗　xiǎo zǔzōng　"little ancestor" (to whom one must pay respects) (an ironic term used to scold someone in exasperation)
19. 流言蜚語　流言蜚语　liú-yán fēi-yǔ　malicious gossip (cf. 流言, Note VII.12)

秦楠： 爸，你自己身體也不好，不要再爲了我……

秦父： 不，你不要考慮我。我是不怕人家指責我這個做父親的。問題是，今天我們雖然是社會主義國家，可舊的傳統觀念還很嚴重，特別像你現在這樣的處境，我就怕你……

秦楠： 爸，爲了帶冬冬回來，我想了好幾個晚上。現在既然把他帶回來了，流言蜚語也好，造謠中傷也好，我都不怕。我心靈上受過創傷，我不能把痛苦加在孩子的身上。冬冬是我的兒子，他有權力和他母親在一起。我是他的媽媽，我有責任愛護他。

秦父： 孩子，你能這樣想，我就放心了。

Qin Nan cries as Dongdong peeps from behind a partition.

Scene 44 ————————————

One day Dongdong and another boy in the neighborhood get into a fight over Dongdong's ball. Qin Nan comes and pulls them apart. An altercation between the adults ensues.

冬冬： 啊，我的球，我的球！

男男： 什麼你的球，我要玩兒！我偏要玩兒！

冬冬： 我的球，這是我的球。

男男： 什麼你的球？我要玩兒。我要玩兒嘛！你的球，我要玩兒！

Qin Nan rushes over.

秦楠： 哎，好好玩兒。怎麼打起來了？快起來，你也起來！

男男： 我要玩兒。我要玩兒！

冬冬： 我不要！

秦楠： 別打了，別打了，快放手！

---

*20.	考慮	考虑	kǎolǜ	to consider
21.	指責	指责	zhǐzé	to fault, to censure, to criticize
*22.	做…的	做…的	zuò...de	one who is in the role of...(做父親的: one who is a father)
*23.	社會主義	社会主义	shèhuì-zhǔyì	socialism
*24.	傳統	传统	chuántǒng	tradition
25.	嚴重	严重	yánzhòng	grave, serious
*26.	既然	既然	jìrán	since, given the fact that... (cf. Grammatical Note VII.6.)

秦楠： 爸，你自己身体也不好，不要再为了我……
秦父： 不，你不要考虑我。我是不怕人家指责我这个做父亲的。问题是，今天我们虽然是社会主义国家，可旧的传统观念还很严重，特别象你现在这样的处境，我就怕你……
秦楠： 爸，为了带冬冬回来，我想了好几个晚上。现在既然把他带回来了，流言蜚语也好，造谣中伤也好，我都不怕。我心灵上受过创伤，我不能把痛苦加在孩子的身上。冬冬是我的儿子，他有权力和他母亲在一起。我是他的妈妈，我有责任爱护他。
秦父： 孩子，你能这样想，我就放心了。

Qin Nan cries as Dongdong peeps from behind a partition.

Scene 44 ————————————

One day Dongdong and another boy in the neighborhood get into a fight over Dongdong's ball. Qin Nan comes and pulls them apart. An altercation between the adults ensues.

冬冬： 啊，我的球，我的球！
男男： 什么你的球，我要玩儿！我偏要玩儿！
冬冬： 我的球，这是我的球。
男男： 什么你的球？我要玩儿。我要玩儿嘛！你的球，我要玩儿！

Qin Nan rushes over.

秦楠： 哎，好好玩儿。怎么打起来了？快起来，你也起来！
男男： 我要玩儿。我要玩儿！
冬冬： 我不要！
秦楠： 别打了，别打了，快放手！

27.	造謠中傷	造谣中伤	zào≠yáo zhòng≠shāng	to fabricate rumors and spread slander
^28.	心靈	心灵	xīnlíng	heart and soul, spirit
^29.	創傷	创伤	chuāngshāng	wound
*30.	愛護	爱护	àihù	to love and protect, to cherish, to take good care of
*31.	偏要	偏要	piānyào	to insist on..., to demand obstinately

冬冬： 媽媽，他打我，他搶我的球！

男男： 你的球？你是野種！野種！

Granny You, Zhou Dama and other neighbors gather. A crowd forms.

冬冬： 你才是野種！野種！

尤奶奶：哎，你們孩子怎麼能這麼罵人哪！誰是野種？誰是野種？我們孩子的爸爸媽媽可都是明媒正娶的。說我們家是野種，到底誰是野種？你說！你們家的孩子才是真正的野種哪！

周大媽：孩子吵架轉眼就沒事了，大人何必跟着慪氣呢？

Pandemonium breaks out, everyone talks at once.

鄰居們：就是嘛！…是她的孩子先罵人的。這老太太怎麼那麼不講理啊？

周大媽：你先帶孩子回去吧！…你也少說兩句了…好了，好了。別說了，走走走。

32.	明媒正娶	明媒正娶	míng méi zhèng qǔ	"openly introduced by a go-between and properly married," to be properly and legally married
*33.	吵架	吵架	chǎo≠jià	to quarrel

討論問題：

1） 小高在第十五幕給毛毛的勸告有沒有效？ 毛毛要怎麼樣考驗考驗"她"呢？
2） 小高和高母第一次看到冬冬，他們有什麼反應 (fǎnyìng: reaction)？ 你猜他們心裡怎麼想？
3） 你想冬冬的爸爸是真的死了嗎？
4） 小高現在對秦楠的態度 (tàidu: attitude) 怎麼樣了？ 外面的流言對他有什麼影響沒有？
5） 高母提醒小高"千萬不能糊塗。" 她說的"糊塗"是什麼意思？ 你想小高真的會糊塗嗎？
6） 秦楠把冬冬帶到上海以後，生活上順利 (shùnlì: smooth-going) 不順利？ 從哪一點我們能看出秦楠是個有勇氣的人？
7） 男男怎麼"知道"冬冬是"野種"呢？ 冬冬知道不知道"野種"是什麼意思？ 他怎麼也罵男男是"野種"呢？

冬冬： 妈妈，他打我，他抢我的球！

男男： 你的球？你是野种！野种！

Granny You, Zhou Dama and other neighbors gather. A crowd forms.

冬冬： 你才是野种！野种！

尤奶奶：哎，你们孩子怎么能这么骂人哪！谁是野种？谁是野种？我们孩子的爸爸妈妈可都是明媒正娶的。说我们家是野种，到底谁是野种？你说！你们家的孩子才是真正的野种哪！

周大妈：孩子吵架转眼就没事了，大人何必跟着怄气呢？

Pandemonium breaks out, everyone talks at once.

邻居们：就是嘛！…是她的孩子先骂人的。这老太太怎么那么不讲理啊？

周大妈：你先带孩子回去吧！…你也少说两句了…好了，好了。别说了，走走走。

^34. 轉眼	转眼	zhuǎn≠yǎn	in a "turn of the eye," in a flash, in a twinkling
*35. 何必	何必	hébì	(rhetorical) why must...? (cf. Grammatical Note VII.9.)
36. 慪氣	怄气	òu≠qì	to be irritated, to sulk

讨论问题：

1) 小高在第十五幕给毛毛的劝告有没有效？ 毛毛要怎么样考验考验"她"呢？
2) 小高和高母第一次看到冬冬，他们有什么反应 (fǎnyìng: reaction)？ 你猜他们心里怎么想？
3) 你想冬冬的爸爸是真的死了吗？
4) 小高现在对秦楠的态度 (tàidu: attitude) 怎么样了？ 外面的流言对他有什么影响没有？
5) 高母提醒小高"千万不能糊涂。" 她说的"糊涂"是什么意思？ 你想小高真的会糊涂吗？
6) 秦楠把冬冬带到上海以后，生活上顺利 (shùnlì: smooth-going) 不顺利？ 从哪一点我们能看出秦楠是个有勇气的人？
7) 男男怎么"知道"冬冬是"野种"呢？ 冬冬知道不知道"野种"是什么意思？ 他怎么也骂男男是"野种"呢？

SEGMENT VIII

Scene 45

Qin Nan takes Dongdong home and spanks him even though he was not at fault. She tells him not to play with the boy.

秦楠：　上次他已經打過你，叫你不要跟他玩兒，為什麼不聽媽的話？為什麼不聽……為什麼不聽話？

秦父：　你幹什麼，你？

秦楠：　以後不許你玩兒球啦！

冬冬：　我又沒跟他玩，他搶我球，還罵我野種！

秦父：　誰欺負你了？

冬冬：　男男，還有尤奶奶！

秦父：　太不像話了！

秦楠：　爸！

秦父：　我去找街道黨委。

秦楠：　爸，算了！

秦父：　不管怎麼說，對孩子怎麼能這樣呢？街道黨委會管的！

He pushes past Qin Nan and goes off.

Feeling guilty about spanking Dongdong, Qin Nan holds him in her arms and cries.

Scene 46

Zhihua is alone by the waterfront puffing away at a cigarette. He is obviously troubled by something.

That evening, Qin Nan goes to the home of Zhou Dama, who has invited her over to comfort her and to give her some advice. At Zhou Dama's door...

---

*1.	欺負	欺负	qīfu	to bully, to take advantage of
˜2.	不像話	不象话	bú xiànghuà	unseemly, outrageous

SEGMENT VIII

Scene 45 ——————————

Qin Nan takes Dongdong home and spanks him even though he was not at fault. She tells him not to play with the boy.

秦楠： 上次他已经打过你，叫你不要跟他玩儿，为什么不听妈的话？为什么不听……为什么不听话？
秦父： 你干什么，你？
秦楠： 以后不许你玩儿球啦！
冬冬： 我又沒跟他玩，他抢我球，还骂我野种！
秦父： 谁欺负你了？
冬冬： 男男，还有尤奶奶！
秦父： 太不象话了！
秦楠： 爸！
秦父： 我去找街道党委。
秦楠： 爸，算了！
秦父： 不管怎么说，对孩子怎么能这样呢？街道党委会管的！

He pushes past Qin Nan and goes off.
Feeling guilty about spanking Dongdong, Qin Nan holds him in her arms and cries.

Scene 46 ——————————

Zhihua is alone by the waterfront puffing away at a cigarette. He is obviously troubled by something.

That evening, Qin Nan goes to the home of Zhou Dama, who has invited her over to comfort her and to give her some advice. At Zhou Dama's door...

---

^3. 街道黨委	街道党委	jiēdào dǎng-wěi	neighborhood Party committee (a unit of the Communist Party that maintains community order and welfare)

周大媽：孩子睡了？
秦楠：　剛睡。
周大媽：你進來，進來。
秦楠：　您找我有什麼事？

Maomao is studying English. Zhou Dama hints to him to go elsewhere so she and Qin Nan can speak in private.

周大媽：哎，毛毛。
毛毛：　啊，好。 (picks up his books and leaves.)
周大媽：坐吧，坐吧。小秦哪，我都憋了好些日子了，一直想找你談談，可有些話……
秦楠：　您有話儘管說好了。
周大媽：咱們娘倆今天是關着房門說話，我有什麼說什麼，你有什麼也別瞞着我。我想問你，你是不是上了男人的當了？
秦楠：　那都是過去的事了，一時也說不清楚。不過，您相信我，我沒做過虧心的事。沒有！
周大媽：是，是，我是相信你。你是個好姑娘。可你以後的日子怎麼辦哪？還拖着個孩子。
秦楠：　現在我把孩子帶在身邊，和爸爸一起過，我覺得很好。
周大媽：哎呀，怎麼能這麼想呢？你還年輕。再說，外面七嘴八舌的，我真替你難過。
秦楠：　日子長了，他們說膩了，也就不說了。
周大媽：小秦哪，你不知道，一個女人沒有丈夫活在世上，苦得很，累得很。
(Qin Nan starts to cry; Zhou Dama's eyes also well up. Zhou Dama takes a wash cloth, wipes her own eyes, then hands it over to Qin Nan.)
有件事我想提一提。我覺得小高這孩子不錯，人老實，能幹，待人又厚道。他在我面前不只一次提到你，說你人好。他心裡想什麼……我知道。
秦楠：　小高對我是不錯，他媽媽對我也很好。不過，自從冬冬來了以後，…怎麼說呢？

4.	憋	憋	biē	to hold in or suppress (anger, excitement, etc.)
5.	有話儘管說	有话尽管说	yǒu huà jǐnguǎn shuō	to say whatever is on one's mind without holding back (cf. 儘管, Note I.7)
6.	娘倆	娘俩	niáng liǎ	two women, woman-to-woman
*7.	瞞	瞒	mán	to hide (the truth or facts) from
*8.	上當	上当	shàng≠dàng	to be duped, to be taken advantage of (by...) (cf. Grammatical Note VIII.2.)
*9.	虧心	亏心	kuīxīn	unconscionable, shameful
*10.	拖	拖	tuō	to drag along, to delay

周大妈：孩子睡了？
秦楠：　刚睡。
周大妈：你进来，进来。
秦楠：　您找我有什么事？

Maomao is studying English. Zhou Dama hints to him to go elsewhere so she and Qin Nan can speak in private.

周大妈：哎，毛毛。
毛毛：　啊，好。 (picks up his books and leaves.)
周大妈：坐吧，坐吧。小秦哪，我都憋了好些日子了，一直想找你谈谈，可有些话……
秦楠：　您有话尽管说好了。
周大妈：咱们娘俩今天是关着房门说话，我有什么说什么，你有什么也别瞒着我。我想问你，你是不是上了男人的当了？
秦楠：　那都是过去的事了，一时也说不清楚。不过，您相信我，我沒做过亏心的事。沒有！
周大妈：是，是，我是相信你。你是个好姑娘。可你以后的日子怎么办哪？还拖着个孩子。
秦楠：　现在我把孩子带在身边，和爸爸一起过，我觉得很好。
周大妈：哎呀，怎么能这么想呢？你还年轻。再说，外面七嘴八舌的，我真替你难过。
秦楠：　日子长了，他们说腻了，也就不说了。
周大妈：小秦哪，你不知道，一个女人沒有丈夫活在世上，苦得很，累得很。

(Qin Nan starts to cry; Zhou Dama's eyes also well up. Zhou Dama takes a wash cloth, wipes her own eyes, then hands it over to Qin Nan.)

有件事我想提一提。我觉得小高这孩子不错，人老实，能干，待人又厚道。他在我面前不只一次提到你，说你人好。他心里想什么……我知道。

秦楠：　小高对我是不错，他妈妈对我也很好。不过，自从冬冬来了以后，…怎么说呢？

---

*11.	年輕	年轻	niánqīng	lit., "light in years," young
12.	七嘴八舌	七嘴八舌	qīzuǐ bāshé	"seven mouths and eight tongues," wagging tongues, many speakers vying to be heard
^13.	日子長了	日子长了	rìzi chángle	過了很多天（很久）以後
*14.	V-膩	V-腻	V-nì	to grow tired of V-ing
^15.	世	世	shì	世界
*16.	累	累	lèi	exhausting, exhausted
*17.	老實	老实	lǎoshí	sincere, honest, "solid," reliable
^18.	待人	待人	dài≠rén	to treat people (in a certain way)
^19.	厚道	厚道	hòudào	sincere and kind

周大媽：噢，這也難怪嘛。人家就只有這麼一個寶貝兒子。
秦楠： 周媽媽，毛毛還在外面等你呢。
周大媽：別管他。我的意見是，只要小高他本人同意，……
秦楠： 啊，我還要去趕裁兩件衣服，我走了。
周大媽：下午尤大媽的事不要放在心上，街道黨委批評她們了。孩子，別再苦自己了。小高的事，你要考慮。

Scene 47 ——————————

One day Qin Nan is taking a customer's measurements at her sewing stall when Dongdong runs out of the house and interrupts her work.

冬冬： 媽媽，這是好人還是壞人啊？
秦楠： 是好人，玩兒去吧。

Dongdong is curious about the tools that Zhihua uses. He wants to touch them but Zhihua stops him.

高志華：哎，別動，髒！
秦楠： 冬冬走開！叔叔幹活兒呢，啊？自己到屋裡看小人書去。
郵遞員：高志華，信！

(Brief dialogue between Qin Nan and customer, irrelevant to plot.)
The letter is from Xiao Jian, who has written to thank Zhihua for taking care of his sister.

信： 小高，接到我妹妹的來信，知道你經常去照顧她。我非常感動。你的友情使我更堅定了重新作人的決心。蕭健。

*20.	難怪	难怪	nánguài	(adv.) "difficult to blame," cannot blame, understandable; no wonder
*21.	寶貝	宝贝	bǎobèi	precious
^22.	裁	裁	cái	to cut (cloth for making a garment)
^23.	放在心上	放在心上	fàng zài xīn-shàng	"to hold in one's heart," to beset one's mind, to worry about
*24.	批評	批评	pīpíng	to criticize
*25.	動	动	dòng	to touch, to move

周大妈：噢，这也难怪嘛。人家就只有这么一个宝贝儿子。
秦楠：　周妈妈，毛毛还在外面等你呢。
周大妈：别管他。我的意见是，只要小高他本人同意，……
秦楠：　啊，我还要去赶裁两件衣服，我走了。
周大妈：下午尤大妈的事不要放在心上，街道党委批评她们了。孩子，别再苦自己了。小高的事，你要考虑。

Scene 47 ———————————

One day Qin Nan is taking a customer's measurements at her sewing stall when Dongdong runs out of the house and interrupts her work.

冬冬：　妈妈，这是好人还是坏人啊？
秦楠：　是好人，玩儿去吧。

Dongdong is curious about the tools that Zhihua uses. He wants to touch them but Zhihua stops him.

高志华：哎，别动，脏！
秦楠：　冬冬走开！叔叔干活儿呢，啊？自己到屋里看小人书去。
邮递员：高志华，信！

(Brief dialogue between Qin Nan and customer, irrelevant to plot.)
The letter is from Xiao Jian, who has written to thank Zhihua for taking care of his sister.

信：　小高，接到我妹妹的来信，知道你经常去照顾她。我非常感动。你的友情使我更坚定了重新作人的决心。肖健。

---

*26. 走開	走开	zǒu≠kāi	to walk away, get away; "get away from here!"
*27. 照顧	照顾	zhàogù	to take care of, to care for, to give special consideration to
*28. 感動	感动	gǎndòng	to move (the emotions); moved, touched
^29. 友情	友情	yǒu-qíng	sincere friendship
*30. 堅定	坚定	jiāndìng	firm, resolute; to be determined
*31. 決心	决心	juéxīn	determination (cf. 下决心, Note III.15)

Zhihua is puzzled by the letter because he has not taken care of Xiao Yun. He rushes to the desk, takes the first letter from Xiao Jian out of the drawer and finds Xiao Yun's address. He decides to see her and find out what lies behind the message.

高志華：(to himself) 大廠西小弄九號。

Scene 48 ————————

When Zhihua arrives at Xiao Yun's place, a painting class is in progress in Xiao Yun's room.

老師： 要理解作者的意圖。雖然有枯枝，有殘雪，但畢竟是春天來了，萬花繁榮的季節很快就會來到。

Zhihua knocks on the door.

蕭雲： 請進來，是要刻圖章嗎？
高志華：不，不，你們忙，我等會兒。
老師： 那好，今天就到這兒吧。下星期早點來。
中： 蕭雲，我們走了，再見！
蕭雲： 再見！

Scene 49 ————————

Zhihua is shocked to discover that Xiao Yun is handicapped.

高志華：你是蕭雲？
蕭雲： 是啊！
高志華：我是高志華。

32.	意圖	意图	yìtú	intention
33.	枯枝	枯枝	kū-zhī	withered branches
34.	殘雪	残雪	cán-xuě	remnant of snow
35.	畢竟	毕竟	bìjìng	到底，究竟，after all, all in all

Zhihua is puzzled by the letter because he has not taken care of Xiao Yun. He rushes to the desk, takes the first letter from Xiao Jian out of the drawer and finds Xiao Yun's address. He decides to see her and find out what lies behind the message.

高志华：(to himself) 大厂西小弄九号。

Scene 48 ——————————

When Zhihua arrives at Xiao Yun's place, a painting class is in progress in Xiao Yun's room.

老师：　要理解作者的意图。虽然有枯枝，有残雪，但毕竟是春天来了，万花繁荣的季节很快就会来到。

Zhihua knocks on the door.

肖云：　请进来，是要刻图章吗？
高志华：不，不，你们忙，我等会儿。
老师：　那好，今天就到这儿吧。下星期早点来。
中：　　肖云，我们走了，再见！
肖云：　再见！

Scene 49 ——————————

Zhihua is shocked to discover that Xiao Yun is handicapped.

高志华：你是肖云？
肖云：　是啊！
高志华：我是高志华。

36.	萬花繁榮	万花繁荣	wàn-huā fánróng	"ten thousand flowers flourishing," everything in bloom
^37.	季節	季节	jìjié	season

蕭雲：　你就是高志華。哎呀，來，快請坐吧！
高志華：不，不，不，你不要起來！不要起來！
蕭雲：　應該說，我們早就認識了。
高志華：我不知道你是……真對不起，一直沒有來看你！
蕭雲：　那有什麼，你讓秦楠來關心我，不是一樣嗎？

Zhihua is shocked at this revelation.

高志華：什麼，秦楠？
蕭雲：　是啊，她每個星期都來看我，幫我洗衣服，洗被子，收拾房間。對了，還買了許多我喜歡的書和畫。喏，這兩枝筆，也是她送給我的。我非常感謝你讓我認識了秦楠。我跟她深談了兩次，我才發現她是那麼純正，那麼善良。我想你一定很了解她。命運對她太不公平了。她心靈上有那麼深的創傷，可還是那樣地關心我，我心裡感到溫暖極了。哎，你坐呀！

Zhihua walks over to the portrait of Xiao Jian.

高志華：你常給你哥哥寫信嗎？
蕭雲：　寫，一個星期寫一封。我鼓勵他，希望他能夠早點兒回來。你關心我的事，我也告訴他了。不過，我沒提秦楠，她叫我不要告訴他。
高志華：那你有什麼事要我做嗎？
蕭雲：　沒有。我生活得很好。居委會很照顧我。我還有許多青年朋友。怎麼，秦楠沒有告訴過你？
高志華：啊？告訴了。(Here Zhihua tells a fib.) 你的腿？
蕭雲：　小兒麻痹症，三歲的時候就不會走路了！看，現在已經習慣了。我知道，世界大得很，可我，只能關在小屋子裡。
高志華：蕭雲，真對不起你，一直沒有很好地關心過你。
蕭雲：　你怎麼這麼說？
高志華：不，這樣，過兩天我來看你。

---

*38. 感謝	感谢	gănxiè	to be grateful
39. 純正	纯正	chúnzhèng	pure and upright
*40. 了解	了解	liăojiě	to understand
*41. 溫暖	温暖	wēnnuăn	warm
*42. 鼓勵	鼓励	gŭlì	to encourage, to urge

肖云：　你就是高志华。哎呀，来，快请坐吧！
高志华：不，不，不，你不要起来！不要起来！
肖云：　应该说，我们早就认识了。
高志华：我不知道你是……真对不起，一直沒有来看你！
肖云：　那有什么，你让秦楠来关心我，不是一样吗？

Zhihua is shocked at this revelation.

高志华：什么，秦楠？
肖云：　是啊，她每个星期都来看我，帮我洗衣服，洗被子，收拾房间。对了，还买了许多我喜欢的书和画。喏，这两枝笔，也是她送给我的。我非常感谢你让我认识了秦楠。我跟她深谈了两次，我才发现她是那么纯正，那么善良。我想你一定很了解她。命运对她太不公平了。她心灵上有那么深的创伤，可还是那样地关心我，我心里感到温暖极了。哎，你坐呀！

Zhihua walks over to the portrait of Xiao Jian.

高志华：你常给你哥哥写信吗？
肖云：　写，一个星期写一封。我鼓励他，希望他能够早点儿回来。你关心我的事，我也告诉他了。不过，我沒提秦楠，她叫我不要告诉他。
高志华：那你有什么事要我做吗？
肖云：　沒有。我生活得很好。居委会很照顾我。我还有许多青年朋友。怎么，秦楠沒有告诉过你？
高志华：啊？告诉了。(Here Zhihua tells a fib.) 你的腿？
肖云：　小儿麻痹症，三岁的时候就不会走路了！看，现在已经习惯了。我知道，世界大得很，可我，只能关在小屋子里。
高志华：肖云，真对不起你，一直沒有很好地关心过你。
肖云：　你怎么这么说？
高志华：不，这样，过两天我来看你。

---

^43. 腿	腿	tuǐ	leg
44. 小兒麻痹症	小儿麻痹症	xiǎoér mábì-zhèng	infantile paralysis, polio
*45. 關	关	guān	to be shut in

Feeling guilty for not having taken care of Xiao Yun before, Zhihua decides to build a special tricycle for her. He rushes to a shop to look for parts, then goes home to thank Qin Nan for secretly taking care of Xiao Yun.

Scene 50 ——————————

Arriving home, Zhihua is again annoyed to see Dongdong with Qin Nan. Qin Nan, on her part, looks up at Zhihua but does not greet or even acknowledge him.

冬冬： 媽媽，這是好人還是壞人哪？
秦楠： 是好人。
冬冬： 媽媽，怎麼都是好人啊？
秦楠： 是好人嘛！
高志華：秦楠，我真沒想到蕭健的妹妹是個殘廢。
秦楠： 噢，你去看過她了？
高志華：我應該感謝你，替我做了我應該做的事。
秦楠： 什麼？
高志華：本來蕭健來信是讓我去……

Dongdong interrupts their conversation. Zhihua is visibly annoyed.

冬冬： 媽媽，這個人是誰呀？
秦楠： 是這個孩子的爸爸。
冬冬： 也是好人，對吧？
秦楠： 是的。(to Zhihua) 啊，你剛才說什麼？
高志華：我說蕭健的事真把我氣得要命。上次給我來的信，我只看了一半就…唉！我真不應該，可你，我應該感謝你。
秦楠： 這有什麼？蕭健也是我的朋友，他的妹妹我也應該照顧的。
高志華：可要不是接到蕭健的信，我根本不知道這件事，是剛才見了蕭雲我才……

---

^46. SV 得要命 SV 得要命 SV de yàomìng ...to the extreme (cf. Grammatical Note VIII.8.)

Feeling guilty for not having taken care of Xiao Yun before, Zhihua decides to build a special tricycle for her. He rushes to a shop to look for parts, then goes home to thank Qin Nan for secretly taking care of Xiao Yun.

Scene 50 ——————————

Arriving home, Zhihua is again annoyed to see Dongdong with Qin Nan. Qin Nan, on her part, looks up at Zhihua but does not greet or even acknowledge him.

冬冬：　妈妈，这是好人还是坏人哪？
秦楠：　是好人。
冬冬：　妈妈，怎么都是好人啊？
秦楠：　是好人嘛！
高志华：秦楠，我真没想到肖健的妹妹是个残废。
秦楠：　噢，你去看过她了？
高志华：我应该感谢你，替我做了我应该做的事。
秦楠：　什么？
高志华：本来肖健来信是让我去……

Dongdong interrupts their conversation. Zhihua is visibly annoyed.

冬冬：　妈妈，这个人是谁呀？
秦楠：　是这个孩子的爸爸。
冬冬：　也是好人，对吧？
秦楠：　是的。(to Zhihua) 啊，你刚才说什么？
高志华：我说肖健的事真把我气得要命。上次给我来的信，我只看了一半就…唉！我真不应该，可你，我应该感谢你。
秦楠：　这有什么？肖健也是我的朋友，他的妹妹我也应该照顾的。
高志华：可要不是接到肖健的信，我根本不知道这件事，是刚才见了肖云我才……

---

*47. 根本	根本	gēnběn	(adv., usually used with a negative verb phrase) fundamentally, ...at all, simply, at the bottom of the matter (cf. Grammatical Note VIII.9.)

Dongdong again interrupts them, much to Zhihua's annoyance。

冬冬： 媽媽。

秦楠： (to Zhihua) 你說你的。

高志華：你先跟孩子說完了我再說吧。

秦楠： 不，你說你的。

高志華：我看到蕭雲是個殘廢，心裡很難過，明明是你在照顧她，可你却告訴她是我在…我…我…

Zhihua looks over at Qin Nan and finds her playing affectionately with Dongdong and not listening to him. Realizing Zhihua's annoyance, Qin Nan again turns her attention to him.

秦楠： 你說蕭雲什麼？

高志華：以後再說吧！(gets up dejectedly and walks off to do his own work.)

---

*48. 明明 明明 míngmíng clearly, obviously

討論問題：

1) 秦楠為什麼打冬冬？ 是因為冬冬不聽話嗎？
2) 在中國社會上街道黨委能起什麼作用 (qǐ...zuòyòng: to have an effect)？ 秦父去找街道黨委會不會有用？ 你覺得美國社會應該不應該也建立 (jiànlì: to establish) 一些"街道委員會"？
3) 周大媽主動叫秦楠到她家去談。她對秦楠的態度 (tàidu: attitude) 怎麼樣？ 要跟秦楠說些什麼？ 為什麼她們兩個都哭了？
4) 秦楠有沒有把她過去的一切 (yíqiè: everything) 告訴周大媽？ 為什麼？ 周大媽勸她考慮"小高的事"，她的反應 (fǎnyìng: reaction) 怎麼樣？ 為什麼？
5) 志華看了蕭健的信，為什麼立刻就去看蕭雲？ 上次蕭健給他寫的信，他不是扔 (rēng: to throw away) 了嗎？ 那他現在怎麼知道那封信還在抽屜 (chōuti: drawer) 裡呢？
6) 蕭雲畫的那幅畫有什麼意義 (yìyì: significance)？ 它表現出 (biǎoxiànchū: to manifest) 她的什麼人生觀 (rénshēng-guān: philosophy of life)？
7) 志華從蕭雲的談話中發現了些什麼事？ 你想這對他有什麼影響？ 他決定作什麼？
8) 為什麼秦楠沒告訴志華她常去看蕭雲？ 為什麼她也不願意讓蕭健知道？
9) 志華回家後想跟秦楠說什麼？ 他們的談話順利 (shùnlì: smooth-going) 嗎？ 你猜志華心裡有什麼感受 (gǎnshòu: feeling)？

Dongdong again interrupts them, much to Zhihua's annoyance。

冬冬：　妈妈。
秦楠：　(to Zhihua) 你说你的。
高志华：你先跟孩子说完了我再说吧。
秦楠：　不，你说你的。
高志华：我看到肖云是个残废，心里很难过，明明是你在照顾她，可你却告诉她是我在…我…我…

Zhihua looks over at Qin Nan and finds her playing affectionately with Dongdong and not listening to him. Realizing Zhihua's annoyance, Qin Nan again turns her attention to him.

秦楠：　你说肖云什么？
高志华：以后再说吧！(gets up dejectedly and walks off to do his own work.)

---

^49. 却	却	què	(adv.) on the contrary (cf. Grammatical Note VIII.10.)

讨论问题：

1) 秦楠为什么打冬冬？ 是因为冬冬不听话吗？
2) 在中国社会上街道党委能起什么作用 (qǐ...zuòyòng: to have an effect)？ 秦父去找街道党委会不会有用？ 你觉得美国社会应该不应该也建立 (jiànlì: to establish)一些"街道委员会"？
3) 周大妈主动叫秦楠到她家去谈。她对秦楠的态度 (tàidu: attitude) 怎么样？ 要跟秦楠说些什么？ 为什么她们两个都哭了？
4) 秦楠有沒有把她过去的一切 (yíqiè: everything) 告诉周大妈？ 为什么？ 周大妈劝她考虑"小高的事"，她的反应 (fǎnyìng: reaction) 怎么样？ 为什么？
5) 志华看了肖健的信，为什么立刻就去看肖云？ 上次肖健给他写的信，他不是扔 (rēng: to throw away) 了吗？ 那他现在怎么知道那封信还在抽屉 (chōuti: drawer) 里呢？
6) 肖云画的那幅画有什么意义 (yìyì: significance)？ 它表现出 (biǎoxiànchū: to manifest) 她的什么人生观 (rénshēng-guān: philosophy of life)？
7) 志华从肖云的谈话中发现了些什么事？ 你想这对他有什么影响？ 他决定作什么？
8) 为什么秦楠沒告诉志华她常去看肖云？ 为什么她也不愿意让肖健知道？
9) 志华回家后想跟秦楠说什么？ 他们的谈话顺利 (shùnlì: smooth-going) 吗？ 你猜志华心里有什么感受 (gǎnshòu: feeling)？

SEGMENT IX

Scene 50 (cont.) ——————————

冬冬：　媽媽，你講啊，講啊！

Zhihua looks for something on the floor.

高志華：我的大螺絲帽呢？

Dongdong walks over to him and pulls the nut out of his pocket.

冬冬：　叔叔，是不是這個呀？

Zhihua explodes with accumulated irritation. He snatches the nut from Dongdong's hand, making him cry.

高志華：你怎麼亂拿我的東西？
秦楠：　(to Zhihua) 你這是幹什麼？你對我有意見直說好了！幹嘛把氣撒在孩子身上？
高志華：秦楠，你千萬別誤會！
秦楠：　我誤會什麼？自從冬冬來了以後，我知道你們看不起我，看不起孩子，討厭我們。(to Dongdong) 冬冬，到對面弄堂玩去，不要走遠了。媽媽一會兒就來。啊？
高志華：秦楠，我絕沒有這個意思。
秦楠：　沒這個意思？幹嘛對孩子撒氣？
高志華：我覺得你把一顆心都放在孩子身上了。
秦楠：　奇怪！我是他母親，我的心當然在他身上，這有什麼不對？
高志華：秦楠，我希望你明白我的意思。

1.	螺絲帽	螺丝帽	luósī-mào	(帽: hat) nut (as in "nut and bolt")
*2.	亂	乱	luàn	(adv.) recklessly, in an unruly or disorderly way
*3.	對…有意見	对…有意见	duì... yǒu yìjian	to have an opinion or objection regarding...
4.	撒氣	撒气	sā≠qì	to vent anger (here the V-O compound 撒氣 is split and rearranged to fit the 把-O V 在... pattern)

SEGMENT IX

Scene 50 (cont.) ————————————

冬冬：　妈妈，你讲啊，讲啊！

Zhihua looks for something on the floor.

高志华：我的大螺丝帽呢？

Dongdong walks over to him and pulls the nut out of his pocket.

冬冬：　叔叔，是不是这个呀？

Zhihua explodes with accumulated irritation. He snatches the nut from Dongdong's hand, making him cry.

高志华：你怎么乱拿我的东西？
秦楠：　(to Zhihua) 你这是干什么？你对我有意见直说好了！干嘛把气撒在孩子身上？
高志华：秦楠，你千万别误会！
秦楠：　我误会什么？自从冬冬来了以后，我知道你们看不起我，看不起孩子，讨厌我们。
　　　　(to Dongdong) 冬冬，到对面弄堂玩去，不要走远了。妈妈一会儿就来。啊？
高志华：秦楠，我绝沒有这个意思。
秦楠：　沒这个意思？干嘛对孩子撒气？
高志华：我觉得你把一颗心都放在孩子身上了。
秦楠：　奇怪！我是他母亲，我的心当然在他身上，这有什么不对？
高志华：秦楠，我希望你明白我的意思。

---

*5. 討厭	讨厌	tǎoyàn	to dislike, to despise, to find repugnant; disgusting
*6. 絕	绝	jué	(same as 絕對, usually used with a negative verb) absolutely (cf. Grammatical Note IX.1.)
^7. 一顆心	一颗心	yì kē xīn	"whole heart," all of one's thoughts and attention

秦楠：　我明白你的意思。你們家幫過我的忙，我很感謝。我走，我現在就走！
高志華：秦楠，你不要這樣！你不能這樣，你不要走，你不能走！
秦楠：　你？
高志華：我希望你理解我，不要走！

Qin Nan has been packing her things preparing to leave. She is trying to put away the sewing machine, when unconsciously, Zhihua clutches her hand to stop her. When they realize what is happening, they are both embarrassed, and Qin Nan pushes his hand off her other hand.

Scene 51——————————

Dongdong runs into the house crying, followed by Nannan in close pursuit.
冬冬：　媽媽……
男男：　野種！小野種！野種！小野種！
秦楠：　冬冬怎麼了？！
高志華：(to Nannan) 滾！

Nannan spits spitefully, then turns and runs away.

冬冬：　媽媽，什麼叫野種？他們為什麼要罵我野種？

Presently, Mother Gao walks in, sizes up the situation, and dejectedly walks upstairs.

Scene 52 ——————————

Her attitude toward Qin Nan having changed greatly, Zhihua's mother now tries to make a match between Zhihua and another girl. She shows a photo of this girl to Zhihua and asks him to meet her at a rendezvous that she has already arranged. But Zhihua refuses to go and counters all her arguments.

---

*8. 滾	滾	gǔn	"Roll!" Get out of here! Beat it! (very rough, spoken in great anger)

秦楠： 我明白你的意思。你们家帮过我的忙，我很感谢。我走，我现在就走！
高志华：秦楠，你不要这样！你不能这样，你不要走，你不能走！
秦楠： 你？
高志华：我希望你理解我，不要走！

Qin Nan has been packing her things preparing to leave. She is trying to put away the sewing machine, when unconsciously, Zhihua clutches her hand to stop her. When they realize what is happening, they are both embarrassed, and Qin Nan pushes his hand off her other hand.

Scene 51——————————

Dongdong runs into the house crying, followed by Nannan in close pursuit.
冬冬： 妈妈……
男男： 野种！小野种！野种！小野种！
秦楠： 冬冬怎么了？！
高志华：(to Nannan) 滚！

Nannan spits spitefully, then turns and runs away.

冬冬： 妈妈，什么叫野种？他们为什么要骂我野种？

Presently, Mother Gao walks in, sizes up the situation, and dejectedly walks upstairs.

Scene 52 ——————————

Her attitude toward Qin Nan having changed greatly, Zhihua's mother now tries to make a match between Zhihua and another girl. She shows a photo of this girl to Zhihua and asks him to meet her at a rendezvous that she has already arranged. But Zhihua refuses to go and counters all her arguments.

高志華：(Referring to the photo) 媽您拿着，我不去！
高母： 哎，約好了怎麼能不去呀？
高志華：我就是不去！
高母： 今天我乾脆跟你挑明了說。小秦的事，趁早給我死了這條心。
高志華：哎呀，我不是跟您說過了嗎，我的事您別管！
高母： 我非管不可！以前我不知道小秦是有孩子的，可人家是還沒有結婚的大姑娘！
高志華：我最討厭您說這種話了！
高母： 不管怎麼說，人家在國營單位，小秦還是個體戶。
高志華：你也看不起個體戶哇，我不就是個個體戶麼？國營單位、個體戶都是爲國家出力，沒有高低！
高母： 兩個都是個體戶，將來怎麼辦？連孩子的勞保都沒有。你能保證個體戶的政策就不變啦？變了怎麼辦？
高志華：個體戶的政策是會變的。粉碎四人幫以後，各方面的政策都在變，您說是變好了，還是變壞了？
高母： 當然是變好了。不…不過我的意思是太不保險了，那萬一要是變……
高志華：不管怎麼變，靠勞動吃飯，靠勞動把國家搞好，靠勞動讓人家過好日子，媽，靠勞動，這個是永遠不會變的。
高母： 那當然，我的意思是，有一個在國營單位不是更好嗎？
高志華：哎呀！國營單位不是也得靠勞動，靠技術。您說不是嗎？
高母： 好好好好，我說不過你。
高志華：媽，您就別跟我兜圈子了。說穿了吧，過去您是不知道秦楠有孩子，就說人家這也好，那也好。現在知道了，就看不起人家了。
高母： 隨你怎麼說，媽這是爲你好，你可千萬不要糊塗！
高志華：我不糊塗，小妹來信不是也說嗎？只要人好，這才是最主要的。

---

9. 挑明	挑明	tiǎo≠míng	to reveal, to put everything out on the table
*10. 趁早	趁早	chènzǎo	while it is still early, before it is too late
*11. 死心	死心	sǐ≠xīn	to give up an idea or hope forever
*12. 國營	国营	guó-yíng	state operated
*13. 單位	单位	dānwèi	unit, work unit
14. 勞保	劳保	láobǎo	short for 勞動保險, labor insurance (a kind of social security)
*15. 保證	保证	bǎozhèng	to guarantee
*16. 政策	政策	zhèngcè	policy
^17. 粉碎	粉碎	fěnsuì	to smash, to pulverize

高志华：(Referring to the photo) 妈您拿着，我不去！
高母： 哎，约好了怎么能不去呀？
高志华：我就是不去！
高母： 今天我干脆跟你挑明了说。小秦的事，趁早给我死了这条心。
高志华：哎呀，我不是跟您说过了吗，我的事您别管！
高母： 我非管不可！以前我不知道小秦是有孩子的，可人家是还没有结婚的大姑娘！
高志华：我最讨厌您说这种话了！
高母： 不管怎么说，人家在国营单位，小秦还是个体户。
高志华：你也看不起个体户哇，我不就是个个体户么？国营单位、个体户都是为国家出力，沒有高低！
高母： 两个都是个体户，将来怎么办？连孩子的劳保都沒有。你能保证个体户的政策就不变啦？变了怎么办？
高志华：个体户的政策是会变的。粉碎四人帮以后，各方面的政策都在变，您说是变好了，还是变坏了？
高母： 当然是变好了。不…不过我的意思是太不保险了，那万一要是变……
高志华：不管怎么变，靠劳动吃饭，靠劳动把国家搞好，靠劳动让人家过好日子，妈，靠劳动，这个是永远不会变的。
高母： 那当然，我的意思是，有一个在国营单位不是更好吗？
高志华：哎呀！国营单位不是也得靠劳动，靠技术。您说不是吗？
高母： 好好好好，我说不过你。
高志华：妈，您就别跟我兜圈子了。说穿了吧，过去您是不知道秦楠有孩子，就说人家这也好，那也好。现在知道了，就看不起人家了。
高母： 随你怎么说，妈这是为你好，你可千万不要糊涂！
高志华：我不糊涂，小妹来信不是也说吗？只要人好，这才是最主要的。

---

^18.	四人幫	四人帮	sì-rén-bāng	Gang of Four
*19.	保險	保险	bǎo≠xiǎn	safe, secure; insurance
*20.	技術	技术	jìshù	skills
*21.	說不過	说不过	shuōbuguò	unable to best one's opponent in an argument (cf. Grammatical Note IX.4.)
22.	兜圈子	兜圈子	dōu quānzi	to go around in circles (getting nowhere), to beat around the bush (not getting to the crux of the matter)
^23.	說穿	说穿	shuō≠chuān	to get to the truth of the matter, to say what the matter is really all about, to put it bluntly

高母： 不行，我不能讓外人對我們家指指戳戳的，多難聽啊？
高志華：跟外人有什麼相干？這是我自己的事！
高母： 可你是我兒子，你得聽媽的！
高志華：媽，我什麼都聽您的，可就是這件事，我不能讓你的舊思想來決定我的命運。
高母： 你…你…

Their argument is interrupted by someone calling Zhihua from downstairs.

某人： 小高！
高志華：來了！

Scene 53 ————————

Zhihua's argument with his mother has made him realize the depth of his feelings for Qin Nan. In order to demonstrate his acceptance of Dongdong, he takes him to an amusement park. On a "spaceship" ride...

高志華：冬冬，高興嗎？
冬冬： 高興！
高志華：怕不怕？
冬冬： 叔叔抱緊我，我就不怕了！
高志華：冬冬，昨天叔叔惹你哭了，是叔叔不好！
冬冬： 是冬冬不好，冬冬不應該亂拿叔叔的東西，媽媽回去也罵我啦！
高志華：不，是叔叔不好。

Zhihua snuggles his chin on Dongdong's face.

冬冬： 哎喲！鬍子，鬍子。

---

24. 指指戳戳	指指戳戳	zhǐzhǐ chuōchuō	to rudely point and jab the finger, to censure

高母： 不行，我不能让外人对我们家指指戳戳的，多难听啊？
高志华：跟外人有什么相干？这是我自己的事！
高母： 可你是我儿子，你得听妈的！
高志华：妈，我什么都听您的，可就是这件事，我不能让你的旧思想来决定我的命运。
高母： 你…你…

Their argument is interrupted by someone calling Zhihua from downstairs.

某人： 小高！
高志华：来了！

Scene 53 ——————————

Zhihua's argument with his mother has made him realize the depth of his feelings for Qin Nan. In order to demonstrate his acceptance of Dongdong, he takes him to an amusement park. On a "spaceship" ride...

高志华：冬冬，高兴吗？
冬冬： 高兴！
高志华：怕不怕？
冬冬： 叔叔抱紧我，我就不怕了！
高志华：冬冬，昨天叔叔惹你哭了，是叔叔不好！
冬冬： 是冬冬不好，冬冬不应该乱拿叔叔的东西，妈妈回去也骂我啦！
高志华：不，是叔叔不好。

Zhihua snuggles his chin on Dongdong's face.

冬冬： 哎哟！胡子，胡子。

---

^25. 相干	相干	xiānggān	關係 (cf. Grammatical Note IX.5.)
*26. 决定	决定	juédìng	to decide, to determine

Zhihua spots Maomao and his girlfriend on the other side of the same ride.

高志華：哎，毛毛。
冬冬：　哎！ (laughter)
高志華：(laughter) 叫，叫，快！
冬冬：　叔叔抱緊我！

Scene 54 ———————————

Zhihua's mother, a widow with only one son, can't bear the thought of Zhihua marrying a woman with a dubious past. Having failed to convince Zhihua to discontinue his relationship with Qin Nan, she now tries to get Qin Nan to move her sewing stall out of her home. In the Gaos' home...

高母：　志華回來沒有？
秦楠：　沒有。
高母：　這孩子，昨晚上很晚才回來…到現在還沒見他人。
秦楠：　噢，今天一清早，他到我家來，把冬冬帶去玩了。
高母：　什麼？帶你孩子出去玩兒去了？
秦楠：　嗯。

Zhihua's mother is visibly upset and agitated. After puttering around the house distractedly, she decides to confront Qin Nan with the issue at hand.

高母：　小秦，你過來！你…你坐下。小秦，有些話，我…我不知道該不該講 。
秦楠：　高媽媽，你有什麼就說什麼吧。如果我有什麼不對的地方……
高母：　你…你沒有什麼不對的。我…我是說……你知道，我是年輕守寡，只有志華這麼一個兒子，他還沒有成家。我…我是爲你好，你的縫紉攤要是能找個好地方……

---

^27. 抱緊	抱紧	bào≠jǐn	to hold tight (cf. 抱, Note III.28)
*28. 惹	惹	rě	to provoke
29. 鬍子	胡子	húzi	beard, stubble
^30. 一清早	一清早	yì qīngzǎo	cf. 一大清早, Note II.10

Zhihua spots Maomao and his girlfriend on the other side of the same ride.

高志华：哎，毛毛。
冬冬： 哎！(laughter)
高志华：(laughter) 叫，叫，快！
冬冬： 叔叔抱紧我！

Scene 54 ——————————

Zhihua's mother, a widow with only one son, can't bear the thought of Zhihua marrying a woman with a dubious past. Having failed to convince Zhihua to discontinue his relationship with Qin Nan, she now tries to get Qin Nan to move her sewing stall out of her home. In the Gaos' home...

高母： 志华回来沒有？
秦楠： 沒有。
高母： 这孩子，昨晚上很晚才回来…到现在还沒见他人。
秦楠： 噢，今天一清早，他到我家来，把冬冬带去玩了。
高母： 什么？带你孩子出去玩儿去了？
秦楠： 嗯。

Zhihua's mother is visibly upset and agitated. After puttering around the house distractedly, she decides to confront Qin Nan with the issue at hand.

高母： 小秦，你过来！你…你坐下。小秦，有些话，我…我不知道该不该讲 。
秦楠： 高妈妈，你有什么就说什么吧。如果我有什么不对的地方……
高母： 你…你沒有什么不对的。我…我是说……你知道，我是年轻守寡，只有志华这么一个儿子，他还沒有成家。我…我是为你好，你的缝纫摊要是能找个好地方……

---

31. 守寡	守寡	shǒu≠guǎ	"to keep widowhood," to become and to remain a widow
*32. 成家	成家	chéng≠jiā	"to form a family," to get married

秦楠： 高媽媽，別說了，我懂你的意思，我一定另外找個地方。
高母： 小秦，你千萬別生我的氣呀！我可不是存心攆你呀。
秦楠： 我知道。

Coming out of the Gaos' house, Qin Nan, now quite dejected, meets Zhihua and Dongdong as they return from the amusement park.

冬冬： 媽媽，媽媽，叔叔帶我去坐大飛船！
秦楠： 冬冬，我們回家去。
高志華：(to Qin Nan) 怎麼回事？
秦楠： 沒什麼。以後我來搬我的東西。
高志華：爲什麼？ (to his mother) 媽，到底是怎麼回事？媽，你跟秦楠說了些什麼？

33. 存心	存心	cúnxīn	intentionally, deliberately
34. 攆	撵	niǎn	to oust, to drive out
^35. 飛船	飞船	fēichuán	spaceship

討論問題：

1) 爲什麼志華罵冬冬？
2) 志華請秦楠"千萬別誤會。" 秦楠誤會了沒有？ 如果有，那你說她誤會了什麼？
3) 在第五十幕，秦楠表現出她對高志華的態度是怎麼樣的？ 你想她理解志華嗎？
4) 高母爲什麼在這個時候要給高志華介紹新的對像呢？ 一般來說 (yìbān lái shuō: generally speaking)，你覺得在中國社會的情況 (qíngkuàng: situation, circumstance) 下，這種認識對像的法子怎麼樣？
5) 高母到底 (dàodǐ: at the bottom of it all) 爲什麼反對志華和秦楠好？
6) 一般來說，志華對他的母親怎麼樣？ 他是不是一個孝順 (xiàoshùn: filial) 的兒子？
7) 爲什麼志華帶冬冬去玩兒去了？ 他們怎麼會碰見 (pèngjian: to encounter) 毛毛跟他的女朋友的？
8) 高母說她不是存心攆秦楠。 你想秦楠相信她嗎？ 你認爲 (rènwéi: to consider, deem) 秦楠對高母的反應 (fǎnyìng: reaction) 怎麼樣？

秦楠： 高妈妈，别说了，我懂你的意思，我一定另外找个地方。

高母： 小秦，你千万别生我的气呀！我可不是存心撵你呀。

秦楠： 我知道。

Coming out of the Gaos' house, Qin Nan, now quite dejected, meets Zhihua and Dongdong as they return from the amusement park.

冬冬： 妈妈，妈妈，叔叔带我去坐大飞船！

秦楠： 冬冬，我们回家去。

高志华：(to Qin Nan) 怎么回事？

秦楠： 沒什么。以后我来搬我的东西。

高志华：为什么？ (to his mother) 妈，到底是怎么回事？妈，你跟秦楠说了些什么？

讨论问题：

1) 为什么志华骂冬冬？
2) 志华请秦楠"千万别误会。" 秦楠误会了沒有？ 如果有，那你说她误会了什么？
3) 在第五十幕，秦楠表现出她对高志华的态度是怎么样的？ 你想她理解志华吗？
4) 高母为什么在这个时候要给高志华介绍新的对象呢？ 一般来说 (yìbān lái shuō: generally speaking)，你觉得在中国社会的情况 (qíngkuàng: situation, circumstance) 下，这种认识对象的法子怎么样？
5) 高母到底 (dàodǐ: at the bottom of it all) 为什么反对志华和秦楠好？
6) 一般来说，志华对他的母亲怎么样？ 他是不是一个孝顺 (xiàoshùn: filial) 的儿子？
7) 为什么志华带冬冬去玩儿去了？ 他们怎么会碰见 (pèngjian: to encounter) 毛毛跟他的女朋友的？
8) 高母说她不是存心撵秦楠。 你想秦楠相信她吗？ 你认为 (rènwéi: to consider, deem) 秦楠对高母的反应 (fǎnyìng: reaction) 怎么样？

SEGMENT X

Scene 55 ———————————

Zhihua is very angry about what his mother has done. He goes to talk with Yinghua, who encourages him to stand up to their mother. On the bleachers of an empty stadium...

高英華 (from some distance)：哥！哥！………

(with 志華 on bleachers) 啊，媽怎麼能這樣對待秦楠呢？這不是太傷人家心了嗎？

高志華：媽要是再反對呀，我就乾脆不回家了。

高英華：嗯，我贊成你這樣做，爲了自己的幸福，就是要和媽的封建思想鬥到底。除非再把秦楠請回來，不然，你不要回家，用不了兩天，媽就該着急了。不過，哥，你爲什麼不把心裡的話早點告訴她呢？我們應該理解秦楠這樣的人，在愛情方面她一定是很自卑的，她不相信會有人愛她，她更沒有勇氣敢去愛人。你說我說得對嗎，哥？

高志華：對。

高英華：那她過去究竟……你問過她沒有？

高志華：沒有必要問她，只是聽冬冬說，他的爸爸死了。

高英華：哎呀！媽怎麼能跟秦楠講這樣的話呢？

Scene 56 ———————————

Yinghua uses high pressure tactics to persuade her mother to stop interfering with Zhihua's relationship with Qin Nan. At the Gaos' home...

高母： 我是不該說那樣的話，傷了她的心。我心裡也不好受，可你哥哥…

---

*1. 傷心	伤心	shāng≠xīn	to hurt (someone's) feelings, to feel hurt or grieved
*2. 反對	反对	fǎnduì	to oppose, to object
*3. 贊成	赞成	zànchéng	to be in favor of, to support (an idea)
^4. 幸福	幸福	xìngfú	good fortune, happiness
^5. 封建	封建	fēngjiàn	"feudal"
*6. 鬥	斗	dòu	to struggle against, to combat
*7. V-到底	V-到底	V-dàodǐ	(to do something) to the end, to the very bottom of the matter (cf. Grammatical Note X.3.)

SEGMENT X

Scene 55

Zhihua is very angry about what his mother has done. He goes to talk with Yinghua, who encourages him to stand up to their mother. On the bleachers of an empty stadium...

高英华 (from some distance)：哥！哥！………

(with 志華 on bleachers) 啊，妈怎么能这样对待秦楠呢？这不是太伤人家心了吗？

高志华：妈要是再反对呀，我就干脆不回家了。

高英华：嗯，我赞成你这样做，为了自己的幸福，就是要和妈的封建思想斗到底。除非再把秦楠请回来，不然，你不要回家，用不了两天，妈就该着急了。不过，哥，你为什么不把心里的话早点告诉她呢？我们应该理解秦楠这样的人，在爱情方面她一定是很自卑的，她不相信会有人爱她，她更沒有勇气敢去爱人。你说我说得对吗，哥？

高志华：对。

高英华：那她过去究竟……你问过她沒有？

高志华：沒有必要问她，只是听冬冬说，他的爸爸死了。

高英华：哎呀！妈怎么能跟秦楠讲这样的话呢？

Scene 56

Yinghua uses high pressure tactics to persuade her mother to stop interfering with Zhihua's relationship with Qin Nan. At the Gaos' home...

高母：　我是不该说那样的话，伤了她的心。我心里也不好受，可你哥哥…

---

*8. 除非	除非	chúfēi	(MA) unless (cf. Grammatical Note X.4.)
*9. 用不了	用不了	yòngbuliǎo	to require less than..., no need (to..., for...)
*10. 着急	着急	zhāojí	worried, anxious
*11. 爱情	爱情	àiqíng	love
^12. 自卑	自卑	zìbēi	to have an inferiority complex
13. 不好受	不好受	bù hǎoshòu	to feel bad (好受 is usually used in the negative form)

高英華：我就認為哥做得對，他是不會輕易喜歡一個人的。媽！不是你親口跟我說的嗎？秦楠又賢惠又能幹。怎麼，人家有了孩子，就不賢惠，不能幹啦？你這明明是封建思想在作怪。爸死得早，你拖着我們吃盡了苦，你最應該理解秦楠的處境。再說，只要哥哥心甘情願，你又管他幹什麼？媽媽，哥哥一直是很孝順您的，就是因為您反對，他飯也吃不好，覺也睡不着，人都瘦成這樣了，你就不心疼他。哎呀，媽，人家後天就去北京參加全國錦標賽了，我是去爭冠軍的，你要我背家裡的思想包袱去跑百米，我跑得動呀？

高母：　死丫頭，我說不過你。好，你哥的事我不管了，好了吧？

高英華：哎呀，我的好媽媽，你早就不該管了。

高母：　這樣，你去找小秦，就說我說的，她的縫紉攤子不用搬走了。

高英華：哎呀，媽，來不及了，我只請了一個小時假，媽，你讓哥哥去嘛。我走啦！媽，你說話可要算數哇！再見！

Scene 57 ————————

At another corner of the Gaos' home...

高英華：哥，媽投降了。現在，你該主動向秦楠猛烈進攻了。好，北京回來見，祝你成功！

Exits Yinghua, enters Mother Gao.

---

*14.	認為	认为	rènwéi	to be of the opinion that...
*15.	輕易	轻易	qīngyì	lightly, frivolously, rashly
^16.	親口	亲口	qīn-kǒu	"with one's own mouth," to say something personally (oneself, i.e., not through an intermediary)
^17.	作怪	作怪	zuò≠guài	to play tricks, to make trouble
^18.	V-盡	V-尽	V-jìn	...to the utmost, ...to the limit
19.	心甘情願	心甘情愿	xīngān qíngyuàn	to be perfectly willing (to make a sacrifice, etc.)
^20.	孝順	孝顺	xiàoshùn	(SV or V) filial; to show filial respect
*21.	瘦	瘦	shòu	thin
^22.	心疼	心疼	xīnténg	to love dearly (to the point of feeling badly if something bad happens to the loved one)
*23.	爭	争	zhēng	to vie for, to strive for

高英华：我就认为哥做得对，他是不会轻易喜欢一个人的。妈！不是你亲口跟我说的吗？秦楠又贤惠又能干。怎么，人家有了孩子，就不贤惠，不能干啦？你这明明是封建思想在作怪。爸死得早，你拖着我们吃尽了苦，你最应该理解秦楠的处境。再说，只要哥哥心甘情愿，你又管他干什么？妈妈，哥哥一直是很孝顺您的，就是因为您反对，他饭也吃不好，觉也睡不着，人都瘦成这样了，你就不心疼他。哎呀，妈，人家后天就去北京参加全国锦标赛了，我是去争冠军的，你要我背家里的思想包袱去跑百米，我跑得动呀？

高母：死丫头，我说不过你。好，你哥的事我不管了，好了吧？

高英华：哎呀，我的好妈妈，你早就不该管了。

高母：这样，你去找小秦，就说我说的，她的缝纫摊子不用搬走了。

高英华：哎呀，妈，来不及了，我只请了一个小时假，妈，你让哥哥去嘛。我走啦！妈，你说话可要算数哇！再见！

Scene 57 ——————————

At another corner of the Gaos' home...

高英华：哥，妈投降了。现在，你该主动向秦楠猛烈进攻了。好，北京回来见，祝你成功！

Exits Yinghua, enters Mother Gao.

24.	背包袱	背包袱	bēi bāofu	to carry a burden on the back (used metaphorically here)
*25.	米	米	mǐ	meter (unit of measure)
*26.	來不及	来不及	láibují	there is not enough time, it is too late to...
*27.	小時	小时	xiǎoshí	鐘頭
*28.	請假	请假	qǐng≠jià	to request a leave of absence
29.	說話…算數	说话…算数	shuō≠huà suàn≠shù	what one says counts, to mean what one says
^30.	投降	投降	tóuxiáng	to surrender
31.	猛烈	猛烈	měngliè	fierce
32.	進攻	进攻	jìngōng	to launch an offensive
*33.	祝	祝	zhù	to wish (someone good luck, etc.)
*34.	成功	成功	chénggōng	success; to succeed

高母： (to Zhihua) 去，把小秦叫來！
高志華：我不去！
高母： 哎呀，去！

Qin Nan, looking very distraught, comes to the Gaos' place looking for Dongdong.

秦楠： 冬冬來過沒有？
高志華：啊，沒有啊！
秦楠： 哎呀！
高母： 小秦，出什麼事了？
秦楠： 冬冬不見了。弄堂前前後後我都找遍了。
高母： 別急別急！快去找！快去找！走走，走！

Scene 58 ————————

Zhihua, his mother, and Qin Nan rush about the city in separate directions looking for Dongdong. Thinking that Dongdong may have had an accident, Zhihua goes to the police station to check whether there has been an accident involving a five-year-old boy. At the police station...

高志華：哎，同志，有沒有見到一個五歲的小男孩兒？
警察： 有，他只會說自己叫冬冬。
高志華：對，是叫冬冬。孩子呢？
警察： 半小時以前，在馬路上被腳踏車撞傷了，已經送中心醫院，快去吧！
高志華：噢，謝謝！

Scene 59 ————————

Qin Nan is informed of the situation and also rushes to the hospital. At the hospital...

---

*35. 不見	不见	bújiàn	to disappear
36. V-遍	V-遍	-biàn	(BF) everywhere (cf. Grammatical Note X.6.)
^37. 馬路	马路	mǎlù	lit., "horse road"; street, road; main road (as opposed to a side street)

高母： (to Zhihua) 去，把小秦叫来！
高志华：我不去！
高母： 哎呀，去！

Qin Nan, looking very distraught, comes to the Gaos' place looking for Dongdong.

秦楠： 冬冬来过沒有？
高志华：啊，沒有啊！
秦楠： 哎呀！
高母： 小秦，出什么事了？
秦楠： 冬冬不见了。弄堂前前后后我都找遍了。
高母： 别急别急！快去找！快去找！走走，走！

Scene 58 ————————

Zhihua, his mother, and Qin Nan rush about the city in separate directions looking for Dongdong. Thinking that Dongdong may have had an accident, Zhihua goes to the police station to check whether there has been an accident involving a five-year-old boy. At the police station...

高志华：哎，同志，有沒有见到一个五岁的小男孩儿？
警察： 有，他只会说自己叫冬冬。
高志华：对，是叫冬冬。孩子呢？
警察： 半小时以前，在马路上被脚踏车撞伤了，已经送中心医院，快去吧！
高志华：噢，谢谢！

Scene 59 ————————

Qin Nan is informed of the situation and also rushes to the hospital. At the hospital...

---

38. 撞傷	撞伤	zhuàng≠shāng	to bump into and injure, to be bumped into and injured
39. 中心醫院	中心医院	Zhōngxīn Yīyuàn	Central Hospital

秦楠：　冬冬怎麼樣了？

高志華：不要緊了，小腿蹭破點皮，縫了幾針。怕引起感染，要在觀察室裡觀察一天。現在已經睡着了。

醫生：　你們是孩子的父母嗎？要登個記，請跟我來！

秦楠：　孩子的病不要緊吧？

醫生：　不要緊的。沒傷着筋骨。我看明天就可以出院了。

秦楠：　噢，謝謝。

Zhihua's mother also comes to the hospital when she learns of the accident.

秦楠：　高媽媽！

高母：　好了，小秦，找到就放心了。我去看看冬冬去。(goes to see Dongdong.)

Qin Nan leans forward, as though about to faint.

高志華：欸，你怎麼了？

秦楠：　沒什麼，有點暈。

高志華：快坐下。我看你是太累了。

Mother Gao returns.

高母：　小秦，孩子睡得很好，不要緊的。

高志華：媽，秦楠不舒服，您帶她回去吧！

高母：　怎麼了？小秦？

秦楠：　沒事兒。大概剛才有點緊張。

高母：　那就讓志華留在這兒照顧冬冬。

秦楠：　不。

高志華：你放心吧。我會好好照顧他的。

秦楠：　我不要緊的。

40.	小腿	小腿	xiǎo-tuǐ	calf of the leg
41.	蹭破	蹭破	cèng≠pò	to scrape (the skin) and open a wound
*42.	縫	缝	féng	to sew
^43.	針	针	zhēn	needle, stitches
*44.	引起	引起	yǐn≠qǐ	to cause, to give rise to
45.	感染	感染	gǎnrǎn	to infect; infection

秦楠： 冬冬怎么样了？

高志华：不要紧了，小腿蹭破点皮，缝了几针。怕引起感染，要在观察室里观察一天。现在已经睡着了。

医生： 你们是孩子的父母吗？要登个记，请跟我来！

秦楠： 孩子的病不要紧吧？

医生： 不要紧的。没伤着筋骨。我看明天就可以出院了。

秦楠： 噢，谢谢。

Zhihua's mother also comes to the hospital when she learns of the accident.

秦楠： 高妈妈！

高母： 好了，小秦，找到就放心了。我去看看冬冬去。 (goes to see Dongdong.)

Qin Nan leans forward, as though about to faint.

高志华：欸，你怎么了？

秦楠： 没什么，有点晕。

高志华：快坐下。我看你是太累了。

Mother Gao returns.

高母： 小秦，孩子睡得很好，不要紧的。

高志华：妈，秦楠不舒服，您带她回去吧！

高母： 怎么了？小秦？

秦楠： 没事儿。大概刚才有点紧张。

高母： 那就让志华留在这儿照顾冬冬。

秦楠： 不。

高志华：你放心吧。我会好好照顾他的。

秦楠： 我不要紧的。

46.	觀察室	观察室	guānchá-shì	observation room
*47.	登記	登记	dēngjì	to register
48.	筋骨	筋骨	jīngǔ	tendons and bones
*49.	出院	出院	chū≠yuàn	出醫院，離開醫院
^50.	暈	晕	yūn	dizzy
*51.	不舒服	不舒服	bùshūfu	to not feel well

高母：　走吧。走吧。
高志華：媽，送她回去。
高母：　好，走吧，走吧，走吧。回去，回去。

Scene 60 ——————————

That night, in quiet darkness, Qin Nan recalls the advice that Zhou Dama has given her before.

周大媽的聲音：孩子，不要再苦自己了，小高的事你要考慮！

Scene 61 ——————————

The next day, Zhihua and Dongdong wait in the hospital for Qin Nan to come pick up Dongdong. At Dongdong's sickbed...

冬冬：　叔叔，你再帶我去坐大飛船好嗎？
高志華：好哇，你的腿還疼嗎？
冬冬：　還有一點點兒疼。媽媽怎麼還不來呀？
高志華：媽媽在電話裡說，一會兒就來接你。

Scene 62 ——————————

Zhihua steps out for a minute; Dongdong's hospital roommate comes over and asks questions about Zhihua.

病友：　他是你爸爸嗎？
冬冬：　什麼？
病友：　我問那個人是你爸爸嗎？
冬冬：　嗯，就是我的爸爸！是我的爸爸又怎麼樣？
病友：　你爸爸好，我爸爸不好。他呀，從來也不給我削蘋果。

---

^52. 疼	疼	téng	to hurt, to be in pain
53. …又怎麼樣	…又怎么样	...yòu zěnmeyàng	so what if..., so what about it? (cf. Grammatical Note X.9.)

高母：　走吧。走吧。
高志华：妈，送她回去。
高母：　好，走吧，走吧，走吧。回去，回去。

Scene 60 ——————————

That night, in quiet darkness, Qin Nan recalls the advice that Zhou Dama has given her before.

周大妈的声音：孩子，不要再苦自己了，小高的事你要考虑！

Scene 61 ——————————

The next day, Zhihua and Dongdong wait in the hospital for Qin Nan to come pick up Dongdong. At Dongdong's sickbed...

冬冬：　叔叔，你再带我去坐大飞船好吗？
高志华：好哇，你的腿还疼吗？
冬冬：　还有一点点儿疼。妈妈怎么还不来呀？
高志华：妈妈在电话里说，一会儿就来接你。

Scene 62 ——————————

Zhihua steps out for a minute; Dongdong's hospital roommate comes over and asks questions about Zhihua.

病友：　他是你爸爸吗？
冬冬：　什么？
病友：　我问那个人是你爸爸吗？
冬冬：　嗯，就是我的爸爸！是我的爸爸又怎么样？
病友：　你爸爸好，我爸爸不好。他呀，从来也不给我削苹果。

---

54. 削	削	xiāo	to pare (fruit)
55. 蘋果	苹果	píngguǒ	apple

Zhihua comes back and gives the roommate an apple.

高志華：拿着吧！
病友：　謝謝叔叔！

Scene 63 ———————

Meanwhile, Qin Nan comes to the hospital to pick up Dongdong. The doctor mistakes Zhihua for Qin Nan's husband and tells her that he has been very nice to Dongdong.

醫生：　是來接孩子的吧？
秦楠：　孩子可以出院了吧？
醫生：　可以。五天以後再來拆線。
秦楠：　謝謝！
醫生：　你愛人真不錯。
秦楠：　你說什麼？
醫生：　我說你愛人真心疼孩子，昨晚上一宿都沒睡。

Scene 64 ———————

Qin Nan comes into Dongdong's hospital room. From behind a screen, she overhears a conversation between Zhihua and Dongdong. She is very touched to see how much Zhihua loves Dongdong.

冬冬：　叔叔，我撒謊了。
高志華：撒什麼謊？
冬冬：　剛才那個小朋友問我，你是不是我爸爸，我說是的。
高志華：爲什麼要撒謊呢？
冬冬：　我害怕他罵我野種。叔叔，你不會罵我吧？

56.	拆線	拆线	chāi≠xiàn	to remove the stitches
*57.	爱人	爱人	àiren	spouse
58.	一宿	一宿	yì xiǔ	a whole night
59.	撒謊	撒谎	sā≠huǎng	to tell a fib or lie
*60.	害怕	害怕	hàipà	怕

Zhihua comes back and gives the roommate an apple.

高志华：拿着吧！
病友：　谢谢叔叔！

Scene 63 ————————

Meanwhile, Qin Nan comes to the hospital to pick up Dongdong. The doctor mistakes Zhihua for Qin Nan's husband and tells her that he has been very nice to Dongdong.

医生：　是来接孩子的吧？
秦楠：　孩子可以出院了吧？
医生：　可以。五天以后再来拆线。
秦楠：　谢谢！
医生：　你爱人真不错。
秦楠：　你说什么？
医生：　我说你爱人真心疼孩子，昨晚上一宿都没睡。

Scene 64 ————————

Qin Nan comes into Dongdong's hospital room. From behind a screen, she overhears a conversation between Zhihua and Dongdong. She is very touched to see how much Zhihua loves Dongdong.

冬冬：　叔叔，我撒谎了。
高志华：撒什么谎？
冬冬：　刚才那个小朋友问我，你是不是我爸爸，我说是的。
高志华：为什么要撒谎呢？
冬冬：　我害怕他骂我野种。叔叔，你不会骂我吧？

討論問題：

1) 志華爲什麼找他妹妹談他的心事？ 他妹妹給了他什麼幫助？
2) 爲什麼志華説不過他母親而他妹妹就能呢？
3) 爲什麼高母不親自 (qīnzì: personally) 去把秦楠叫回來呢？爲什麼志華也不願意去？ 結果呢？
4) 醫生怎麼會以爲志華是冬冬的父親呢？
5) 那天晚上秦楠怎麼會想起周大媽的勸告？
6) 高母對秦楠和冬冬的態度怎麼會變得那麼快？ 這可能嗎？
7) 爲什麼冬冬撒謊説志華是他的爸爸？ 聽到了冬冬説他撒謊的事，志華跟秦楠會有什麼感受？

讨论问题：

1) 志华为什么找他妹妹谈他的心事？ 他妹妹给了他什么帮助？
2) 为什么志华说不过他母亲而他妹妹就能呢？
3) 为什么高母不亲自 (qīnzì: personally) 去把秦楠叫回来呢？为什么志华也不愿意去？ 结果呢？
4) 医生怎么会以为志华是冬冬的父亲呢？
5) 那天晚上秦楠怎么会想起周大妈的劝告？
6) 高母对秦楠和冬冬的态度怎么会变得那么快？ 这可能吗？
7) 为什么冬冬撒谎说志华是他的爸爸？ 听到了冬冬说他撒谎的事，志华跟秦楠会有什么感受？

SEGMENT XI

Scene 65 ———————————

Walking out of the hospital, Zhihua, carrying Dongdong in his arms, wants to tell Qin Nan something that he has been holding in his heart. She stops him short because she wants him to know everything about her past before he makes any decisions.

高志華：秦楠，我心裡一直有句話想跟你說…
秦楠：　不，不要說了，你還不了解我的過去。等你了解了再……
冬冬：　叔叔，走啊，走啊！
高志華：噢！
冬冬：　叔叔，你再帶我去坐大飛船，好嗎？
高志華：好，好。

Scene 66 ———————————

Arriving in Qin Nan's home, Zhihua puts Dongdong on the bed.

秦楠：　謝謝你了。
高志華：謝什麼？
冬冬：　叔叔，書……
高志華：今晚你還去我們家做活嗎？
秦楠：　啊，晚上沒活兒，我不去了。
高志華：那好，我回家了。冬冬再見！
冬冬：　叔叔再見。
秦楠：　小高！
高志華：什麼事？

Qin Nan gets a notebook from a chest and hands it to Zhihua.

---

1. 做活	做活	zuò≠huó	幹活，工作
*2. 筆記本	笔记本	bǐjì-běn	notebook

SEGMENT XI

Scene 65 ——————————

Walking out of the hospital, Zhihua, carrying Dongdong in his arms, wants to tell Qin Nan something that he has been holding in his heart. She stops him short because she wants him to know everything about her past before he makes any decisions.

高志华：秦楠，我心里一直有句话想跟你说…
秦楠： 不，不要说了，你还不了解我的过去。等你了解了再……
冬冬： 叔叔，走啊，走啊！
高志华：噢！
冬冬： 叔叔，你再带我去坐大飞船，好吗？
高志华：好，好。

Scene 66 ——————————

Arriving in Qin Nan's home, Zhihua puts Dongdong on the bed.

秦楠： 谢谢你了。
高志华：谢什么？
冬冬： 叔叔，书……
高志华：今晚你还去我们家做活吗？
秦楠： 啊，晚上没活儿，我不去了。
高志华：那好，我回家了。冬冬再见！
冬冬： 叔叔再见。
秦楠： 小高！
高志华：什么事？

Qin Nan gets a notebook from a chest and hands it to Zhihua.

秦楠： 你等等。這是我過去的筆記本。你拿去看吧！
高志華：好。

After Zhihua leaves, Qin Nan looks at herself in a hand mirror. For the first time in many years, she feels herself coming to life again. Dongdong is puzzled by her behavior.

冬冬： 媽媽，你幹什麼？

Scene 67 ——————

Returning to his own home, Zhihua opens Qin Nan's diary and finds a letter to him from her. As he reads the letter, Qin Nan's past is gradually revealed to him.

秦楠的信：小高，痛苦的往事是不堪回首的，但經過再三考慮，決定寫這封信給你，談談我的過去吧！一九六九年春，在爸爸被關進牛棚的第三天，知青上山下鄉的狂潮催逼着我離開了痛哭流涕的媽媽，在淮北的廣闊天地裡開始了我接受再教育的新生活。在我們這個集體戶裡，有個男同學叫孟彬。他從小失去母親。他父親帶着繼母很早就離開中國去加拿大經商，他一直跟着祖父相依為命。文化大革命剛開始，他的祖父就以裡通

ˆ3. 往事	往事	wǎngshì	從前的事情
4. 不堪…	不堪…	bùkān...	cannot bear to...
5. 回首	回首	huí≠shǒu	"to turn the head around," to look back
ˆ6. 再三	再三	zàisān	repeated, repeatedly
ˆ7. 關進	关进	guān≠jìn	to be locked up in, to be incarcerated
8. 牛棚	牛棚	niúpéng	"ox shed," a makeshift prison set up in a work unit
*9. 知青	知青	zhīqīng	short for 知識青年 "educated youths" (here, specifically the junior high and high school graduates who were sent to the countryside during the Cultural Revolution)
ˆ10. 上山下鄉	上山下乡	shàng≠shān xià≠xiāng	to go up the mountain and down to the countryside (as part of the rustication movement)
11. 狂潮	狂潮	kuángcháo	"wild tides," frenzied movement
12. 催逼	催逼	cuībī	to compel, to press
ˆ13. 痛哭	痛哭	tòngkū	to weep bitterly

秦楠：　你等等。这是我过去的笔记本。你拿去看吧！
高志华：好。

After Zhihua leaves, Qin Nan looks at herself in a hand mirror. For the first time in many years, she feels herself coming to life again. Dongdong is puzzled by her behavior.

冬冬：　妈妈，你干什么？

Scene 67 ——————————

Returning to his own home, Zhihua opens Qin Nan's diary and finds a letter to him from her. As he reads the letter, Qin Nan's past is gradually revealed to him.

秦楠的信：小高，痛苦的往事是不堪回首的，但经过再三考虑，决定写这封信给你，谈谈我的过去吧！一九六九年春，在爸爸被关进牛棚的第三天，知青上山下乡的狂潮催逼着我离开了痛哭流涕的妈妈，在淮北的广阔天地里开始了我接受再教育的新生活。在我们这个集体户里，有个男同学叫孟彬。他从小失去母亲。他父亲带着继母很早就离开中国去加拿大经商，他一直跟着祖父相依为命。文化大革命刚开始，他的祖父就以里通

---

^14.	流涕	流涕	liú≠tì	to shed tears
15.	淮北	淮北	Huáiběi	an area in Anhui province
^16.	再教育	再教育	zài jiàoyù	reeducation
^17.	集體户	集体户	jítǐ-hù	a collective
*18.	從小	从小	cóngxiǎo	從小(孩兒)的時候
19.	失去	失去	shīqù	to lose, to be bereft of
20.	繼母	继母	jìmǔ	stepmother
21.	加拿大	加拿大	Jiānádà	Canada
^22.	經商	经商	jīng≠shāng	to engage in business
23.	相依爲命	相依为命	xiāng yī wéi mìng	to lean on each other for survival, to be emotionally dependent on each other
*24.	文化大革命	文化大革命	wénhuà dà gémìng	the Great Cultural Revolution
*25.	以	以	yǐ	by, through, with, due to
26.	裡通外國	里通外国	lǐ tōng wài guó	to have illicit relations with a foreign country (e.g., being a secret agent)

外國的罪名被隔離審查。因此我和他都屬於被人歧視的黑七類子女。沒有人敢接近我們。共同的遭遇促使我們兩個人經常在一起，相互同情，相互安慰。

Scene 68 ————————

Flashback. Qin Nan and Meng Bin by a pile of straw. Dejected, Meng Bin lights up a cigarette.

秦楠： 你怎麼抽起煙來了？你不該這樣對待生活！
孟彬： 可生活是怎麼對待我們呢？念了那麼多年書，跑到這兒來修地球，命運哪！

Scene 69 ————————

Continuation of Qin Nan's letter to Zhihua:

秦楠的信：他相信人生的遭遇都受着命運的支配。而命運是不可抗拒的。單調的勞動，枯燥的生活就這樣拖着我們渡過了一個春天，又一個春天。

Scene 70 ————————

Flashback. Qin Nan and Meng Bin riding on the back of an oxcart.

秦楠： 春天又來了！你不要太悲觀，我想將來一切都會好的！
孟彬： 好？我才不做這樣的夢！你我是永遠闖不過政審這一關的。

---

^27. 罪名	罪名	zuìmíng	charge, accusation
*28. 屬於	属于	shǔyú	to belong to...
*29. 歧視	歧视	qíshì	to discriminate against, to look down on
30. 黑七類	黑七类	hēi qī lèi	the seven "black" elements, i.e., the seven undesirable elements in society
*31. 接近	接近	jiējìn	to approach, to get close to...
*32. 共同	共同	gòngtóng	to share in common
^33. 遭遇	遭遇	zāoyù	bitter circumstances, hard lot; to meet with (bad circumstances)
34. 促使	促使	cùshǐ	to spur, to impel, to cause
*35. 相互	相互	xiānghù	mutually
^36. 安慰	安慰	ānwèi	to console

外国的罪名被隔离审查。因此我和他都属于被人歧视的黑七类子女。沒有人敢接近我们。共同的遭遇促使我们两个人经常在一起，相互同情，相互安慰。

Scene 68 ——————————

Flashback. Qin Nan and Meng Bin by a pile of straw. Dejected, Meng Bin lights up a cigarette.

秦楠： 你怎么抽起烟来了？你不该这样对待生活！
孟彬： 可生活是怎么对待我们呢？念了那么多年书，跑到这儿来修地球，命运哪！

Scene 69 ——————————

Continuation of Qin Nan's letter to Zhihua:

秦楠的信：他相信人生的遭遇都受着命运的支配。而命运是不可抗拒的。单调的劳动，枯燥的生活就这样拖着我们渡过了一个春天，又一个春天。

Scene 70 ——————————

Flashback. Qin Nan and Meng Bin riding on the back of an oxcart.

秦楠： 春天又来了！你不要太悲观，我想将来一切都会好的！
孟彬： 好？我才不做这样的梦！你我是永远闯不过政审这一关的。

---

*37.	抽煙	抽烟	chōu≠yān	to smoke
^38.	支配	支配	zhīpèi	control, domination; to control, to dominate, to govern
^39.	抗拒	抗拒	kàngjù	to resist
*40.	單調	单调	dāndiào	monotonous
^41.	枯燥	枯燥	kūzào	dull, wearisome
^42.	渡過	渡过	dù≠guò	to pass (time)
*43.	悲觀	悲观	bēi-guān	pessimistic
*44.	夢	梦	mèng	dream
45.	闖過	闯过	chuǎng≠guò	to charge and break through
46.	政審	政审	zhèng-shěn	short for 政治審查, political investigation
^47.	關	关	guān	an impasse, a barrier, a difficulty

Scene 71 ————————

Continuation of Qin Nan's letter to Zhihua.

秦楠自述：光陰像流水一樣，年復一年，悄悄地流去。我們的生活，像滾在土路上的牛車輪子那麼艱難而遲緩。就在這漫長的日子裡，我和他逐漸地產生了感情。在人生的道路上，我永遠忘不了一九七七年的春節。那是打倒四人幫以後的第一個春節。全國在歡騰，而我們的處境還沒有什麼改變。除夕那天晚上，雪下得特別大，其他同學早就上調回城了，只剩下我和孟彬兩個人，在痛苦中渡了個歡樂的春節。

Scene 72 ————————

Flashback. New Year's Eve, Qin Nan and Meng Bin are alone in a dark room. A snowstorm rages outside.

秦楠： 別再喝了！
孟彬： 不,不，再喝最後一杯！來，慶祝打倒四人幫。他們把我們害得太苦了！
秦楠： 時間不早了，你早點休息吧！我回去了。
孟彬： 外面雪這麼大，你不要回去了！
秦楠： 不！

Scene 73 ————————

Continuation of Qin Nan's letter to Zhihua:

---

^48.	自述	自述	zìshù	an account in one's own words (from the diary)
49.	光陰	光阴	guāngyīn	(formal, poetic) time
50.	年復一年	年复一年	nián fù yì nián	year after year (復: repeat, again)
51.	悄悄地	悄悄地	qiāoqiāo-de	quietly, without fanfare
^52.	輪子	轮子	lúnzi	wheel
^53.	艱難	艰难	jiānnán	difficult, arduous
54.	遲緩	迟缓	chíhuǎn	slow
^55.	漫長	漫长	màncháng	long, endless
^56.	逐漸	逐渐	zhújiàn	gradually

Scene 71 ———————————

Continuation of Qin Nan's letter to Zhihua.

秦楠自述：光阴象流水一样，年复一年，悄悄地流去。我们的生活，象滚在土路上的牛车轮子那么艰难而迟缓。就在这漫长的日子里，我和他逐渐地产生了感情。在人生的道路上，我永远忘不了一九七七年的春节。那是打倒四人帮以后的第一个春节。全国在欢腾，而我们的处境还没有什么改变。除夕那天晚上，雪下得特别大，其他同学早就上调回城了，只剩下我和孟彬两个人，在痛苦中渡了个欢乐的春节。

Scene 72 ———————————

Flashback. New Year's Eve, Qin Nan and Meng Bin are alone in a dark room. A snowstorm rages outside.

秦楠：　别再喝了！
孟彬：　不,不，再喝最后一杯！来，庆祝打倒四人帮。他们把我们害得太苦了！
秦楠：　时间不早了，你早点休息吧！我回去了。
孟彬：　外面雪这么大，你不要回去了！
秦楠：　不！

Scene 73 ———————————

Continuation of Qin Nan's letter to Zhihua:

---

*57.	感情	感情	gǎnqíng	affection, emotional attachment; feelings, emotions
^58.	春節	春节	chūn-jié	Spring Festival, Chinese New Year
*59.	打倒	打倒	dǎ≠dǎo	to overthrow, to strike down
60.	歡騰	欢腾	huānténg	jubilation, great rejoicing
^61.	除夕	除夕	chúxī	New Year's Eve
*62.	調	调	diào	to transfer
*63.	剩下	剩下	shèng≠xia	to remain, to be left (cf. 剩, p. 19.37)
^64.	歡樂	欢乐	huānlè	快樂
*65.	慶祝	庆祝	qìngzhù	to celebrate (an occasion)
*66.	害	害	hài	to do harm to..., to impair, to cause trouble to...

秦楠自述：命運之神有意地捉弄我們。七七年五月，也就是我懷孕後的第三個月，上海外事局突然通知孟彬，説他的父親在加拿大替他和他的祖父辦好了移民手續，出國護照很快就可以拿到了。

Scene 74 ——————————

Flashback. Qin Nan hangs laundry while Meng Bin talks with her about his plan.

秦楠： 那我？

孟彬： 我已經想好了，等我到了加拿大以後，先安頓一下，馬上就回來接你。要是孩子生下來了，就帶你和孩子一起去。啊？你怎麼了？

秦楠： 我怎麼覺得好像在做夢？

孟彬： 不，秦楠，這不是夢，不是夢。

Scene 75 ——————————

Continuation of Qin Nan's letter to Zhihua:

秦楠自述：兩個月以後，孟彬和他的祖父到加拿大去了。我天天流着眼淚等待着他的消息。我等啊，等啊，等到孩子快要臨產的時候，還是音信全無。我不敢相信孟彬會欺騙我，但我已感到我的前途是多麼可怕。天哪！我該怎麼辦？我實在沒臉在生產隊生下我的孩子，只好遷居到蘇州鄉下我舅舅家裡。那年冬天是我二十多年來感到最寒冷的冬天，連我的心都結上了冰。就在這刺骨的嚴寒裡，孩子生下來了。

---

*67.	有意地	有意地	yǒuyì-de	deliberately, intentionally
68.	捉弄	捉弄	zhuōnòng	to tease, to make fun of
*69.	懷孕	怀孕	huái≠yùn	to become pregnant
^70.	外事局	外事局	wàishì-jú	Foreign Affairs Bureau
*71.	突然	突然	tūrán	忽然, suddenly
^72.	移民	移民	yí≠mín	"to move people," to immigrate or emigrate
*73.	手續	手续	shǒuxù	procedures, formalities
*74.	護照	护照	hùzhào	passport
*75.	安頓	安顿	āndùn	to settle, to stabilize
^76.	眼淚	眼泪	yǎnlèi	tears

秦楠自述：命运之神有意地捉弄我们。七七年五月，也就是我怀孕后的第三个月，上海外事局突然通知孟彬，说他的父亲在加拿大替他和他的祖父办好了移民手续，出国护照很快就可以拿到了。

Scene 74

Flashback. Qin Nan hangs laundry while Meng Bin talks with her about his plan.

秦楠： 那我？

孟彬： 我已经想好了，等我到了加拿大以后，先安顿一下，马上就回来接你。要是孩子生下来了，就带你和孩子一起去。啊？你怎么了？

秦楠： 我怎么觉得好象在做梦？

孟彬： 不，秦楠，这不是梦，不是梦。

Scene 75

Continuation of Qin Nan's letter to Zhihua:

秦楠自述：两个月以后，孟彬和他的祖父到加拿大去了。我天天流着眼泪等待着他的消息。我等啊，等啊，等到孩子快要临产的时候，还是音信全无。我不敢相信孟彬会欺骗我，但我已感到我的前途是多么可怕。天哪！我该怎么办？我实在沒脸在生产队生下我的孩子，只好迁居到苏州乡下我舅舅家里。那年冬天是我二十多年来感到最寒冷的冬天，连我的心都结上了冰。就在这刺骨的严寒里，孩子生下来了。

---

^77.	等待	等待	děngdài	等
78.	臨產	临产	lín-chǎn	(臨: about to...) about to give birth
79.	音信全無	音信全无	yīnxìn quán wú	to have absolutely no news
*80.	前途	前途	qiántú	future, prospect
^81.	生產隊	生产队	shēngchǎn-duì	production team (a unit within a commune)
82.	遷居	迁居	qiān≠jū	(formal) 搬家
^83.	寒冷	寒冷	hánlěng	非常冷
^84.	結冰	结冰	jié≠bīng	to form ice, to freeze over
85.	刺骨	刺骨	cìgǔ	bone-piercing (extremely cold)
86.	嚴寒	严寒	yánhán	非常非常冷

討論問題：

1） 在第六十五幕，秦楠爲什麼沒讓志華說完他要說的話？
2） 爲什麼秦楠讓高志華看她的筆記本？ 志華走了以後，她又爲什麼照鏡子 (zhǎo jìngzi: to look in the mirror) 呢？ 她心裡想什麼？
3） 秦楠和孟彬是怎麼產生感情 (chǎnshēng gǎnqíng: to develop feelings of love) 的？ 如果他們沒有共同的遭遇，那他們的關係會怎麼樣？
4） 一九七七年的春節秦楠過得“歡樂”嗎？
5） 孟彬將要去加拿大的時候有什麼計劃 (jìhuà: plan)？ 他跟秦楠說的是他真實的計劃嗎？
6） 秦楠臨產的時候有哪幾條路可走？ 你認爲她的選擇 (xuǎnzé: choice) 怎麼樣？

讨论问题：

1) 在第六十五幕，秦楠为什么没让志华说完他要说的话？
2) 为什么秦楠让高志华看她的笔记本？ 志华走了以后，她又为什么照镜子 (zhào jìngzi: to look in the mirror) 呢？ 她心里想什么？
3) 秦楠和孟彬是怎么产生感情 (chǎnshēng gǎnqíng: to develop feelings of love) 的？ 如果他们没有共同的遭遇，那他们的关系会怎么样？
4) 一九七七年的春节秦楠过得“欢乐”吗？
5) 孟彬将要去加拿大的时候有什么计划 (jìhuà: plan)？ 他跟秦楠说的是他真实的计划吗？
6) 秦楠临产的时候有哪几条路可走？ 你认为她的选择 (xuǎnzé: choice) 怎么样？

SEGMENT XII

Scene 76 ————————————

Someone knocks at the door. Zhihua opens it to find Qin Nan. She has come on the pretext that she must finish a garment that night.

高志華：噢，是你。
秦楠：　我忘了，這件衣服，今天晚上一定要趕出來的。
高志華：好，那你做，你做吧。

Zhihua goes upstairs feeling puzzled. He sits there for a while, then realizes that he does not hear the sound of the sewing machine downstairs. He goes down to see why.

高志華：秦楠，你怎麼了？
秦楠：　我的信，你看完了嗎？
高志華：那個孟彬，以後就再也沒有音信了嗎？
秦楠：　在冬冬快滿兩週歲的時候，我插隊的公社給我轉來了他從加拿大給我的第一封信，也是最後一封。(hands Zhihua the letter which she received from Meng Bin two years after Dongdong was born.) 你也看看吧！

The letter:

孟彬的信：今天，良心逼使我不得不給你寫這封信。我必須痛苦地告訴你，我來到加拿大不到兩個月，就和我的表姐結婚了。* 因為這門親事直接影響到我父親經營的事業，在這個命運面前，我是無法抗拒的。秦楠，寬恕我吧！我們的孩子是男孩還是女孩？代我

---

*In Chinese culture, marriage between cousins of different surnames has always been quite acceptable.

^1.	趕出來	赶出来	gǎn≠chū≠lái	to rush to finish a job
2.	滿…週歲	满…周岁	mǎn... zhōusuì	to fully reach the age of... (as opposed to the generous approximation often used by the Chinese)
*3.	良心	良心	liángxīn	conscience
4.	逼使	逼使	bīshǐ	逼, to force, to urge

SEGMENT XII

Scene 76 ——————————

Someone knocks at the door. Zhihua opens it to find Qin Nan. She has come on the pretext that she must finish a garment that night.

高志华：噢，是你。
秦楠： 我忘了，这件衣服，今天晚上一定要赶出来的。
高志华：好，那你做，你做吧。

Zhihua goes upstairs feeling puzzled. He sits there for a while, then realizes that he does not hear the sound of the sewing machine downstairs. He goes down to see why.

高志华：秦楠，你怎么了？
秦楠： 我的信，你看完了吗？
高志华：那个孟彬，以后就再也沒有音信了吗？
秦楠： 在冬冬快满两周岁的时候，我插队的公社给我转来了他从加拿大给我的第一封信，也是最后一封。(hands Zhihua the letter which she received from Meng Bin two years after Dongdong was born.) 你也看看吧！

The letter:

孟彬的信：今天，良心逼使我不得不给你写这封信。我必须痛苦地告诉你，我来到加拿大不到两个月，就和我的表姐结婚了。* 因为这门亲事直接影响到我父亲经营的事业，在这个命运面前，我是无法抗拒的。秦楠，宽恕我吧！我们的孩子是男孩还是女孩？代我

---

*5. 必須	必须	bìxū	必得
*6. 表姐	表姐	biǎojiě	older female cousin (on mother's side of the family)
*7. 門	门	mén	M for marriage
^8. 親事	亲事	qīnshì	結婚的事情
*9. 經營	经营	jīngyíng	to operate or manage (a business or enterprise)
*10. 事業	事业	shìyè	enterprise, business
11. 寬恕	宽恕	kuānshù	to forgive

吻吻他吧！如果金錢能夠彌補我的過失，我將盡力地滿足你的要求。把我永遠地忘了吧！孟彬。

高志華：原來他還活着。

秦楠：可他在我心裡早就死了。當時我看了他這封信，一心就想去死，可我懷裡抱着兩歲的孩子。孩子是無罪的，他那雙天真的眼睛喚醒了我一個作母親的責任。爲了冬冬，爲了我的父親，我才逼着自己活下來。

高志華：秦楠，這些年你太苦了。秦楠，別再爲過去的事難過了。

秦楠：小高，你一直對我很好。不過你回答我，你這是出於對我的憐憫嗎？

高志華：什麼？

秦楠：你因爲可憐我和冬冬是孤兒寡母。

高志華：不，不，你怎麼會這麼想？

秦楠：我怕，我真怕。我和孟彬就是被一股可怕的勢力硬捏合在一起的。當時，我們彼此在絶望中尋找憐憫，尋找寄托。經過這麼多年的波折，我才理解，那不是愛情。不是，今天我再也不願意走這條痛苦的路了。

高志華：我懂，秦楠。自從我認識了你，特別是見到蕭雲以後，我認爲你很尊重自己的感情，可是有的人把什麼都説成是命運，其實，他心裡只有自己，根本就不考慮會給別人帶來多大的不幸。

秦楠：孟彬就是這樣的人！以前我也曾相信過他説過的所謂命運。後來，我才看透，他是個最自私的人。你相信命運嗎？

12.	吻	吻	wěn	to kiss
^13.	彌補	弥补	míbǔ	to make up for (a shortcoming), to compensate for
^14.	過失	过失	guòshī	error, fault, transgression
*15.	盡力	尽力	jìn≠lì	to one's best ability
*16.	滿足	满足	mǎnzú	to satisfy
*17.	要求	要求	yāoqiú	demand
*18.	一心	一心	yìxīn	"single-heartedly," wholeheartedly
^19.	懷	怀	huái	bosom
^20.	無罪	无罪	wú≠zuì	guiltless, innocent
21.	喚醒	唤醒	huàn≠xǐng	to awaken by calling
^22.	出於	出于	chūyú	to arise from...
23.	憐憫	怜悯	liánmǐn	pity, compassion
^24.	孤兒	孤儿	gū'ér	orphan
^25.	寡母	寡母	guǎmǔ	widowed mother
26.	股	股	gǔ	M for such things as odor, spirit, power, anger, excitement, etc.

吻吻他吧！如果金钱能够弥补我的过失，我将尽力地满足你的要求。把我永远地忘了吧！孟彬。

高志华：原来他还活着。

秦楠：可他在我心里早就死了。当时我看了他这封信，一心就想去死，可我怀里抱着两岁的孩子。孩子是无罪的，他那双天真的眼睛唤醒了我一个作母亲的责任。为了冬冬，为了我的父亲，我才逼着自己活下来。

高志华：秦楠，这些年你太苦了。秦楠，别再为过去的事难过了。

秦楠：小高，你一直对我很好。不过你回答我，你这是出于对我的怜悯吗？

高志华：什么？

秦楠：你因为可怜我和冬冬是孤儿寡母。

高志华：不，不，你怎么会这么想？

秦楠：我怕，我真怕。我和孟彬就是被一股可怕的势力硬捏合在一起的。当时，我们彼此在绝望中寻找怜悯，寻找寄托。经过这么多年的波折，我才理解，那不是爱情。不是，今天我再也不愿意走这条痛苦的路了。

高志华：我懂，秦楠。自从我认识了你，特别是见到肖云以后，我认为你很尊重自己的感情，可是有的人把什么都说成是命运，其实，他心里只有自己，根本就不考虑会给别人带来多大的不幸。

秦楠：孟彬就是这样的人！以前我也曾相信过他说过的所谓命运。后来，我才看透，他是个最自私的人。你相信命运吗？

---

*27. 硬	硬	yìng	forcibly (making someone do something against his/her will or best judgment), obstinately
28. 捏合	捏合	niēhé	to act as a go-between, to pull together (two parties)
^29. 絶望	绝望	jué≠wàng	to have given up all hope, to despair
30. 尋找	寻找	xúnzhǎo	找
^31. 寄托	寄托	jìtuō	spiritual sustenance, something to hang on to for moral support; to entrust (to the care of someone)
32. 波折	波折	bōzhé	twists and turns
*33. 尊重	尊重	zūnzhòng	to respect, to value
*34. 不幸	不幸	búxìng	misfortune; unfortunately
*35. 曾…	曾…	céng...	to have...in the past (cf. Grammatical Note XII.9.)
*36. 所謂	所谓	suǒwèi	so-called
37. 看透	看透	kàn≠tòu	to see through
*38. 自私	自私	zìsī	selfish

高志華：要說命運嘛，我只相信國家好了，我們就好了。這就是我們的命運。

秦楠： 國家好了，我們就好了。

高志華：是的，我們的國家一定會好的。

秦楠： 嗯，一定的。*

高志華：你笑什麼？

秦楠： 奇怪，我今天怎麼把什麼都跟你說了？

高志華：我明白。

秦楠： 你明白什麼？

高志華：反正我明白，你也明白。

At a loss for words, Qin Nan and Zhihua look deeply into each other's eyes.

— END —

---

*The last four lines carry heavy political overtones and fit poorly in context. They reflect the necessity of paying lip service to the state's dictates for the arts rather than the filmmaker's lack of artistry.

討論問題：

1) 秦楠那天晚上說沒活要做，後來又怎麼有件衣服要趕出來呢？
2) 在冬冬出院回家的路上，秦楠告訴志華說他還不了解她的過去，那時他還不了解什麼？
3) 爲什麼秦楠用信件 (xìnjiàn: letters) 來讓志華了解她的情況而沒直接 (zhíjiē: directly) 跟他說呢？ 你認爲 (rènwéi: to consider, deem) 她的這個做法怎麼樣？
4) 志華知道了秦楠過去的一切 (yíqiè: everything) 以後，你想他會有什麼感受？ 他對秦楠表示出 (biǎoshìchū: to express) 什麼反應 (fǎnyìng: reaction)？ 你認爲這個反應自然 (zìrán: natural) 不自然？
5) 爲什麼秦楠會認爲志華對她好是出於憐憫呢？ 爲什麼她怕會是這樣？
6) 爲什麼志華說"我只相信國家好了，我們就好了，這就是我們的命運。"？ 這句話跟電影的情節 (qíngjié: plot) 有什麼相干？
7) 最後志華和秦楠都"明白"了。他們明白了什麼？ 你明白他們的意思嗎？ 爲什麼他們不直說他們明白了什麼呢？
8) 請談一談在中國社會上，一個沒丈夫的母親的情況。死了丈夫的、離了婚的、和沒結過婚的，她們的情況在哪些方面一樣，在哪些方面不一樣？ 在美國呢？

高志华：要说命运嘛，我只相信国家好了，我们就好了。这就是我们的命运。

秦楠：　国家好了，我们就好了。

高志华：是的，我们的国家一定会好的。

秦楠：　嗯，一定的。*

高志华：你笑什么？

秦楠：　奇怪，我今天怎么把什么都跟你说了？

高志华：我明白。

秦楠：　你明白什么？

高志华：反正我明白，你也明白。

At a loss for words, Qin Nan and Zhihua look deeply into each other's eyes.

— END —

讨论问题：

1) 秦楠那天晚上说没活要做，后来又怎么有件衣服要赶出来呢？
2) 在冬冬出院回家的路上，秦楠告诉志华说他还不了解她的过去，那时他还不了解什么？
3) 为什么秦楠用信件 (xìnjiàn: letters) 来让志华了解她的情况而没直接 (zhíjiē: directly) 跟他说呢？ 你认为 (rènwéi: to consider, deem) 她的这个做法怎么样？
4) 志华知道了秦楠过去的一切 (yíqiè: everything) 以后，你想他会有什么感受？ 他对秦楠表示出 (biǎoshìchū: to express) 什么反应 (fǎnyìng: reaction)？ 你认为这个反应自然 (zìrán: natural) 不自然？
5) 为什么秦楠会认为志华对她好是出于怜悯呢？ 为什么她怕会是这样？
6) 为什么志华说"我只相信国家好了，我们就好了，这就是我们的命运。"？ 这句话跟电影的情节 (qíngjié: plot) 有什么相干？
7) 最后志华和秦楠都"明白"了。他们明白了什么？ 你明白他们的意思吗？ 为什么他们不直说他们明白了什么呢？
8) 请谈一谈在中国社会上，一个没丈夫的母亲的情况。死了丈夫的、离了婚的、和没结过婚的，她们的情况在哪些方面一样，在哪些方面不一样？ 在美国呢？

PRIORITY VOCABULARY IN COMPLEX FORM

Codes used in annotations: * top priority vocabulary
ˆ secondary priority vocabulary

Segment I:

Top Priority Vocabulary:

啊 (呀，哪)		儘管	工錢	肯	怎麼好意思	弄
燒	遲	幹	理解	都	對像	擠
收	趟	要不	對面	沒…的事	要回來	沒事
來信	緊張	上班	廠	還不是	…什麼	反正
碰到	限	妨礙	交通	窄	挪	…就是了
乾脆	牌	賺				

Secondary Priority Vocabulary:

喲	早點	合身	舅舅	生活費	…下來	還債
噢	代課	鑰匙	啦	當心	執照	哎
師傅	哎呀	個體戶	哇	腳踏車	沒收	愣
瞧	神	爐子	幹嘛	呵	特地	嘿
廣闊天地	戰友	擱	礙事	對過	摘	命運
踩	踏	倆				

Segment II:

Top Priority Vocabulary:

趕	顧客	交給	代	開	關	人家
碗	解決	出事	換	當時	剩	老太婆
逼	身邊	…才對	尺寸	咱們	千萬	誤會
騙	衣裳	取	放手	條	褲子	…底
退休	試試	合適				

Secondary Priority Vocabulary:

松	一大清早	夠…的	嘛	改天	差不多了	颱風
打雷	搞清	有說有笑	疙瘩	解開	隔離	審查
插隊	落戶	揭發	老伴	幹活	開導	嗯
睡懶覺	可是 (indeed)		打(從)	好嘞	上市	奶奶
死…	不要臉	阿姨	脫下來	扣子	挺	頂替

Segment III:

Top Priority Vocabulary:

約	一起	還是 (after all)		搞	裝	矛盾	面
前	偷	一…二…	勞動	送	提	抱	
孫子	補	懂事	能幹	厲害	提意見	相處	
樂觀	熱	開水	襯衫	猜	白…		

Secondary Priority Vocabulary:

零件	還…啊	輛	名牌	下決心	一刀兩斷	搶
志氣	又來了	補	省事	戴上	擦汗	文靜

Segment IV:

Top Priority Vocabulary:

一輩子	痛苦	主見	究竟	V 什麼(O)	天真	處境
公平	對待	勢力	統治	勇氣	英雄	中華
聊	治	名貴	改革	參加	同志們	口氣
把握	印象	正經	主動	班		

Secondary Priority Vocabulary:

迴避	折磨	忍心	操心	哼	善良	泡
特效	特產	體制	教練	哈哈	獲得	他媽
過癮	笑米米	胡說	老大難	胡鬧		

Segment V:

Top Priority Vocabulary:

聽話	趁	頭髮	濕	吃力	專門	放假
包	免得	吵	説定	後悔	勸告	犯罪
處理	接受	改造	唯一	關心	託	其他
包括…在內	殘廢	出門	通知	恨	原諒	情況
重新	鄰居					

Secondary Priority Vocabulary:

趕緊	湊巧	經常	段	毛衣	架	平時
活該	教養	寬大	醜	驚奇	摔跤	黨支部
書記	鎖	慢走				

Segment VI:

Top Priority Vocabulary:

離婚	搬	想像	徹底	改正	到處	鬧
公安局	批準	保障	公社	醫院	偷偷	至少
倒	顧	偏偏	乖	嫁	一下子	肯定

Secondary Priority Vocabulary:

高才生	右派	瘋	諒解	睜眼	望	哭哭啼啼
烏七八糟	今後	叫	外公	親親	巧克力糖	

Segment VII:

Top Priority Vocabulary:

考驗	…死了	丈夫	沈默	碰上	提醒	糊塗
考慮	做…的	社會主義	傳統	既然	愛護	偏要
吵架	何必					

Secondary Priority Vocabulary:

V-死	叔叔	火柴	意想不到	憂鬱	流言
…一聲(兒)	吃飽了飯沒事幹		心靈	創傷	轉眼

Segment VIII:

Top Priority Vocabulary:

欺負　瞞　上當　拖　年輕　…膩　累
老實　難怪　寶貝　批評　動　走開　感動
堅定　照顧　決心　感謝　了解　溫暖　鼓勵
闖　根本　明明

Secondary Priority Vocabulary:

不像話　街道黨委　虧心　日子長了　世　待人　厚道
放在心上　裁　友情　畢竟　季節　…得要命　腿
却

Segment IX:

Top Priority Vocabulary:

亂　對…有意見　討厭　絶　滚　趁早　死心
國營　單位　保證　政策　保險　技術　説不
過　決定　惹　成家

Secondary Priority Vocabulary:

一顆心　粉碎　四人幫　説穿　相干　抱緊　一清早
飛船

Segment X:

Top Priority Vocabulary:

傷心　反對　贊成　鬥　V-到底　除非　用不了
着急　愛情　認爲　輕易　瘦　爭　米
來不及　小時　請假　祝　成功　不見　縫
引起　登記　出院　不舒服　愛人　害怕

Secondary Priority Vocabulary:

幸福　封建　自卑　親口　作怪　V-盡　孝順
心疼　投降　馬路　針　暈　疼　蘋果

Segment XI:

Top Priority Vocabulary:

筆記本	知青	從小	文化大革命	以	屬於	歧視
接近	共同	抽煙	單調	悲觀	相互	夢
感情	打倒	調	剩下	害	有意地	懷孕
突然	手續	護照	安頓	前途	慶祝	

Secondary Priority Vocabulary:

往事	再三	闖進	上山下鄉	痛哭	流涕	再教育
集體戶	經商	罪名	遭遇	安慰	支配	抗拒
枯燥	渡過	關 (impasse)	自述	輪子	艱難	漫長
逐漸	春節	除夕	歡樂	外事局	移民	眼淚
等待	生產隊	寒冷	結冰			

Segment XII:

Top Priority Vocabulary:

良心	必須	表姐	門 (M)	經營	事業	盡力
滿足	要求	一心	硬 (forcibly)	尊重	不幸	曾
所謂	自私					

Secondary Priority Vocabulary:

趕出來	親事	彌補	過失	懷 (bosom)	無罪	出於
孤兒	寡母	絶望	寄托			

PRIORITY VOCABULARY IN SIMPLIFIED FORM

Codes used in annotations: * top priority vocabulary
^ secondary priority vocabulary

Segment I:

Top Priority Vocabulary:

啊（呀，哪）		尽管	工钱	肯	怎么好意思	弄
烧	迟	干	理解	都	对象	挤
收	趟	要不	对面	沒…的事	要回来	沒事
来信	紧张	上班	厂	还不是	…什么	反正
碰到	限	妨碍	交通	窄	挪	…就是了
干脆	牌	赚				

Secondary Priority Vocabulary:

哟	早点	合身	舅舅	生活费	…下来	还债
噢	代课	钥匙	啦	当心	执照	哎
师傅	哎呀	个体户	哇	脚踏车	沒收	愣
瞧	神	炉子	干嘛	呵	特地	嘿
广阔天地	战友	搁	碍事	对过	摘	命运
踩	踏	俩				

Segment II:

Top Priority Vocabulary:

赶	顾客	交给	代	开	关	人家
碗	解决	出事	换	当时	剩	老太婆
逼	身边	…才对	尺寸	咱们	千万	误会
骗	衣裳	取	放手	条	裤子	…底
退休	试试	合适				

Secondary Priority Vocabulary:

松	一大清早	够…的	嘛	改天	差不多了	刮风
打雷	搞清	有说有笑	疙瘩	解开	隔离	审查
插队	落户	揭发	老伴	干活	开导	嗯
睡懒觉	可是 (indeed)		打(从)	好嘞	上市	奶奶
死…	不要脸	阿姨	脱下来	扣子	挺	顶替

Segment III:

Top Priority Vocabulary:

约	一起	还是 (after all)		搞	装	矛盾	面
前	偷	一…二…	劳动	送	提	抱	
孙子	补	懂事	能干	厉害	提意见	相处	
乐观	热	开水	衬衫	猜	白…		

Secondary Priority Vocabulary:

零件	还…啊	辆	名牌	下决心	一刀两断	抢
志气	又来了	补	省事	戴上	擦汗	文静

Segment IV:

Top Priority Vocabulary:

一辈子	痛苦	主见	究竟	V 什么(O)	天真	处境
公平	对待	势力	统治	勇气	英雄	中华
聊	治	名贵	改革	参加	同志们	口气
把握	印象	正经	主动	班		

Secondary Priority Vocabulary:

回避	折磨	忍心	操心	哼	善良	泡
特效	特产	体制	教练	哈哈	获得	他妈
过瘾	笑米米	胡说	老大难	胡闹		

Segment V:

Top Priority Vocabulary:

听话　趁　头发　湿　吃力　专门　放假
包　免得　吵　说定　后悔　劝告　犯罪
处理　接受　改造　唯一　关心　托　其他
包括…在内　残废　出门　通知　恨　原谅　情况
重新　邻居

Secondary Priority Vocabulary:

赶紧　凑巧　经常　段　毛衣　架　平时
活该　教养　宽大　丑　惊奇　摔跤　党支部
书记　锁　慢走

Segment VI:

Top Priority Vocabulary:

离婚　搬　想象　彻底　改正　到处　闹
公安局　批准　保障　公社　医院　偷偷　至少
倒　顾　偏偏　乖　嫁　一下子　肯定

Secondary Priority Vocabulary:

高才生　右派　疯　谅解　睁眼　望　哭哭啼啼
乌七八糟　今后　叫　外公　亲亲　巧克力糖

Segment VII:

Top Priority Vocabulary:

考验　…死了　丈夫　沈默　碰上　提醒　糊涂
考虑　做…的　社会主义　传统　既然　爱护　偏要
吵架　何必

Secondary Priority Vocabulary:

V-死　叔叔　火柴　意想不到　忧郁　流言
…一声(儿)　吃饱了饭没事干　心灵　创伤　转眼

Segment VIII:

Top Priority Vocabulary:

欺负	瞒	上当	拖	年轻	…腻	累
老实	难怪	宝贝	批评	动	走开	感动
坚定	照顾	决心	感谢	了解	温暖	鼓励
关	根本	明明				

Secondary Priority Vocabulary:

不象话	街道党委	亏心	日子长了	世	待人	厚道
放在心上	裁	友情	毕竟	季节	…得要命	腿
却						

Segment IX:

Top Priority Vocabulary:

乱	对…有意见	讨厌	绝	滚	趁早	死心
国营	单位	保证	政策	保险	技术	说不
过	决定	惹	成家			

Secondary Priority Vocabulary:

一颗心	粉碎	四人帮	说穿	相干	抱紧	一清早
飞船						

Segment X:

Top Priority Vocabulary:

伤心	反对	赞成	斗	V-到底	除非	用不了
着急	爱情	认为	轻易	瘦	争	米
来不及	小时	请假	祝	成功	不见	缝
引起	登记	出院	不舒服	爱人	害怕	

Secondary Priority Vocabulary:

幸福	封建	自卑	亲口	作怪	V-尽	孝顺
心疼	投降	马路	针	晕	疼	苹果

Segment XI:

Top Priority Vocabulary:

笔记本	知青	从小	文化大革命	以	属于	歧视
接近	共同	抽烟	单调	悲观	相互	梦
感情	打倒	调	剩下	害	有意地	怀孕
突然	手续	护照	安顿	前途	庆祝	

Secondary Priority Vocabulary:

往事	再三	关进	上山下乡	痛哭	流涕	再教育
集体户	经商	罪名	遭遇	安慰	支配	抗拒
枯燥	渡过	关 (impasse)	自述	轮子	艰难	漫长
逐渐	春节	除夕	欢乐	外事局	移民	眼泪
等待	生产队	寒冷	结冰			

Segment XII:

Top Priority Vocabulary:

良心	必须	表姐	门 (M)	经营	事业	尽力
满足	要求	一心	硬 (forcibly)	尊重	不幸	曾
所谓	自私					

Secondary Priority Vocabulary:

赶出来	亲事	弥补	过失	怀 (bosom)	无罪	出于
孤儿	寡母	绝望	寄托			

VOCABULARY INDEX

Codes: Roman numeral - segment number
Arabic numeral - item number
RW - "Cast of Characters" (p. 1)
(RW is short for rénwù 人物 "character, personnage.")
* - vocabulary item of primary importance
^ - vocabulary item of secondary importance
+ - item has been truncated in this index to fit within the column

A

a	*啊	*啊	I.12
Āyí	^阿姨	^阿姨	II.79
ā; ài	^哎	^哎	I.37
āiyā	^哎呀	^哎呀	I.40
àihù	^愛護	^爱护	VII.30
àiqíng	*愛情	*爱情	X.11
àiren	*愛人	*爱人	X.57
ài≠shì	^礙事	^碍事	I.90
āndùn	*安頓	*安顿	XI.75
Ānhuī	安徽	安徽	V.38
ānwèi	^安慰	^安慰	XI.36

B

bǎwò	^把握	^把握	IV.42
bái-	*白-	*白-	III.48
bǎi≠tān	擺攤	摆摊	I.19
bān	*班	*班	IV.59
bān	*搬	*搬	VI.05
bāo	*包	*包	V.18
bāokuò... zài nèi	^包括… 在内	^包括… 在内	V.48
bǎobèi	*寶貝	*宝贝	VIII.21
bǎozhàng	^保障	^保障	VI.19
bǎozhèng	^保證	^保证	IX.15
bǎo≠xiǎn	^保險	^保险	IX.19
bào	^抱	^抱	III.28
bào≠jǐn	^抱緊	^抱紧	IX.27
bēi bāofu	背包袱	背包袱	X.24
bēi-guān	^悲觀	^悲观	XI.43
bèng	蹦	蹦	II.60
bèngbeng tiàotiao	蹦蹦跳跳	蹦蹦跳跳	II.94
bī	*逼	*逼	II.41
bīshǐ	逼使	逼使	XII.04
bǐjì-běn	*筆記本	*笔记本	XI.02
bìjìng	^畢竟	^毕竟	VIII.35
bìxū	*必須	*必须	XII.05
biàn	V-遍	V-遍	X.36
biǎojiě	*表姐	*表姐	XII.06
biē	憋	憋	VIII.04
bìngyǒu	病友	病友	RW
bōzhé	波折	波折	XII.32
bǔ	^補	^补	III.30
bǔ-yào	補藥	补药	IV.32
bù hǎoshòu	不好受	不好受	X.13
bújiàn	*不見	*不见	X.35
bújiàn búsàn	不見不散	不见不散	II.70
bùkān...	不堪…	不堪…	XI.04
bùshūfu	*不舒服	*不舒服	X.51
bú xiànghuà	^不像話	^不象话	VIII.02
búxìng	^不幸	^不幸	XII.34
bùyán bùyǔ	不言不語	不言不语	III.46
búyào liǎn	^不要臉	^不要脸	II.77

C

cā hàn	^擦汗	^擦汗	III.36
cāi	*猜	*猜	III.44
cái duì	*…才對	*…才对	II.50

cái	^裁	^裁	VIII.22
cáiyī-bǎn	裁衣板	裁衣板	II.02
cǎi	^踩	^踩	I.98
cānjiā	*參加	*参加	IV.35
cán-xuě	殘雪	残雪	VIII.34
cánfèi	^殘廢	^残废	V.51
cāngkù	倉庫	仓库	II.69
cāo⫽xīn	^操心	^操心	IV.10
céng...	*曾…	*曾…	XII.35
cèng⫽pò	蹭破	蹭破	X.41
chā⫽duì	^插隊	^插队	II.35
chàbuduōle	^差不多了	^差不多了	II.17
chāi⫽xiàn	拆線	拆线	X.56
chànhuǐ	懺悔	忏悔	VI.12
chángnián lěiyuè	長年累月	长年累月	IV.05
chǎng	*廠	*厂	I.63
chǎo	*吵	*吵	V.22
chǎo⫽jià	^吵架	^吵架	VII.33
chèdǐ	^徹底	^彻底	VI.07
chénmò	^沈默	^沈默	VII.10
chèn	^趁	^趁	V.03
chènróng jiá'ǎo	襯絨夾襖	衬绒夹袄	II.53
chènshān	^襯衫	^衬衫	III.43
chènzǎo	^趁早	^趁早	IX.10
chénggōng	*成功	*成功	X.34
chéng⫽jiā	*成家	*成家	IX.32
chīlì	*吃力	*吃力	V.11
chī⫽bǎole fàn +	^吃飽了飯 +	^吃饱了饭 +	VII.17
chí	*遲	*迟	I.15
chíhuǎn	遲緩	迟缓	XI.54
chǐcùn	*尺寸	*尺寸	II.54
Chóngmíng Nóngchǎng	崇明農場	崇明农场	II.92
chóngxīn...	*重新	*重新	V.61
chōu⫽yān	^抽煙	^抽烟	XI.37
chǒu	^醜	^丑	V.47
chū-fàn	初犯	初犯	V.34
chūyú	^出於	^出于	XII.22
chū⫽mén	*出門	*出门	V.52
chū⫽shì	*出事	*出事	II.28
chū⫽yuàn	*出院	*出院	X.49
chúfēi	*除非	*除非	X.08
chúxī	^除夕	^除夕	XI.61
chǔjìng	*處境	*处境	IV.15
chǔlǐ	*處理	*处理	V.37
chuántǒng	*傳統	*传统	VII.24
chuāngshāng	^創傷	^创伤	VII.29
chuǎng⫽guò	闖過	闯过	XI.45
chūn-jié	^春節	^春节	XI.58
chúnzhèng	純正	纯正	VIII.39
cìgǔ	刺骨	刺骨	XI.85
cóngxiǎo	*從小	*从小	XI.18
còuqiǎo	^湊巧	^凑巧	V.06
cùshǐ	促使	促使	XI.34
cuībī	催逼	催逼	XI.12
cúnxīn	存心	存心	IX.33

D

dǎ	^打	^打	II.59
dǎ⫽dǎo	^打倒	^打倒	XI.59
dǎ⫽léi	^打雷	^打雷	II.20
dà gūniang jiā	大姑娘家	大姑娘家	II.82
Dàchǎng Xī Xiǎolòng	大廠西小弄	大厂西小弄	V.42
dàmā	大媽	大妈	I.02
dài...	*代	*代	II.05
dài⫽kè	^代課	^代课	I.24
dài⫽rén	^待人	^待人	VIII.18
dài⫽shang	^戴上	^戴上	III.35
dāndiào	^單調	^单调	XI.40
dānwèi	*單位	*单位	IX.13
dāngshí	*當時	*当时	II.32
dāngxīn	^當心	^当心	I.32
dǎng-zhībù	^黨支部	^党支部	V.67
dào	*倒	*倒	VI.31
dàochù	*到處	*到处	VI.10
...dàodǐ	*V-到底	*V-到底	X.07
dào⫽shǒu	到手	到手	III.14
dēngjì	^登記	^登记	X.47
děngdài	^等待	^等待	XI.77
dèng	蹬	蹬	V.10
dǐ	*-底	*-底	II.90
diào	*調	*调	XI.62
dīng	釘	钉	II.88

guāi	*乖	*乖	VI.35
guān	*關	*关	II.07
guān	*關	*关	VIII.45
guān	^關	^关	XI.47
guān⸗jìn	^關進	^关进	XI.07
guān⸗xīn	*關心	*关心	V.44
guānchá-shì	觀察室	观察室	X.46
guǎnlǐguán	管理員	管理员	RW
guànjūn	冠軍	冠军	IV.40
guāngyīn	光陰	光阴	XI.49
guǎngkuò tiāndì	^廣闊天地	^广阔天地	I.80
Guǎngxī	廣西	广西	I.56
guǐ yātou	鬼丫頭	鬼丫头	I.51
gǔn	^滾	^滚	IX.08
Guō Nǎinai	郭奶奶	郭奶奶	RW
guó-yíng	^國營	^国营	IX.12
guòshī	^過失	^过失	XII.14
guò⸗yǐn	^過癮	^过瘾	IV.48

H

hāhā	^哈哈	^哈哈	IV.44
hái...a	^還…啊	^还…啊	III.07
háibushì	*還不是	*还不是	I.69
háishì	^還是	^还是	III.03
hài	咳	咳	II.18
hài	*害	*害	XI.66
hàipà	^害怕	^害怕	X.60
hánlěng	^寒冷	^寒冷	XI.83
hǎn	喊	喊	II.51
hǎo lei!	^好嘞!	^好嘞!	II.72
hē	^呵	^呵	I.66
hébì	*何必	*何必	VII.35
héshēn	^合身	^合身	I.05
héshì	*合適	*合适	II.97
hēi	^嘿	^嘿	I.77
hēi qī lèi	黑七類	黑七类	XI.30
hèn	^恨	^恨	V.55
hng	^哼	^哼	IV.11
hòudào	^厚道	^厚道	VIII.19
hòuhuǐ	*後悔	*后悔	V.31
húnào	^胡鬧	^胡闹	IV.57
húshuō	^胡説	^胡说	IV.52
hútu	*糊塗	*糊涂	VII.16
húzi	鬍子	胡子	IX.29
hùzhào	*護照	*护照	XI.74
huātou	花頭	花头	II.81
huái	^懷	^怀	XII.19
huái⸗yùn	^懷孕	^怀孕	XI.69
Huáiběi	淮北	淮北	XI.15
huānlè	^歡樂	^欢乐	XI.64
huānténg	歡騰	欢腾	XI.60
huán⸗zhài	^還債	^还债	I.21
huàn	*換	*换	II.31
huàn⸗xǐng	喚醒	唤醒	XII.21
huángyú-chē	黄魚車	黄鱼车	I.100
huíbì	^迴避	^回避	IV.01
huí⸗shǒu	回首	回首	XI.05
húntun	餛飩	馄饨	II.24
huógāi	^活該	^活该	V.30
huǒchái	^火柴	^火柴	VII.06
huòdé	^獲得	^获得	IV.46

J

jítǐ-hù	^集體户	^集体户	XI.17
jíxùn	集訓	集训	I.57
jǐ	*擠	*挤	I.31
jìjié	^季節	^季节	VIII.37
jìmǔ	繼母	继母	XI.20
jìrán	*既然	*既然	VII.26
jìshù	*技術	*技术	IX.20
jìtuō	^寄托	^寄托	XII.31
Jiānádà	加拿大	加拿大	XI.21
jiāwù-huó	家務活	家务活	II.86
jià	^架	^架	V.21
jià	^嫁	^嫁	VI.42
jiāndìng	^堅定	^坚定	VIII.30
jiānnán	^艱難	^艰难	XI.53
jiǎng⸗sǐ	講死	讲死	III.04
jiāogěi	*交給	*交给	II.04
jiāotōng	*交通	*交通	I.87
jiǎotà-chē	^脚踏車	^脚踏车	I.45
jiào	^叫	^叫	VI.36
jiàoliàn	^教練	^教练	IV.38
jiàoyǎng	^教養	^教养	V.35
jiēdào dǎng-wěi	^街道黨委	^街道党委	VIII.03
jiēfā	^揭發	^揭发	II.42

K

L

lín-chǎn	臨產	临产	XI.78
línjū	*鄰居	*邻居	V.70
línjū	鄰居	邻居	RW
língjiàn	^零件	^零件	III.06
liú-yán	^流言	^流言	VII.12
liú-yán fēi-yǔ	流言蜚語	流言蜚语	VII.19
liú≠tì	^流涕	^流涕	XI.14
lòngtáng	弄堂	弄堂	I.88
lòngtáng-kǒu	弄堂口	弄堂口	II.13
lúzi	^爐子	^炉子	I.61
luàn	*亂	*乱	IX.02
lúnzi	^輪子	^轮子	XI.52
luósī-mào	螺絲帽	螺丝帽	IX.01
luò≠hù	^落戶	^落户	II.36

M

ma	^嘛	^嘛	II.12
mǎlù	^馬路	^马路	X.37
mǎtóu	碼頭	码头	II.68
mán	^瞞	^瞒	VIII.07
mǎn...zhōusuì	滿…週歲	满…周岁	XII.02
mǎnzú	*滿足	*满足	XII.16
mànchána	^漫長	^漫长	XI.55
mànzǒu	^慢走	^慢走	V.71
mánghe	忙合	忙合	II.22
Máomao	毛毛	毛毛	RW
máo-yī	^毛衣	^毛衣	V.17
máodùn	*矛盾	*矛盾	III.17
mào	冒	冒	V.63
méi...de shì	*沒…的事	*沒…的事	I.46
méishì	*沒事	*沒事	I.50
méi-qiú	煤球	煤球	V.66
mēn zài xīnlǐ	悶在心裡	闷在心里	IV.06
mén	*門	*门	XII.07
měngliè	猛烈	猛烈	X.31
mèng	*夢	*梦	XI.44
Mèng Bīn	孟彬	孟彬	RW
míbǔ	^彌補	^弥补	XII.13
mǐ	*米	*米	X.25
miǎnde	^免得	^免得	V.19
miàn	面	面	II.56
miànqián	^面前	^面前	III.18
míng méi zhèng qǔ	明媒正娶	明媒正娶	VII.32
míngmíng	*明明	*明明	VIII.48
míng-pái	^名牌	^名牌	III.11
míngguì	*名貴	*名贵	IV.31
mìngkǔ	命苦	命苦	II.26
mìngyùn	^命運	^命运	I.97
mòbukāi	抹不開	抹不开	II.44
mòshōu	^沒收	^沒收	I.47
mǒurén	某人	某人	RW

N

na	*哪	*哪	I.06
nǎinai	^奶奶	^奶奶	II.75
nánguài	*難怪	*难怪	VIII.20
Nánnan	男男	男男	RW
nào	*鬧	*闹	VI.11
nào bièniu	鬧別扭	闹别扭	III.25
nénggàn	*能幹	*能干	III.32
ǹg	^嗯	^嗯	II.45
nǐ máng	你忙	你忙	VII.05
...nì	*V-膩	*V-腻	VIII.14
nián fù yìnián	年復一年	年复一年	XI.50
niánqīng	*年輕	*年轻	VIII.11
niǎn	攆	撵	IX.34
niáng	娘	娘	VI.25
niáng liǎ	娘倆	娘俩	VIII.06
niēhé	捏合	捏合	XII.28
niúpéng	牛棚	牛棚	XI.08
nòng	*弄	*弄	I.13
nǚ-pái	女排	女排	IV.45
nuó	*挪	*挪	I.92
nuò	喏	喏	VII.07

O

o	^噢	^噢	I.23
òuqì	慪氣	怄气	VII.36

shīqù	失去	失去	XI.19
shì	^世	^世	VIII.15
shìlì	*勢力	*势力	IV.18
shìshi	*試試	*试试	II.96
shìyè	*事業	*事业	XII.10
shōu	*收	*收	I.34
shǒu-qiāng	手槍	手枪	V.02
shǒuxù	*手續	*手续	XI.73
shǒu≠guǎ	守寡	守寡	IX.31
shòu	*瘦	*瘦	X.21
shūjì	^書記	^书记	V.68
shūshu	^叔叔	^叔叔	VII.04
shǔyú	*屬於	*属于	XI.28
shuāi≠jiāo	^摔跤	^摔跤	V.62
shuì lǎn jiào	^睡懶覺	^睡懒觉	II.52
shuōbuguò	*說不過	*说不过	IX.21
shuō≠chuān	^說穿	^说穿	IX.23
shuō≠dìng	*說定	*说定	V.25
shuō≠huà... suàn≠shù	說話…算數	说话…算数	X.29
sī-zhāng	私章	私章	VI.18
...sǐ	^V-死	^V-死	VII.01
sǐ yātou	死丫頭	死丫头	I.54
sǐ...	^死…	^死…	II.76
...sǐle	*SV死了	*SV死了	VII.03
sǐ≠xīn	^死心	^死心	IX.11
sì-rén-bāng	^四人幫	^四人帮	IX.18
sìjiǎo-shé	四腳蛇	四脚蛇	IV.29
sōng	^鬆	^松	II.09
sòng	*送	*送	III.24
sòng≠huò	送貨	送货	I.70
Sūzhōu	蘇州	苏州	II.15
sūnzi	*孫子	*孙子	III.29
suǒ	^鎖	^锁	V.69
suǒwèi	*所謂	*所谓	XII.36

T

tā mā	^他媽	^他妈	IV.47
tà	^踏	^踏	I.99
tà-bǎn	踏板	踏板	V.09
tàntan	探探	探探	IV.58
tàng	*趟	*趟	I.36
tǎoyàn	^討厭	^讨厌	IX.05
tào bèizi	套被子	套被子	V.64
tè-chǎn	^特產	^特产	IV.30
tè-xiào	^特效	^特效	IV.28
tèdì	^特地	^特地	I.71
téng	^疼	^疼	X.52
tí	*提	*提	III.27
tí yìjian	^提意見	^提意见	III.37
tíxǐng	^提醒	^提醒	VII.14
tǐzhì	^體制	^体制	IV.33
tiānzhēn	*天真	*天真	IV.14
tiánjìng-duì	田徑隊	田径队	II.95
tiáo	*條	*条	II.83
tiǎo≠míng	挑明	挑明	IX.09
tīng≠huà	*聽話	*听话	V.01
tǐng	^挺	^挺	II.89
tǐng≠zhù	挺住	挺住	V.58
tōngzhī	*通知	*通知	V.54
tóngzhì-men	*同志們	*同志们	IV.37
tǒngzhì	*統治	*统治	IV.19
tòngkū	^痛哭	^痛哭	XI.13
tòngkǔ	*痛苦	*痛苦	IV.04
tōu	*偷	*偷	III.19
tōutōu	^偷偷	^偷偷	VI.23
tóufa	^頭髮	^头发	V.07
tóuxiáng	^投降	^投降	X.30
tūrán	*突然	*突然	XI.71
tuántuán-zhuàn	團團轉	团团转	IV.55
tuī...yibǎ	推…一把	推…一把	II.71
tuǐ	^腿	^腿	VIII.43
tuì≠xiū	*退休	*退休	II.91
tuō	*託	*托	V.45
tuō	*拖	*拖	VIII.10
tuō≠shǒu	脫手	脱手	III.05
tuō≠xialai	^脫下來	^脱下来	II.85

W

wa	^哇	^哇	I.42
wài-gōng	^外公	^外公	VI.37
wàishì-jú	^外事局	^外事局	XI.70
wān≠guòlái	彎過來	弯过来	I.72
wǎn	*碗	*碗	II.23

wàn-huā fánróng	萬花繁榮	万花繁荣	VIII.36
wǎngshì	^往事	^往事	XI.03
wàng	望	望	V.43
wàng	^望	^望	VI.27
wéiyī	*唯一	*唯一	V.41
wēnnuǎn	^溫暖	^温暖	VIII.41
wénhuà dà gémìng	*文化大革命	*文化大革命	XI.24
wénjìng	^文靜	^文静	III.45
wěn	吻	吻	XII.12
wǒ shuō ne	我說呢	我说呢	II.65
wūqī bāzāo	^烏七八糟	^乌七八糟	VI.29
wú shì bu+	無事不+	无事不+	I.75
wú≠zuì	^無罪	^无罪	XII.20
wùhuì	*誤會	*误会	II.63

X

xià juéxīn	^下決心	^下决心	III.15
...xialai	^…下來	^…下来	I.20
xiánhuì	賢惠	贤惠	III.47
xiánròu	鹹肉	咸肉	I.62
xiàn	*限	*限	I.84
xiànquān	線圈	线圈	II.08
xiāng yī wéi mìng	相依為命	相依为命	XI.23
xiāngchǔ	^相處	^相处	III.38
xiānggān	^相干	^相干	IX.25
xiānghù	*相互	*相互	XI.35
xiǎngxiàng	*想像	*想象	VI.06
xiāo	削	削	X.54
Xiāo Jiàn	^蕭健	^肖健	RW
Xiāo Yún	^蕭雲	^肖云	RW
Xiǎo Tián	小田	小田	V.65
xiǎo zǔzōng	小祖宗	小祖宗	VII.18
xiǎo-tuǐ	小腿	小腿	X.40
xiǎoér mábì-zhèng	小兒麻痺症	小儿麻痹症	VIII.44
xiǎorén-shū	小人書	小人书	VI.40
xiǎoshí	*小時	*小时	X.27
xiǎozi	小子	小子	I.67
xiǎozǔ	小組	小组	I.35
xiàomīmī	^笑咪咪	^笑咪咪	IV.50

xiàoshùn	^孝順	^孝顺	X.20
xīngān qíngyuàn	心甘情願	心甘情愿	X.19
xīnlíng	^心靈	^心灵	VII.28
xīnténg	^心疼	^心疼	X.22
xìngfú	^幸福	^幸福	X.04
xiū dìqiú	修地球	修地球	I.81
xuétou	噱頭	噱头	II.61
xúnzhǎo	尋找	寻找	XII.30

Y

ya	*呀	*呀	I.11
yánhán	嚴寒	严寒	XI.86
yánzhòng	嚴重	严重	VII.25
yǎnlèi	^眼淚	^眼泪	XI.76
yángméi	楊梅	杨梅	II.73
yāoqiú	*要求	*要求	XII.17
yǎo≠yá	咬牙	咬牙	V.57
yàobu	*要不	*要不	I.39
...yàomìng	^SV得要命	^SV得要命	VIII.46
yào≠huílai	*要回來	*要回来	I.49
yàoshi	^鑰匙	^钥匙	I.26
yězhǒng	野種	野种	VI.44
yíbèizi	*一輩子	*一辈子	IV.03
yí dà qīngzǎo	^一大清早	^一大清早	II.10
yìdāo liǎngduàn	^一刀兩斷	^一刀两断	III.16
yī..., èr...	^一…, 二…	^一…, 二…	III.20
yì kē xīn	^一顆心	^一颗心	IX.07
yìqǐ	*一起	*一起	III.02
yì qīngzǎo	^一清早	^一清早	IX.30
...yì shēng(r)	^V …一聲(兒)	^V …一声(儿)	VII.15
yíxiàzi	^一下子	^一下子	VI.43
yìxīn	*一心	*一心	XII.18
yì xiǔ	一宿	一宿	X.58
yīshang	*衣裳	*衣裳	II.66
yīshēng	醫生	医生	RW
yīyuàn	*醫院	*医院	VI.22
yí≠mín	^移民	^移民	XI.72
yǐ	*以	*以	XI.25

yìtú	意圖	意图	VIII.32
yìxiǎng búdào	^意想不到	^意想不到	VII.08
yīnxìn quán wú	音信全無	音信全无	XI.79
yǐn≠qǐ	^引起	^引起	X.44
yìnxiàng	*印象	*印象	IV.49
yīngxióng	^英雄	^英雄	IV.21
yìng	^硬	^硬	XII.27
yō	^喲	^哟	I.01
yǒngqì	*勇氣	*勇气	IV.20
yòngbuliǎo	^用不了	^用不了	X.09
yōuyù	^憂鬱	^忧郁	VII.11
Yóu Nǎinai	尤奶奶	尤奶奶	RW
yóudìyuán	郵遞員	邮递员	RW
yǒu-qíng	^友情	^友情	VIII.29
yǒu guǐ	有鬼	有鬼	III.13
yǒu huà jǐn-guǎn shuō	有話儘管說	有话尽管说	VIII.05
yǒushuō yǒuxiào	^有說有笑	^有说有笑	II.27
yǒuyì-de	*有意地	*有意地	XI.67
yòu lái le	^又來了	^又来了	III.26
yòu zěnmeyàng	…又怎麼樣	…又怎么样	X.53
yòu-pài	^右派	^右派	VI.04
yú	餘	余	I.22
yuánliàng	*原諒	*原谅	V.56
yuē	*約	*约	III.01
yūn	^暈	^晕	X.50

Z

zá-pái	雜牌	杂牌	III.09
zài jiàoyù	^再教育	^再教育	XI.16
zàisān	^再三	^再三	XI.06
zánmen	*咱們	*咱们	II.57
zànchéng	*贊成	*赞成	X.03
zāng-shuǐ	髒水	脏水	VI.30
zāoyù	^遭遇	^遭遇	XI.33
zǎodiǎn	^早點	^早点	I.03
zàofǎn-pài	造反派	造反派	II.40
zào≠yáo zhòng≠shāng	造謠中傷	造谣中伤	VII.27
zěnme hǎo yìsi	*怎麼好意思	*怎么好意思	I.10
zhà	炸	炸	V.24
zhāi	^摘	^摘	I.96
zhǎi	*窄	*窄	I.89
zhànyǒu	^戰友	^战友	I.82
zhāngkǒu... bìkǒu...	張口…閉口…	张口…闭口…	III.39
zhàngfu	*丈夫	*丈夫	VII.09
zhāojí	*着急	*着急	X.10
zhàogù	*照顧	*照顾	VIII.27
zhémó	^折磨	^折磨	IV.02
Zhèjiāng Měiyuàn	浙江美院	浙江美院	VI.01
zhēn	^針	^针	X.43
zhēnxī	珍惜	珍惜	V.60
zhēng	*爭	*争	X.23
zhēng≠yǎn	^睜眼	^睁眼	VI.24
zhèng-shěn	政審	政审	XI.46
zhèngcè	*政策	*政策	IX.16
zhèngjing	*正經	*正经	IV.53
zhī	織	织	V.16
zhīpèi	^支配	^支配	XI.38
zhīqīng	*知青	*知青	XI.09
zhízhào	^執照	^执照	I.33
zhǐzé	指責	指责	VII.21
zhǐzhǐ chuōchuō	指指戳戳	指指戳戳	IX.24
zhì	^治	^治	IV.26
zhìqì	^志氣	^志气	III.23
zhìshǎo	*至少	*至少	VI.26
Zhōnghuá	*中華	*中华	IV.22
Zhōngxīn Yīyuàn	中心醫院	中心医院	X.39
zhòng	眾	众	RW
Zhōu Dàmā	周大媽	周大妈	RW
zhújiàn	^逐漸	^逐渐	XI.56
zhǔdòng	*主動	*主动	IV.56
zhǔjiàn	^主見	^主见	IV.07
zhù	^祝	^祝	X.33
zhuānmén...	*專門…	*专门…	V.12
zhuǎn≠yǎn	^轉眼	^转眼	VII.34
zhuàn	^賺	^赚	I.101
zhuànkē	篆刻	篆刻	VI.17
zhuāng	^裝	^装	III.12

LIST OF FIRST CHARACTERS IN THE VOCABULARY INDEX

IN COMPLEX FORM

The lead characters of all entries in the vocabulary index are listed here. Characters are ordered by number of strokes and, within each stroke-number grouping, by the configuration of the first stroke of each character. Thus a character whose pronunciation is not known can first be looked up here, then entries beginning with this character can be found in the alphabetically ordered vocabulary index on the preceding pages.

一畫

一 yī

二畫

一 七 qī
丿 人 rén
乛 了 liǎo
又 yòu

三畫

一 下 xià
丈 zhàng
大 dà
工 gōng
才 cái
丨 上 shàng
口 kǒu
丿 千 qiān
乙 女 nǚ
小 xiǎo

四畫

丶 心 xīn
文 wén
火 huǒ
一 不 bù
友 yǒu
天 tiān
尤 yóu
支 zhī
丨 中 zhōng
日 rì
丿 什 shén
今 jīn
公 gōng
反 fǎn
手 shǒu
毛 máo
牛 niú
乛 尺 chǐ
引 yǐn

五畫

丶 主 zhǔ
必 bì
一 世 shì
可 kě
右 yòu
巧 qiǎo
平 píng
打 dǎ
正 zhèng
丨 叫 jiào
四 sì
田 tián
丿 他 tā
代 dài
冬 dōng
包 bāo
外 wài
失 shī
犯 fàn
生 shēng
用 yòng
白 bái
乙 以 yǐ
出 chū
加 jiā
奶 nǎi
皮 pí
矛 máo

六畫

丶 交 jiāo
守 shǒu
安 ān
忙 máng
米 mǐ
衣 yī
一 共 gòng
再 zài
存 cún
成 chéng
扣 kòu
有 yǒu
死 sǐ
老 lǎo
考 kǎo
至 zhì
丨 光 guāng
同 tóng
吃 chī
回 huí
早 zǎo
丿 印 yìn
名 míng
合 hé
年 nián
自 zì
ㄥ 好 hǎo
收 shōu

七畫

丶 沈 chén
決 jué
沒 méi
沒 mò
究 jiū
良 liáng
一 孝 xiào
弄 lòng
志 zhì
抗 kàng
技 jì
把 bǎ
批 pī
折 zhé
投 tóu
走 zǒu
丨 吭 kēng
吻 wěn
吵 chǎo
呀 ya
男 nán
丿 何 hé
作 zuò
你 nǐ
免 miǎn
我 wǒ
狂 kuáng
私 sī
身 shēn
乙 妨 fáng
忍 rěn
改 gǎi

八畫

丶 刻 kē
底 dǐ
放 fàng
波 bō
治 zhì
泡 pào
疙 gē
社 shè
初 chū
一 事 shì
來 lái
其 qí
刺 cì
到 dào
取 qǔ
幸 xìng
抹 mò
抽 chōu
抱 bào
拖 tuō
拆 chāi
花 huā
表 biǎo
長 cháng
丨 叔 shū

- 呵 hē
- 明 míng
- 歧 qí
- 肯 kěn
- 丿 乖 guāi
- 周 zhōu
- 命 mìng
- 季 jì
- 往 wǎng
- 所 suǒ
- 爭 zhēng
- 知 zhī
- 肺 fèi
- 股 gǔ
- 乛 孟 mèng
- 孤 gū
- 居 jū
- 門 mén
- 阿 ā

九畫

- 、 冠 guàn
- 前 qián
- 恨 hèn
- 流 liú
- 活 huó
- 炸 zhà
- 炮 pào
- 突 tū
- 音 yīn
- 一 厚 hòu
- 封 fēng
- 拼 pīn
- 指 zhǐ
- 挑 tiǎo
- 政 zhèng
- 春 chūn
- 某 mǒu
- 枯 kū
- 珍 zhēn
- 相 xiāng
- 胡 hú
- 英 yīng
- 要 yāo yào
- 面 miàn
- 丨 冒 mào
- 削 xiāo
- 咬 yǎo
- 哎 āi
- 咳 hài
- 哇 wa
- 哈 hā
- 咱 zán
- 省 shěng
- 背 bēi
- 丿 保 bǎo
- 促 cù
- 卻 què
- 待 dài
- 後 hòu
- 怎 zěn
- 段 duàn
- 看 kàn
- 重 chóng
- 風 fēng
- 乛 勇 yǒng
- 既 jì
- 架 jià
- 約 yuē
- 限 xiàn
- 飛 fēi

十畫

- 、 害 hài
- 家 jiā
- 差 chà
- 悄 qiāo
- 料 liào
- 浙 zhè
- 病 bìng
- 疼 téng
- 神 shén
- 祝 zhù
- 窄 zhǎi
- 粉 fěn
- 討 tǎo
- 送 sòng
- 高 gāo
- 託 tuō
- 一 原 yuán
- 套 tào
- 捏 niē
- 捉 zhuō
- 挺 tǐng
- 挪 nuó
- 根 gēn
- 班 bān
- 秦 qín
- 馬 mǎ
- 鬥 dòu
- 丨 哼 hng
- 哭 kū
- 哪 na
- 豈 qǐ
- 迴 huí
- 丿 倆 liǎ
- 借 jiè
- 倒 dào
- 個 gè
- 修 xiū
- 倉 cāng
- 師 shī
- 氣 qì
- 烏 wū
- 特 tè
- 笑 xiào
- 釘 dīng
- 針 zhēn
- 鬼 guǐ
- 乛 娘 niáng
- 孫 sūn
- 書 shū
- 純 chún
- 能 néng
- 退 tuì
- 除 chú

十一畫

- 、 寄 jì
- 情 qíng
- 望 wàng
- 淮 huái
- 淨 jìng
- 郭 guō
- 一 乾 gān
- 堅 jiān
- 執 zhí
- 專 zhuān
- 探 tàn
- 接 jiē
- 推 tuī
- 教 jiào
- 理 lǐ
- 聊 liáo
- 逐 zhú
- 都 dōu
- 頂 dǐng
- 丨 啦 la
- 啊 a
- 唯 wéi
- 國 guó
- 崇 chóng
- 畢 bì
- 眾 zhòng
- 眼 yǎn
- 累 lèi
- 處 chǔ
- 野 yě
- 丿 做 zuò
- 偷 tōu
- 偏 piān
- 兜 dōu
- 動 dòng
- 夠 gòu
- 從 cóng
- 條 tiáo
- 猜 cāi
- 猛 měng
- 移 yí
- 脫 tuō
- 造 zào
- 乛 參 cān
- 張 zhāng
- 統 tǒng
- 通 tōng
- 欸 ēi

十二畫

- 、 勞 láo
- 寒 hán
- 尊 zūn
- 就 jiù
- 愣 lèng
- 曾 céng
- 渡 dù
- 湊 còu
- 痛 tòng
- 善 shàn
- 着 zhāo
- 一 插 chā
- 提 tí
- 揭 jiē
- 換 huàn
- 散 sàn
- 欺 qī
- 殘 cán
- 硬 yìng
- 裁 cái
- 趁 chèn
- 黃 huáng
- 丨 喊 hǎn
- 單 dān
- 喲 yō
- 喚 huàn
- 喏 nuò
- 悲 bēi
- 蛤 gé
- 黑 hēi
- 丿 創 chuàng
- 剩 shèng
- 無 wú
- 牌 pái
- 等 děng
- 筆 bǐ
- 筋 jīn
- 街 jiē
- 進 jìn
- 郵 yóu
- 集 jí
- 飯 fàn
- 乛 尋 xún

	悶	mèn
	登	dēng
	結	jié
	絶	jué
	開	kāi

十三畫

丶	意	yì
	溫	wēn
	煤	méi
	補	bǔ
	裡	lǐ
	試	shì
一	勢	shì
	幹	gàn
	感	gǎn
	想	xiǎng
	惹	rě
	搞	gǎo
	搬	bān
	搶	qiǎng
	楊	yáng
	碰	pèng
	碗	wǎn
	萬	wàn
	落	luò
	逼	bī
	零	líng
	鼓	gǔ
丨	嗯	ǹg
	暈	yūn
	照	zhào
	當	dāng
	睜	zhēng
	罪	zuì
	過	guò
丿	遍	biàn
	亂	luàn
	傳	chuán
	催	cuī
	傷	shāng
	愛	ài
	腳	jiǎo
	舅	jiù
	解	jiě
乙	嫁	jià
	經	jīng
	裝	zhuāng
	隔	gé

十四畫

丶	寡	guǎ
	慢	màn
	慪	òu
	滾	gǔn
	滿	mǎn
	漫	màn
	瘋	fēng
	認	rèn
	誤	wù
	説	shuō
一	夢	mèng
	摘	zhāi
	摔	shuāi
	緊	jǐn
	趕	gǎn
	輕	qīng
丨	嘛	ma
	團	tuán
	對	duì
	睡	shuì
丿	徹	chè
	管	guǎn
	腿	tuǐ
ㄱ	盡	jìn

十五畫

丶	寬	kuān
	審	shěn
	廣	guǎng
	廠	chǎng
	慶	qìng
	憐	lián
	瘦	shòu
	糊	hú
	諒	liàng
	請	qǐng
	調	diào
	鄰	lín
一	厲	lì
	憂	yōu
	撞	zhuàng
	撒	sā
	熱	rè
	碼	mǎ
	賢	xián
	趟	tàng
	輛	liàng
	輪	lún
	遭	zāo
	遷	qiān
	鬧	nào
丨	嘿	hēi
	憋	biē
	踏	tà
	踩	cǎi
丿	篆	zhuàn
	颳	guā
	餘	yú
ㄥ	樂	lè
	線	xiàn

十六畫

丶	燒	shāo
	褲	kù
	親	qīn
一	操	cāo
	蕭	xiāo
	頭	tóu
丨	噱	xué
	噢	o
	戰	zhàn
	瞞	mán
丿	儘	jǐn
	膩	nì
	錦	jǐn
	餛	hún
ㄱ	遲	chí

十七畫

丶	懂	dǒng
	濕	shī
	講	jiǎng
一	戴	dài
	擠	jǐ
	擦	cā
	擱	gē
	臨	lín
	艱	jiān
	醜	chǒu
丨	瞧	qiáo
	虧	kuī
	螺	luó
	賺	zhuàn
	還	hái
	還	huán
丿	獲	huò
乙	彌	mí
	縫	féng

十八畫

丶	離	lí
	雜	zá
一	攆	niǎn
	擺	bǎi
	轉	zhuǎn
	醫	yī
	鬆	sōng
丨	蹦	bèng
丿	鎖	suǒ
乙	織	zhī
	闖	chuǎng

十九畫

丶	懷	huái
一	礙	ài
	難	nán
	騙	piàn
	鬍	hú
丨	蹬	dèng
	蹭	cèng
丿	贊	zàn
ㄱ	關	guān

二十畫

丶	寶	bǎo
	懺	chàn
	爐	lú
一	勸	quàn
	蘋	píng
	蘇	sū
	警	jǐng
丨	嚴	yán
	鹹	xián
	黨	dǎng
ㄥ	繼	jì

二十一畫

丶	護	hù
丿	顧	gù
ㄱ	屬	shǔ

二十二 - 二十七畫

丶	彎	wān
	襯	chèn
一	歡	huān
	聽	tīng
	驚	jīng
	觀	guān
丨	髒	zāng
	體	tǐ
丿	鑰	yào
	鑽	zuān

LIST OF FIRST CHARACTERS IN THE VOCABULARY INDEX

IN SIMPLIFIED FORM

The lead characters of all entries in the vocabulary index are listed here. Characters are ordered by number of strokes and, within each stroke-number grouping, by the configuration of the first stroke of each character. Thus a character whose pronunciation is not known can first be looked up here, then entries beginning with this character can be found in the alphabetically ordered vocabulary index on the preceding pages.

一画

- 一 yī

二画

- 一 厂 chǎng
- 七 qī
- 丿 人 rén
- ㇇ 又 yòu
- 了 liǎo

三画

- 丶 广 guǎng
- 门 mén
- 一 干 gān
- 干 gàn
- 亏 kuī
- 工 gōng
- 下 xià
- 大 dà
- 万 wàn
- 丈 zhàng
- 才 cái
- 丨 上 shàng
- 口 kǒu
- 丿 千 qiān
- 个 gè
- ㇠ 飞 fēi
- 亅 小 xiǎo
- 女 nǚ
- 马 mǎ

四画

- 丶 斗 dòu
- 火 huǒ
- 文 wén
- 认 rèn
- 心 xīn
- 一 开 kāi
- 天 tiān
- 无 wú
- 专 zhuān
- 支 zhī
- 不 bù
- 尤 yóu
- 友 yǒu
- 丨 日 rì
- 中 zhōng
- 丿 仓 cāng
- 从 cóng
- 公 gōng
- 今 jīn
- 毛 máo
- 牛 niú
- 气 qì
- 手 shǒu
- 什 shén
- 反 fǎn
- 风 fēng
- 乌 wū
- ㇇ 劝 quàn
- 尺 chǐ
- 引 yǐn
- 丑 chǒu
- 书 shū

五画

- 丶 头 tóu
- 主 zhǔ
- 必 bì
- 讨 tǎo
- 一 平 píng
- 巧 qiǎo
- 世 shì
- 正 zhèng
- 厉 lì
- 右 yòu
- 打 dǎ
- 可 kě
- 丨 长 cháng
- 叫 jiào
- 四 sì
- 田 tián
- 丿 失 shī
- 白 bái
- 代 dài
- 生 shēng
- 他 tā
- 包 bāo
- 处 chǔ
- 冬 dōng
- 犯 fàn
- 乐 lè
- 外 wài
- 用 yòng
- ㇠ 对 duì
- 矛 máo
- 以 yǐ
- 出 chū
- 加 jiā
- 奶 nǎi
- 皮 pí

六画

- 丶 安 ān
- 关 guān
- 决 jué
- 米 mǐ
- 守 shǒu
- 交 jiāo
- 庆 qìng
- 衣 yī
- 忏 chàn
- 闯 chuǎng
- 忙 máng
- 讲 jiǎng
- 一 动 dòng
- 共 gòng
- 考 kǎo
- 老 lǎo
- 再 zài
- 成 chéng
- 存 cún
- 死 sǐ
- 有 yǒu
- 毕 bì
- 过 guò
- 扣 kòu
- 托 tuō
- 执 zhí
- 至 zhì
- 丨 当 dāng
- 光 guāng
- 师 shī
- 吃 chī
- 回 huí
- 岂 qǐ
- 同 tóng
- 团 tuán
- 早 zǎo
- 丿 创 chuāng
- 合 hé
- 众 zhòng
- 年 nián
- 迁 qiān
- 传 chuán
- 伤 shāng
- 自 zì
- 后 hòu
- 名 míng
- 印 yìn
- 杂 zá
- 争 zhēng
- ㇠ 观 guān
- 欢 huān
- 尽 jǐn, jìn
- 寻 xún
- 收 shōu
- 好 hǎo
- 孙 sūn
- 约 yuē

七画

- 丶 沈 chén
- 究 jiū

没 méi
没 mò
怀 huái
闷 mèn
怄 òu
忧 yōu
补 bǔ
初 chū
良 liáng
一 来 lái
进 jìn
弄 lòng
劳 láo
苏 sū
孝 xiào
严 yán
杨 yáng
志 zhì
走 zǒu
还 hái
还 huán
把 bǎ
护 hù
技 jì
抗 kàng
批 pī
抢 qiǎng
投 tóu
医 yī
折 zhé
丨 肖 xiāo
坚 jiān
呀 ya
吵 chǎo
吭 kēng
里 lǐ
男 nán
听 tīng
吻 wěn
邮 yóu
丿 邻 lín
余 yú
钉 dīng
乱 luàn
私 sī

我 wǒ
针 zhēn
何 hé
你 nǐ
身 shēn
体 tǐ
作 zuò
彻 chè
饭 fàn
狂 kuáng
免 miǎn
条 tiáo
乛 迟 chí
改 gǎi
阿 ā
妨 fáng
忍 rěn
纯 chún

八画

宝 bǎo
波 bō
单 dān
炉 lú
泡 pào
审 shěn
治 zhì
底 dǐ
放 fàng
疙 gē
净 jìng
刻 kē
怜 lián
闹 nào
衬 chèn
社 shè
试 shì
一 表 biǎo
刺 cì
花 huā
苹 píng
其 qí
取 qǔ
事 shì
松 sōng
幸 xìng
码 mǎ
抱 bào
拆 chāi
抽 chōu
到 dào
顶 dǐng
轮 lún
抹 mò
势 shì
拖 tuō
转 zhuǎn
丨 肯 kěn
歧 qí
叔 shū
紧 jǐn
贤 xián
哎 āi
国 guó
呵 hē
明 míng
丿 命 mìng
刮 guā
乖 guāi
季 jì
知 zhī
所 suǒ
往 wǎng
肺 fèi
股 gǔ
周 zhōu
乛 参 cān
艰 jiān
居 jū
弥 mí
张 zhāng
限 xiàn
孤 gū
经 jīng
孟 mèng
线 xiàn
织 zhī

九画

丶 活 huó
流 liú
炮 pào
前 qián
突 tū
炸 zhà
疯 fēng
亲 qīn
弯 wān
音 yīn
恨 hèn
冠 guàn
说 shuō
误 wù
一 春 chūn
珍 zhēn
封 fēng
胡 hú
枯 kū
某 mǒu
却 què
相 xiāng
要 yāo, yào
英 yīng
政 zhèng
残 cán
厚 hòu
面 miàn
咸 xián
挤 jǐ
挪 nuó
拼 pīn
轻 qīng
挑 tiāo
指 zhǐ
丨 省 shěng
削 xiāo
背 bēi
战 zhàn
临 lín
哈 hā
咳 hài
冒 mào
哪 na
哇 wa
咬 yǎo
哟 yō
咱 zán
丿 重 chóng
看 kàn
钥 yào
怎 zěn
保 bǎo
促 cù
段 duàn
俩 liǎ
待 dài
乛 勇 yǒng
既 jì
除 chú
架 jià
结 jié
绝 jué
统 tǒng

十画

丶 差 chà
粉 fěn
害 hài
家 jiā
宽 kuān
料 liào
烧 shāo
送 sòng
窄 zhǎi
浙 zhè
病 bìng
高 gāo
郭 guō
离 lí
疼 téng
悄 qiāo
调 diào
谅 liàng
请 qǐng
神 shén
祝 zhù

一 班 bān
秦 qín
都 dōu
赶 gǎn
根 gēn
获 huò
顾 gù
套 tào
原 yuán
丨 唤 huàn
换 huàn
捏 niē
热 rè
挺 tǐng
捉 zhuō
党 dǎng
啊 a
哼 hng
回 huí
哭 kū
晕 yūn
丿 爱 ài
笔 bǐ
特 tè
笑 xiào
钻 zuān
倒 dào
鬼 guǐ
借 jiè
修 xiū
脏 zāng
乙 难 nán
能 néng
退 tuì
娘 niáng
继 jì

十一画

丶 凑 còu
淮 huái
寄 jì
望 wàng
惊 jīng
情 qíng
一 理 lǐ
教 jiào
聊 liáo
梦 mèng
逐 zhú
接 jiē
辆 liàng
探 tàn
推 tuī
丨 崇 chóng
啦 la
累 lèi
喏 nuò
唯 wéi
眼 yǎn
野 yě
睁 zhēng
丿 移 yí
造 zào
兜 dōu
偏 piān
偷 tōu
做 zuò
猜 cāi
够 gòu
馄 hún
猛 měng
脱 tuō
乙 欸 ēi
通 tōng
属 shǔ

十二画

丶 曾 céng
渡 dù
寒 hán
善 shàn
湿 shī
温 wēn
着 zhao
装 zhuāng
尊 zūn
就 jiù
痛 tòng
愣 lèng
遍 biàn
裤 kù
一 逼 bī
裁 cái
趁 chèn
黄 huáng
落 luò
欺 qī
惹 rě
散 sàn
硬 yìng
插 chā
搁 gē
揭 jiē
提 tí
丨 悲 bēi
蛤 gé
喊 hǎn
黑 hēi
丿 等 děng
筋 jīn
剩 shèng
锁 suǒ
集 jí
舅 jiù
牌 pái
街 jiē
乙 登 dēng
隔 gé
骗 piàn

十三画

丶 满 mǎn
煤 méi
意 yì
一 零 líng
鼓 gǔ
想 xiǎng
碍 ài
感 gǎn
碰 pèng
碗 wǎn
摆 bǎi
搬 bān
搞 gǎo
丨 嗯 ǹg
照 zhào
罪 zuì
丿 锦 jǐn
催 cuī
脚 jiǎo
解 jiě
腻 nì
乙 嫁 jià
缝 féng

十四画

丶 寡 guǎ
滚 gǔn
漫 màn
瘦 shòu
慢 màn
一 摔 shuāi
摘 zhāi
丨 嘛 ma
睡 shuì
赚 zhuàn
丿 管 guǎn
腿 tuǐ

十五画

丶 憋 biē
糊 hú
一 趟 tàng
遭 zāo
撵 niǎn
撒 sā
撞 zhuàng
丨 踩 cǎi
嘿 hēi
瞒 mán
噢 o
踏 tà
丿 篆 zhuàn

十六画

一 操 cāo
丿 赞 zàn
丨 噱 xué

十七画

丶 懂 dǒng
一 戴 dài
擦 cā
丨 螺 luó
瞧 qiáo

十八画

丨 蹦 bèng

十九画

丨 蹭 cèng
蹬 dèng

二十画

一 警 jǐng

大橋下面

二. 句型解釋及練習

Part II: Grammatical Notes and Exercises

CONTENTS OF PART II: GRAMMATICAL NOTES AND EXERCISES

PREFACE TO GRAMMATICAL NOTES AND EXERCISES

The grammatical notes, example sentences, and exercises in this volume are designed to enhance the student's understanding of the dialogues in this film and of the authentic Chinese language in general, and to aid the student in gaining active control of the discourse patterns and key vocabulary items used in the film. In many cases notes and examples go beyond the dialogues in the film, placing the vocabulary and discourse patterns in the larger linguistic context. Many of the items selected for study here are neither purely grammatical patterns nor simple lexical items, as the syntactic and semantic aspects of the language are inextricably interwoven. This semantic-syntactic interdependence, with added dimensions of context sensitivity and emotional connotation, is much more prominent in colloquial speech than in expository prose, and dictionary definitions and textbook explanations are often inadequate to convey the full meaning and nuance of the utterance in its context. In such cases our explanations and examples need to be fleshed out and brought to life by a teacher with native-level proficiency in the language presenting the examples orally, with appropriate intonation, facial expressions, and body language.

This part is divided into the same twelve segments as Part I: Script and Vocabulary Annotations. Each segment contains, on the average, nine discourse patterns. In identifying the patterns to be included, a wide net was cast in order to accommodate students from different textbook backgrounds. Certain high-frequency patterns that are especially difficult for students to absorb, even though they appear in all the basic textbooks, are deliberately included in this volume for "recycling." Individual instructors should feel free to select from the list of discourse patterns to cover in class and to weed out those that seem superfluous for their students.

Within each segment, each discourse pattern is first labeled by a pattern heading, followed in the same line by the contextual example from the film. The pattern is then explained in English and further clarified by two examples (例句) placing the pattern in contexts beyond the film. To help students carry their "passive knowledge" of these patterns into "active usage," exercises of three different kinds are provided under each pattern: 造句, creating sentences using the given pattern; 填充, filling in blanks, either with the given vocabulary or in free form; and 改寫, paraphrasing the given sentence using the given pattern.

Aside from the exercises under each pattern, each segment ends with a set of inclusive translation exercises (翻譯) in which the patterns are represented in random order to foster their active use. In the translations, each sentence should contain at least one of the discourse patterns introduced in the segment.

In all the exercises, an attempt has been made to reinforce the student's newly acquired key vocabulary and to place the discourse patterns and vocabulary in a larger linguistic context beyond that of the film. If there is sufficient class time, all of these exercises, but particularly 填充 and 改寫, as well as the 討論問題 in Part I, can best be done orally to further the student's spoken language proficiency.

SEGMENT I

1) 多/多麼…（呀/啊/哇/哪）！　　你幫我做的飯兜兒多合身哪！ (Part I, p. 2)

The closest English equivalent to this exclamatory pattern is "How...!" The 麼 part of 多麼 is often dispensed with in colloquial speech. The final sentence particle 啊 carries emotional weight, but is optional. The basic form of the particle is "a 啊," but it takes on the following transformations depending on the ending of the preceding syllable.

哇	wa	after u or ao
呀	ya	after a, e, i (except after z, c, s, zh, ch, sh, r), o, ü (including ju, qu, xu)
哪	na	after n
啊	a	after everything but the above

例句： 1) 今天的天氣多好哇！
2) 這張畫多好看哪！

造句 (This exercise is inserted after example sentences under all patterns which students should learn to use actively as well as to understand. If appropriate, provide sufficient context so the meaning of your sentence is clear):

改寫： 例：那個孩子很高興。　　那個孩子多高興啊！
1) 這個孩子很可愛。
2) 那個電影真有意思。
3) 去年夏天，北京特別熱。
4) 她媽媽作的飯好吃極了。

2) 儘管…（好了/吧）　　儘管找我好了。 (p. 2)

儘管 is a movable adverb meaning "as far as one wishes, without holding back, go right ahead and..." In colloquial speech, the sentence usually ends with the optional 好了 or 吧 to give further reinforcement to the sense of being unrestrained. 儘管 is also a colloquial synonym of 雖然, and as such is used as an adverbial conjunction in the following two-clause sentence patterns:

儘管…，（可是/但是）…	Although..., (but)...
…，儘管…	..., even though...

例句： 1) 有什麼不懂的地方，儘管問我好了。
2) 你有什麼心事，儘管跟我說吧。

SEGMENT I

1) 多/多么…（呀/啊/哇/哪）！ 你帮我做的饭兜儿多合身哪！ (Part I, p. 3)

The closest English equivalent to this exclamatory pattern is "How...!" The 么 part of 多么 is often dispensed with in colloquial speech. The final sentence particle 啊 carries emotional weight, but is optional. The basic form of the particle is "a 啊," but it takes on the following transformations depending on the ending of the preceding syllable.

哇	wa	after u or ao
呀	ya	after a, e, i (except after z, c, s, zh, ch, sh, r), o, ü (including ju, qu, xu)
哪	na	after n
啊	a	after everything but the above

例句： 1) 今天的天气多好哇！
2) 这张画多好看哪！

造句 (This exercise is inserted after example sentences under all patterns which students should learn to use actively as well as to understand. If appropriate, provide sufficient context so the meaning of your sentence is clear):

改写： 例：那个孩子很高兴。 那个孩子多高兴啊！
1) 这个孩子很可爱。
2) 那个电影真有意思。
3) 去年夏天，北京特别热。
4) 她妈妈作的饭好吃极了。

2) 尽管…（好了/吧） 尽管找我好了。 (p. 3)

尽管 is a movable adverb meaning "as far as one wishes, without holding back, go right ahead and..." In colloquial speech, the sentence usually ends with the optional 好了 or 吧 to give further reinforcement to the sense of being unrestrained. 尽管 is also a colloquial synonym of 虽然, and as such is used as an adverbial conjunction in the following two-clause sentence patterns:

尽管…，（可是/但是）…	Although..., (but)...
…，尽管…	..., even though...

例句： 1) 有什么不懂的地方，尽管问我好了。
2) 你有什么心事，尽管跟我说吧。

造句：

改寫： 例：要是你喜歡那本書，就告訴我。我替你買。
要是你喜歡那本書，儘管告訴我好了。我替你買。
1) 你們如果來這兒玩兒，就住在我家吧。
2) 別着急，還有半個鐘頭呢，慢慢走吧。
3) 我的書，你們可以隨便看。
4) 我有很多張電影票。誰想看電影，請告訴我。
5) 如果有困難就告訴我，我願意幫助你們。

3) 連…都/也（不）… 你連工錢都不肯收。(p. 2)

The coverb 連 must be coupled with the adverb 都 or 也 to convey the meaning "even (in the adverbial sense)." The pitfall is that students, when actively speaking in Chinese, often equate "even" with 連 and overlook the 都/也 part. This pattern, which should be familiar to intermediate students, is included here for review.

例句： 1) 他學了一年中文了，可是連一個字都不會寫。
2) 昨天我很忙，連晚飯也沒吃。

造句：

改寫： 例：他是美國人，可是他不知道雷根。 他連雷根都不知道。
1) 他一年沒有看見他的老朋友，結果他忘了這個朋友的名字。
2) 學校裡常常演電影，可是他都沒有看過。
3) 我幫了他很多忙，可是他從來不說"謝謝。"
4) 小王有很多有意思的書，可是他一本也不給他的妹妹看。
5) 你知道爲什麼，可是你怎麼一句話都不說呢？

4) 最 早/遲/晚/多/少/好/快, etc. 最遲大後天就回來。(p. 4)

This phrase often functions as an adverbial expression that translates as "at the earliest/the latest/most/best, etc." It functions in two other contexts: a) as a noun modifier, e.g., 最快的車; b) as an expression of manner following a verb, e.g., 他跑得最快.

例句： 1) 我每天晚上最少得睡七個鐘頭的覺，要不然第二天就沒精神。
2) 他家離我這兒有一百英裡，開車去最快也得兩個鐘頭。

造句：

造句：

改写： 例：要是你喜欢那本书，就告诉我。我替你买。
要是你喜欢那本书，尽管告诉我好了。我替你买。
1) 你们如果来这儿玩儿，就住在我家吧。
2) 别着急，还有半个钟头呢，慢慢走吧。
3) 我的书，你们可以随便看。
4) 我有很多张电影票。谁想看电影，请告诉我。
5) 如果有困难就告诉我，我愿意帮助你们。

3) 连…都/也（不）… 你连工钱都不肯收。(p. 3)

The coverb 连 must be coupled with the adverb 都 or 也 to convey the meaning "even (in the adverbial sense)." The pitfall is that students, when actively speaking in Chinese, often equate "even" with 连 and overlook the 都/也 part. This pattern, which should be familiar to intermediate students, is included here for review.

例句： 1) 他学了一年中文了，可是连一个字都不会写。
2) 昨天我很忙，连晚饭也没吃。

造句：

改写： 例：他是美国人，可是他不知道雷根。 他连雷根都不知道。
1) 他一年没有看见他的老朋友，结果他忘了这个朋友的名字。
2) 学校里常常演电影，可是他都没有看过。
3) 我帮了他很多忙，可是他从来不说"谢谢。"
4) 小王有很多有意思的书，可是他一本也不给他的妹妹看。
5) 你知道为什么，可是你怎么一句话都不说呢？

4) 最 早/迟/晚/多/少/好/快，etc. 最迟大后天就回来。(p. 5)

This phrase often functions as an adverbial expression that translates as "at the earliest/the latest/most/best, etc." It functions in two other contexts: a) as a noun modifier, e.g., 最快的车; b) as an expression of manner following a verb, e.g.,他跑得最快.

例句： 1) 我每天晚上最少得睡七个钟头的觉，要不然第二天就没精神。
2) 他家离我这儿有一百英里，开车去最快也得两个钟头。

造句：

改寫： 例：我打算去紐約玩一玩，一個星期後一定回來。
…，最晚一個星期後回來。
1) 我家離學校很近，快點兒走，十分鐘就到了。
2) 美國的字典很貴，便宜的也要五塊錢。
3) 她覺得瘦一點兒好看，所以她每天就吃一碗飯。
4) 這個禮拜我很忙，下個禮拜才能來看你。

5) 還是…吧 還是找個對像，結婚吧。(p. 4)

The 還是 (meaning "still, after all") suggests that the pros and cons of an issue have been taken into account, and the conclusion is being presented in the sentence. The 吧 conveys strong suggestion or urging, and is reinforced by 還是. Note that 還是…吧 is to be treated as one unit even though there may be one or more commas separating verb phrases within it. An example of this is the use of a comma to separate 找個對像 and 結婚 in the example above. 還是 is one of the many expressions that defy precise translation into English (translating it as "after all" results in a certain stiffness in the English). The sense of it is sometimes best conveyed by stress and intonation.

例句： 1) 汽車都很貴，但是在美國很有用，你還是買吧。
2) 自己做飯太麻煩，還是去飯館吃飯吧。

造句：

改寫： 例：我看去杭州吧，西安太遠了。 我看還是去杭州吧，西安太遠了。
1) 你們家人太多，我們家人少，在我們家談更方便。
2) 這件衣服又好又便宜，比那件好，我要買這件。
3) 今天太冷，你最好多穿一點兒。
4) 今天太晚了，你最好明天再去找你的老師。

6) 要不/要是不 要不先收掉你的執照… (p. 6)

In this context, 要不 is short for 要是不, meaning "if (subj.) don't..."
要不 can also be short for 要不然, meaning "otherwise," and functioning as a pivotal phrase in a two-clause sentence, e.g. 你別走，要不，我就生氣了！
要不 and 要是不 should be distinguished from 要不是 "if it weren't for the fact that..." 要不 and 要是不 apply to events in prospect, whereas 要不是 applies to events in retrospect, e.g.:

你<u>要不</u>/<u>要是不</u>來幫忙，我們就作不完了。
If you don't come to help, we will not be able to finish. ("you" may or may not come help)

改写： 例：我打算去纽约玩一玩，一个星期后一定回来。
…，最晚一个星期后回来。
1) 我家离学校很近，快点儿走，十分钟就到了。
2) 美国的字典很贵，便宜的也要五块钱。
3) 她觉得瘦一点儿好看，所以她每天就吃一碗饭。
4) 这个礼拜我很忙，下个礼拜才能来看你。

5) 还是…吧 还是找个对象，结婚吧。 (p. 5)

The 还是 (meaning "still, after all") suggests that the pros and cons of an issue have been taken into account, and the conclusion is being presented in the sentence. The 吧 conveys strong suggestion or urging, and is reinforced by 还是. Note that 还是…吧 is to be treated as one unit even though there may be one or more commas separating verb phrases within it. An example of this is the use of a comma to separate 找个对象 and 结婚 in the example above. 还是 is one of the many expressions that defy precise translation into English (translating it as "after all" results in a certain stiffness in the English). The sense of it is sometimes best conveyed by stress and intonation.

例句： 1) 汽车都很贵，但是在美国很有用，你还是买吧。
2) 自己做饭太麻烦，还是去饭馆吃饭吧。

造句：

改写： 例：我看去杭州吧，西安太远了。 我看还是去杭州吧，西安太远了。
1) 你们家人太多，我们家人少，在我们家谈更方便。
2) 这件衣服又好又便宜，比那件好，我要买这件。
3) 今天太冷，你最好多穿一点儿。
4) 今天太晚了，你最好明天再去找你的老师。

6) 要不/要是不 要不先收掉你的执照… (p. 7)

In this context, 要不 is short for 要是不, meaning "if (subj.) don't..."
要不 can also be short for 要不然, meaning "otherwise," and functioning as a pivotal phrase in a two-clause sentence, e.g. 你别走，要不，我就生气了！
要不 and 要是不 should be distinguished from 要不是 "if it weren't for the fact that..." 要不 and 要是不 apply to events in prospect, whereas 要不是 applies to events in retrospect, e.g.:

你<u>要不</u>/<u>要是不</u>来帮忙，我们就作不完了。
If you don't come to help, we will not be able to finish. ("you" may or may not come help)

<u>要不是</u>你來幫忙，我們就作不完了。

If you hadn't come to help, we would not have been able to finish. ("you" did in fact come help)

例句： 1) 今天天氣太冷了，要不多穿一點兒，一定會生病的。
2) 你要是不喜歡這個飯館，我們可以去另外一個。

造句：

改寫： 例：你如果不說這件事，別人不會知道的。
你要(是)不說這件事，別人不會知道的。
1) 該寫信了，如果再不寫信，家裡人就不放心了。
2) 你如果不想打電話，就去一趟他的宿舍吧。
3) 學生應該做作業，如果你不想做，就別來上課。
4) 下個週末，你如果不去別的地方，請到我家來玩吧。
5) 我覺得今天晚上的電影很好。你如果不想跟我去，我就自己去了。

翻譯 (translate)：
1) If it hadn't rained yesterday, I would have gone. (But in fact, I did not go.)
2) If it doesn't rain tomorrow, I will go for sure. (I may or may not go, depending on the weather.)

7) SV 得很　　她說訓練緊張得很。 (p. 8)

得很 is used to express the intensity of the preceding SV. SV 得很 is quite a bit more intense than 很 SV. There are other phrases that can appear in this pattern:

SV 得利害　　SV 得不得了

Some other expressions of intensity are not linked to the preceding SV by 得:

SV 極了　　SV 透了

例句： 1) 他中午沒有吃飯，餓得很。
2) 那座飯店是新建的，漂亮得很！

造句：

改寫： 例：爸爸的工作忙極了。　　爸爸的工作忙得很。
1) 我的朋友考試考得很好，他很聰明。
2) 這種表是日本進口的，貴極了。
3) 我走了一天的路，真累啊！

要不是你来帮忙，我们就作不完了。

If you hadn't come to help, we would not have been able to finish. ("you" did in fact come help)

例句： 1) 今天天气太冷了，要不多穿一点儿，一定会生病的。

2) 你要是不喜欢这个饭馆，我们可以去另外一个。

造句：

改写： 例：你如果不说这件事，别人不会知道的。

你要(是)不说这件事，别人不会知道的。

1) 该写信了，如果再不写信，家里人就不放心了。

2) 你如果不想打电话，就去一趟他的宿舍吧。

3) 学生应该做作业，如果你不想做，就别来上课。

4) 下个周末，你如果不去别的地方，请到我家来玩吧。

5) 我觉得今天晚上的电影很好。你如果不想跟我去，我就自己去了。

翻译 (translate)：

1) If it hadn't rained yesterday, I would have gone. (But in fact, I did not go.)

2) If it doesn't rain tomorrow, I will go for sure. (I may or may not go, depending on the weather.)

7) SV 得很 她说训练紧张得很。(p. 9)

得很 is used to express the intensity of the preceding SV. SV 得很 is quite a bit more intense than 很 SV. There are other phrases that can appear in this pattern:

SV 得利害 SV 得不得了

Some other expressions of intensity are not linked to the preceding SV by 得:

SV 极了 SV 透了

例句： 1) 他中午沒有吃饭，饿得很。

2) 那座饭店是新建的，漂亮得很！

造句：

改写： 例：爸爸的工作忙极了。 爸爸的工作忙得很。

1) 我的朋友考试考得很好，他很聪明。

2) 这种表是日本进口的，贵极了。

3) 我走了一天的路，真累啊！

4) 很多人都說中國菜好吃極了，是真的嗎？
5) 後天就到春節了，所以這幾天街上買東西的人多極了。

8) 幹嘛/幹嗎/幹什麼　　您幹嘛什麼都留給我呢？ (p. 8)

幹嘛 is a very colloquial way (sometimes to the point of being rude) of saying 怎麼, 爲什麼 or 作什麼. 嘛 is sometimes written with the character 嗎. A slightly less colloquial version of 幹嘛 is 幹什麼.

例句： 1) 你幹嘛把你的功課借給他？
2) 這麼晚了，你出去幹嗎？

造句：

改寫： 例：你爲什麼不去上課？　　你幹嘛不去上課？
1) 你媽媽爲什麼跟你生氣？
2) 他們已經相愛很多年了，爲什麼不結婚呢？
3) 你知道抽煙對身體不好，可是你還抽，爲什麼那麼傻呢？
4) 那個電影不錯，你爲什麼不去看？
5) 從北京到上海不太遠，你爲什麼一定要坐飛機去呢？

9) 還不是…　　我還不是天天送貨。 (p. 8)

This is a rhetorical expression indicating in a rueful tone that not much is new. Here again, the sense can be conveyed much more adequately in English by appropriate stress and intonation rather than by literal translation.

例句： 1) 他每次去商店，還不是用我的自行車。
2) 像他那樣有學問的人，還不是也得去農村勞動。

改寫： 例：這個公司的飛機很好，可是也出過事。
這個公司的飛機很好，還不是也出過事。
1) 我來得那麼早，可是也沒買到新鮮的菜。
2) 這個圖書館很大，可是也沒有這本書。
3) 我作學生的時候，也是天天看書，忙得很。

10) 反正　　反正讓你幫個忙。 (p. 10)

A movable adverb meaning "anyway, anyhow, in any case." Individually, the two characters mean "backward" and "forward," hence the combined meaning "anyway (the thing) is turned."

4) 很多人都说中国菜好吃极了，是真的吗？
5) 后天就到春节了，所以这几天街上买东西的人多极了。

8) 干嘛/干吗/干什么　　　　您干嘛什么都留给我呢？ (p. 9)

干嘛 is a very colloquial way (sometimes to the point of being rude) of saying 怎么, 为什么 or 作什么. 嘛 is sometimes written with the character 吗. A slightly less colloquial version of 干嘛 is 干什么 .

例句：1) 你干嘛把你的功课借给他？
2) 这么晚了，你出去干吗？

造句：

改写：例：你为什么不去上课？　　　你干嘛不去上课？
1) 你妈妈为什么跟你生气？
2) 他们已经相爱很多年了，为什么不结婚呢？
3) 你知道抽烟对身体不好，可是你还抽，为什么那么傻呢？
4) 那个电影不错，你为什么不去看？
5) 从北京到上海不太远，你为什么一定要坐飞机去呢？

9) 还不是…　　　　我还不是天天送货。 (p. 9)

This is a rhetorical expression indicating in a rueful tone that not much is new. Here again, the sense can be conveyed much more adequately in English by appropriate stress and intonation rather than by literal translation.

例句：1) 他每次去商店，还不是用我的自行车。
2) 象他那样有学问的人，还不是也得去农村劳动。

改写：例：这个公司的飞机很好，可是也出过事。
这个公司的飞机很好，还不是也出过事。
1) 我来得那么早，可是也没买到新鲜的菜。
2) 这个图书馆很大，可是也没有这本书。
3) 我作学生的时候，也是天天看书，忙得很。

10) 反正　　　　反正让你帮个忙。 (p. 11)

A movable adverb meaning "anyway, anyhow, in any case." Individually, the two characters mean "backward" and "forward," hence the combined meaning "anyway (the thing) is turned."

例句： 1) 你不去就算了，反正我一個人去也行。
2) 你星期天到我家來玩吧，反正我也沒事。

造句：

改寫： 例：明天下雨或者不下雨，我都不去。 明天下雨或者不下雨，反正我不去。
1) 這件衣服便宜、貴，我都不買。
2) 我幫你買吧！因爲今天我要去商店買東西。
3) 大家都喜歡也沒用，我不喜歡。
4) 這本書是誰寫的都不要緊，這是一本好書。
5) 媽媽不讓我學中文沒有關係，我一定要學中文。

11) …是…，可/可是… 執照是要回來了，可… (p. 10)

This is a two-clause sentence in which the first clause concedes a fact, and the second clause states a countering fact or opinion. The 是 in the first clause is best conveyed in English translation by putting stress on the verb (e.g., "I got the license back"; "I did get the license back."). Sometimes the sense of this 是 can be conveyed by the word "alright" at the end of the first clause (e.g. 她忙是忙，可是… "She's busy alright, but...").

例句： 1) 雪是下了，可是不大。
2) 燈是開了，可是不夠亮。

造句：

改寫： 例：我看了那個電影，可是沒有看懂。 那個電影是看了，可是我沒有看懂。
1) 我吃過飯了，可是沒吃飽。
2) 老師在上課的時候講過這種句子，可是我忘了。
3) 我學過中文，可是那是兩年前的事了。
4) 我有一個表，可是常常不準。

12) 倒也… 這倒也是啊。 (p. 12)

倒也 is a double adverb conveying the sense that the speaker is conceding that his view/assumption/stance/wish was not quite right, and that he has come around to accepting the view/situation stated in the sentence with this double adverb.

例句： 1) 你說的倒也是真的，這個工作就是比那個好。
2) 每天早睡早起，對身體有好處，我想這話倒也有道理啊。

例句： 1) 你不去就算了，反正我一个人去也行。
2) 你星期天到我家来玩吧，反正我也没事。

造句：

改写： 例：明天下雨或者不下雨，我都不去。 明天下雨或者不下雨，反正我不去。
1) 这件衣服便宜、贵，我都不买。
2) 我帮你买吧！因为今天我要去商店买东西。
3) 大家都喜欢也没用，我不喜欢。
4) 这本书是谁写的都不要紧，这是一本好书。
5) 妈妈不让我学中文没有关系，我一定要学中文。

11) …是…，可/可是… 执照是要回来了，可… (p. 11)

This is a two-clause sentence in which the first clause concedes a fact, and the second clause states a countering fact or opinion. The 是 in the first clause is best conveyed in English translation by putting stress on the verb (e.g., "I got the license back"; "I did get the license back."). Sometimes the sense of this 是 can be conveyed by the word "alright" at the end of the first clause (e.g. 她忙是忙，可是… "She's busy alright, but...").

例句： 1) 雪是下了，可是不大。
2) 灯是开了，可是不够亮。

造句：

改写： 例：我看了那个电影，可是没有看懂。 那个电影是看了，可是我没有看懂。
1) 我吃过饭了，可是没吃饱。
2) 老师在上课的时候讲过这种句子，可是我忘了。
3) 我学过中文，可是那是两年前的事了。
4) 我有一个表，可是常常不准。

12) 倒也… 这倒也是啊。 (p. 13)

倒也 is a double adverb conveying the sense that the speaker is conceding that his view/assumption/stance/wish was not quite right, and that he has come around to accepting the view/situation stated in the sentence with this double adverb.

例句： 1) 你说的倒也是真的，这个工作就是比那个好。
2) 每天早睡早起，对身体有好处，我想这话倒也有道理啊。

改寫以下乙說的：例：甲：你沒吃過中國菜，當然不知道中國菜好不好了。
乙：你說得對。　　　你說得倒也對。

1) 甲：你看，開車很容易，我教了你一個下午，你就會了。
乙：是啊，學開車真的不難。
2) 甲：他雖然沒去成北京，可是他去香港玩了幾天。
乙：噢，那也不錯。
3) 甲：要是你不願意現在就工作，那你就在家呆一年，再考一次大學吧。
乙：你說的也是一個辦法，好吧。
4) 甲：很多家庭因爲太有錢了，所以他們的孩子什麼事也不會作。
乙：你說的是一個原因。

INCLUSIVE EXERCISES FOR SEGMENT I:

填充 (Translate the English words or short phrases into Chinese in the contexts provided. Then read the sentences for comprehension):

1) 秦楠三十多歲了還沒 (an "intended")，這件事很多人都不 (comprehend)。
2) 秦楠的爸爸吃過 (light breakfast) 以後，就到學校 (substitute teach) 去了。
3) 他的 ("intended") 又會 (cook) ，又會作衣服。
4) 這件大衣真 (fits)，(fee) 也很便宜。
5) 那個商店很大，所以人總是特別多，(crowded) 得很，要 (be cautious with) 你的錢。
6) 住在我家 (across the way) 的那個人常常忘了帶他的 (key)。
7) 今天早上，他在去 (factory) 的路上，(encounter) 了他的一位老朋友。
8) (not only) 認識，我們很早就是朋友了。
9) 這裡太 (narrow) 了，(set up a stall) 是 (to be a hindrance)。
10) 他們 (set a deadline) 我今天就把攤子 (put away).

翻譯 (The translation exercises are designed to provide practice in using the sentence patterns introduced in each segment. Therefore, each sentence in this section should contain at least one of the sentence patterns introduced in the segment.):

1) Whatever you want me to send you, feel free to write and tell me.
2) I will finish making this dress by Friday at the latest.
3) If you don't ask for your license back, you won't be able to set up your stand anymore.
4) (Colloquial) How come Qin Nan's father doesn't make dinner himself (like a liberated man should)?
5) What's the use of going to college? After graduation, one is still no more than a self-employed person (i.e., still can't get a state-assigned job).
6) - 12): See bottom of facing page.

改写以下乙说的：例：甲：你沒吃过中国菜，当然不知道中国菜好不好了。
乙：你说得对。 你说得倒也对。

1) 甲：你看，开车很容易，我教了你一个下午，你就会了。
乙：是啊，学开车真的不难。
2) 甲：他虽然沒去成北京，可是他去香港玩了几天。
乙：噢，那也不错。
3) 甲：要是你不愿意现在就工作，那你就在家呆一年，再考一次大学吧。
乙：你说的也是一个办法，好吧。
4) 甲：很多家庭因为太有钱了，所以他们的孩子什么事也不会作。
乙：你说的是一个原因。

INCLUSIVE EXERCISES FOR SEGMENT I:

填充 (Translate the English words or short phrases into Chinese in the contexts provided. Then read the sentences for comprehension):

1) 秦楠三十多岁了还沒 (an "intended")，这件事很多人都不 (comprehend)。
2) 秦楠的爸爸吃过 (light breakfast) 以后，就到学校 (substitute teach) 去了。
3) 他的 ("intended") 又会 (cook) ，又会作衣服。
4) 这件大衣真 (fits)，(fee) 也很便宜。
5) 那个商店很大，所以人总是特别多，(crowded) 得很，要 (be cautious with) 你的钱。
6) 住在我家 (across the way) 的那个人常常忘了带他的 (key)。
7) 今天早上，他在去 (factory) 的路上，(encounter) 了他的一位老朋友。
8) (not only) 认识，我们很早就是朋友了。
9) 这里太 (narrow) 了，(set up a stall) 是 (to be a hindrance)。
10) 他们 (set a deadline) 我今天就把摊子 (put away).

翻译 (The translation exercises are designed to provide practice in using the sentence patterns introduced in each segment. Therefore, each sentence in this section should contain at least one of the sentence patterns introduced in the segment.):

1) - 5): See bottom of facing page.
6) Formerly it didn't matter whether one went to work, in any case one had an "iron rice bowl."
7) What you say is right after all. One should be very careful in choosing a potential mate.
8) The lane in front of the Qin's home is very narrow (colloquial).
9) Our school work is intense alright, but sometimes we still have time to play.
10) You had after all better move your stand to across the way.
11) Aiya! How come you even forgot to bring the key?
12) How crowded Shanghai's traffic is!

SEGMENT II

1) 夠 NP SV 的/了 [very colloquial] 這一大清早可夠你忙的啊。 (p. 16)

"It's SV enough for..." This pattern, which has a colloquial flavor, is a variation on the more standard pattern "Subj. 夠 SV 的." The difference in flavor between the two patterns can be seen in the following examples:

這幾天可夠我忙的！ These few days are really busy enough for me!
這幾天我可夠忙的！ These few days I'm really busy enough!

這所新房子夠你舒服了吧！
This new house ought to be comfortable enough for you!
這所新房子，你夠舒服了吧！
You ought to be comfortable enough in this new house!

例句： 1) 她那麼年輕就死了丈夫，一個人帶大三個孩子，真夠她苦的了。
2) 我們在她家住了一個星期，真夠她麻煩的了。

改寫： 例：今天店裡有那麼多的顧客，你一定忙極了。
今天店裡有那麼多的顧客，真夠你忙的。
1) 他今天收到三封信，開心極了。
2) 下星期學生大考，他們非常緊張，所以我決定不再讓他們寫報告了。
3) 他沒考上大學，已經很難過了，你就別再說他了。

2) 差不多了 [colloquial] 你們家毛毛和小陳的事兒差不多了吧？ (p. 16)

差不多 ("almost") is an adverb and is normally followed by a SV or verb phrase. But in the context of a conversation, the SV or verb phrase which logically follows 差不多 may be understood and omitted. In the context of the above example, 差不多了 means "it's just about wrapped up," implying that 毛毛 and 小陳 are just about ready to take the plunge. The exact translation of 差不多了 in each instance depends on the context, e.g.:

你寫的那本書差不多了吧! That book you're writing is just about done, isn't it?
你們休息得差不多了吧！ You've rested just about long enough now, haven't you?

例句： 1) 你功課做得差不多了吧？
2) 下個星期你們要結婚，東西準備得差不多了吧。

SEGMENT II

1) 够 NP SV 的/了 [very colloquial] 这一大清早可够你忙的啊。(p. 17)

"It's SV enough for..." This pattern, which has a colloquial flavor, is a variation on the more standard pattern "Subj. 够 SV 的." The difference in flavor between the two patterns can be seen in the following examples:

这几天可够我忙的！ These few days are really busy enough for me!
这几天我可够忙的！ These few days I'm really busy enough!

这所新房子够你舒服了吧！
This new house ought to be comfortable enough for you!
这所新房子，你够舒服了吧！
You ought to be comfortable enough in this new house!

例句： 1) 她那么年轻就死了丈夫，一个人带大三个孩子，真够她苦的了。
2) 我们在她家住了一个星期，真够她麻烦的了。

改写： 例：今天店里有那么多的顾客，你一定忙极了。
今天店里有那么多的顾客，真够你忙的。
1) 他今天收到三封信，开心极了。
2) 下星期学生大考，他们非常紧张，所以我决定不再让他们写报告了。
3) 他沒考上大学，已经很难过了，你就别再说他了。

2) 差不多了 [colloquial] 你们家毛毛和小陈的事儿差不多了吧？(p. 17)

差不多 ("almost") is an adverb and is normally followed by a SV or verb phrase. But in the context of a conversation, the SV or verb phrase which logically follows 差不多 may be understood and omitted. In the context of the above example, 差不多了 means "it's just about wrapped up," implying that 毛毛 and 小陈 are just about ready to take the plunge. The exact translation of 差不多了 in each instance depends on the context, e.g.:

你写的那本书差不多了吧! That book you're writing is just about done, isn't it?
你们休息得差不多了吧！ You've rested just about long enough now, haven't you?

例句： 1) 你功课做得差不多了吧？
2) 下个星期你们要结婚，东西准备得差不多了吧。

改寫： 例：這件衣裳快做好了吧？ 這件衣裳做得差不多了吧？

1) 你的行李快收拾好了吧？
2) 這個電影快演完了吧？
3) 給顧客做的那條褲子，快做好了吧？
4) 今年夏天，你去了舊金山、紐約、波士頓旅遊，你玩兒夠了吧。

3) 又 一會兒颳風，一會兒下雨，一會兒又打雷。(p. 18)

又 does not always mean "again." Often it is an intensifier, meaning "furthermore, moreover."

例句： 1) 小李本來就聰明好學，去年他家又住了個美國留學生，結果他的英文進步得非常快。
2) 那是一個中午，又沒有風，天氣熱得很。

造句:

改寫： 例：山很高，路也難走，怎麼辦呢？ 山很高，路又難走，怎麼辦呢？

1) 他每天得在外頭工作，還得在家裡做事，累得很。
2) 白天爸爸媽媽都不在家，姐姐也去上學去了。家裡就只有我一個人。
3) 他人很聰明，也願意努力，所以他的中文進步得很快。
4) 學生在學校裡得學這個，得學那個，所以每天都很忙。
5) 他吃得很多，而且也不運動，所以他很胖。

4) 說什麼也 [very colloquial] 她說什麼也抹不開。(p. 18)

Contrary to surface appearance, the subject of 說什麼也 is not 她, but the unstated "one/others." The meaning of the sentence is "No matter what others say, she..." But even this translation sticks too closely to the literal meaning of 說什麼也 ("no matter what...says"). 說什麼也 has come to be used most commonly in its looser meaning of "no matter what,..." Therefore, an even more accurate translation of the above example is "No matter what, she..."

例句： 1)她說那件大衣不好看，說什麼也不肯穿。
2) 那麼多人勸他，可他說什麼也不聽。

改寫： 例：工作太多了，一星期內一定做不完。 說什麼一星期內也做不完。

1) 他睡得很香，沒辦法叫醒他。
2) 這個菜難吃極了，我怎麼也吃不下去。
3) 這兒的活兒太多了，他一個人怎麼也幹不完。
4) 現在太遲了，儘管跑得很快也來不及了。

改写： 例：这件衣裳快做好了吧？ 这件衣裳做得差不多了吧？

1) 你的行李快收拾好了吧？
2) 这个电影快演完了吧？
3) 给顾客做的那条裤子，快做好了吧？
4) 今年夏天，你去了旧金山、纽约、波士顿旅游，你玩儿够了吧。

3) 又 一会儿刮风，一会儿下雨，一会儿又打雷。 (p. 19)

又 does not always mean "again." Often it is an intensifier, meaning "furthermore, moreover."

例句：
1) 小李本来就聪明好学，去年他家又住了个美国留学生，结果他的英文进步得非常快。
2) 那是一个中午，又沒有风，天气热得很。

造句:

改写： 例：山很高，路也难走，怎么办呢？ 山很高，路又难走，怎么办呢？

1) 他每天得在外头工作，还得在家里做事，累得很。
2) 白天爸爸妈妈都不在家，姐姐也去上学去了。家里就只有我一个人。
3) 他人很聪明，也愿意努力，所以他的中文进步得很快。
4) 学生在学校里得学这个，得学那个，所以每天都很忙。
5) 他吃得很多，而且也不运动，所以他很胖。

4) 说什么也 [very colloquial] 她说什么也抹不开。 (p. 19)

Contrary to surface appearance, the subject of 说什么也 is not 她, but the unstated "one/others." The meaning of the sentence is "No matter what others say, she..." But even this translation sticks too closely to the literal meaning of 说什么也 ("no matter what...says"). 说什么也 has come to be used most commonly in its looser meaning of "no matter what,..." Therefore, an even more accurate translation of the above example is "No matter what, she..."

例句：
1)她说那件大衣不好看，说什么也不肯穿。
2) 那么多人劝他，可他说什么也不听。

改写： 例：工作太多了，一星期内一定做不完。 说什么一星期内也做不完。

1) 他睡得很香，沒办法叫醒他。
2) 这个菜难吃极了，我怎么也吃不下去。
3) 这儿的活儿太多了，他一个人怎么也干不完。
4) 现在太迟了，尽管跑得很快也来不及了。

5) …才對　　　總該樂樂呵呵才對嘛。(p. 20)

…才對, literally meaning "only then will it be right," comes at the end of a sentence in Chinese. A literal translation into English is very awkward, e.g. "One should be happy after all, and only then will it be right." Rendering …才對 as "one should/must..." at the beginning of a sentence would produce a much smoother English translation, e.g., "One should be happy after all."

例句：
1) 你應該先作完功課再去玩兒才對嘛!
2) 他是你的朋友，你應該多幫幫他才對嘛!

造句：

改寫：例：他的中文不太好，你應該說慢一點。　　你應該說慢一點才對。
1) 每次出門以前，應該先看看有沒有帶鑰匙。
2) 上課的時候，應該把每一個問題都搞清。
3) 今天的事就應該今天把它作完，不要等明天。
4) 上公共汽車的時候，應該把座位讓給老太婆。
5) 你退了休，就應該在家多幫幫老伴的忙。

6) 說是…　[colloquial]　　　說是上蘇州去了。(p. 20)

說是… tagged on at the beginning of a sentence means "it is said that...," "they say it's...," "...so they say," "...so it's said," conveying suspicion on the part of the speaker that what is said may deviate from the truth. (A variation on 說是… is simply 說…, cf. Scene 11, line 5, 說休息…)

例句：
1) 說是放假，可是還有那麼多作業!
2) 說是看書，可是他的眼睛一直看着電視。

改寫：例：他告訴我六點來，可是現在還沒有來。　　他說是六點來，可現在還沒有來。
1) 他同意洗碗，可是從來不洗，他就是說說。
2) 你告訴我你出去一會兒就回來，可你出去了一個下午才回來。
3) 他以為他懂了這個問題，可是下一次碰到同樣的問題他還是不會作。
4) 張先生說他會用這個錄音機，可是誰知道是不是真的。
5) 人家告訴我他找到合適的工作了，其實是頂替了他母親。

7) 打 (從) [regional]　　咱們倆可是打小學到現在了，你打什麼時候又蹦出來個妹妹呀？(p. 20)

打 is a synonym of 從, but used only in very colloquial northern speech.

5) …才对 总该乐乐呵呵才对嘛。 (p. 21)

…才对, literally meaning "only then will it be right," comes at the end of a sentence in Chinese. A literal translation into English is very awkward, e.g. "One should be happy after all, and only then will it be right." Rendering …才对 as "one should/must..." at the beginning of a sentence would produce a much smoother English translation, e.g., "One should be happy after all."

例句： 1) 你应该先作完功课再去玩儿才对嘛！
2) 他是你的朋友，你应该多帮帮他才对嘛！

造句：

改写： 例：他的中文不太好，你应该说慢一点。 你应该说慢一点才对。
1) 每次出门以前，应该先看看有沒有带钥匙。
2) 上课的时候，应该把每一个问题都搞清。
3) 今天的事就应该今天把它作完，不要等明天。
4) 上公共汽车的时候，应该把座位让给老太婆。
5) 你退了休，就应该在家多帮帮老伴的忙。

6) 说是… [colloquial] 说是上苏州去了。 (p. 21)

说是… tagged on at the beginning of a sentence means "it is said that...," "they say it's...," "...so they say," "...so it's said," conveying suspicion on the part of the speaker that what is said may deviate from the truth. (A variation on 说是… is simply 说…, cf. Scene 11, line 5, 说休息…)

例句： 1) 说是放假，可是还有那么多作业！
2) 说是看书，可是他的眼睛一直看着电视。

改写： 例：他告诉我六点来，可是现在还沒有来。 他说是六点来，可现在还沒有来。
1) 他同意洗碗，可是从来不洗，他就是说说。
2) 你告诉我你出去一会儿就回来，可你出去了一个下午才回来。
3) 他以为他懂了这个问题，可是下一次碰到同样的问题他还是不会作。
4) 张先生说他会用这个录音机，可是谁知道是不是真的。
5) 人家告诉我他找到合适的工作了，其实是顶替了他母亲。

7) 打 (从) [regional] 咱们俩可是打小学到现在了，你打什么时候又蹦出来个妹妹呀？ (p. 21)

打 is a synonym of 从, but used only in very colloquial northern speech.

例句： 1) 打上個星期他就沒來上課。
2) 打初中的時候起，我們就學英文了。

改寫： 例：在美國孩子們從五歲起就開始上學了。
在美國孩子們打五歲起就開始上學了。
1) 從紐約坐飛機到芝加哥，花了三個鐘頭。
2) 從結婚到現在，已經三年了，可是他們還不想要孩子。
3) 他從鄉下回到城裡以後，一直沒找到工作。
4) 你從一大清早就不停地幹活，該累了吧。

8) 一直 她一直住在上海鄉下。 (p. 22)

一直 is an adverb meaning "straight on, straight through." When used in the physical sense, it implies that movement is along a straight line, without turns (e.g., 一直往前走). When used in the temporal sense (as in the above example), it implies that the action or situation is continuous without interruption for the relevant time period or up to the present.

例句： 1) 你在前頭的路口往左拐，再一直走兩英里，就到天安門了。
2) 關於上哪個學校的問題，我們一直談了差不多兩個小時。
3) 飛機一直飛了十五個鐘頭，才從美國飛到中國。

改寫： 例：大雨不停地下了好幾天。 大雨一直下了好幾天。
1) 人數不斷地增加。
2) 他說的話我老是不敢相信。
3) 從去年出了事以後，張老師身體都不好。
4) 晚飯以後，他不停地做他的功課。
5) 我從七點等你，等到現在，已經十點半了你才來。
6) 老李一句話也不說，眼睛看着窗外，很久很久。

9) 死 VP [crude] 別死不要臉，快放手吧！ (p. 22)

Used as an adverb, 死, like the adverbial 老, means "persistently," but 死 is stronger than 老 in that it implies the behavior is carried out with "dead" persistence. A variation of the adverbial 死 is 死也, meaning "..., even if (one) has to die for it." E.g. 我死也要把中文學會 "I must master Chinese even if it means dying for it." Both 死 and 死也 convey extreme persistence or perseverence.

例句： 1) 別死也不起來，老睡懶覺的！
2) 別死喊，我聽得見！

例句： 1) 打上个星期他就没来上课。
2) 打初中的时候起，我们就学英文了。

改写： 例：在美国孩子们从五岁起就开始上学了。
在美国孩子们打五岁起就开始上学了。
1) 从纽约坐飞机到芝加哥，花了三个钟头。
2) 从结婚到现在，已经三年了，可是他们还不想要孩子。
3) 他从乡下回到城里以后，一直没找到工作。
4) 你从一大清早就不停地干活，该累了吧。

8) 一直 她一直住在上海乡下。 (p. 23)

一直 is an adverb meaning "straight on, straight through." When used in the physical sense, it implies that movement is along a straight line, without turns (e.g., 一直往前走). When used in the temporal sense (as in the above example), it implies that the action or situation is continuous without interruption for the relevant time period or up to the present.

例句： 1) 你在前头的路口往左拐，再一直走两英里，就到天安门了。
2) 关于上哪个学校的问题，我们一直谈了差不多两个小时。
3) 飞机一直飞了十五个钟头，才从美国飞到中国。

改写： 例：大雨不停地下了好几天。 大雨一直下了好几天。
1) 人数不断地增加。
2) 他说的话我老是不敢相信。
3) 从去年出了事以后，张老师身体都不好。
4) 晚饭以后，他不停地做他的功课。
5) 我从七点等你，等到现在，已经十点半了你才来。
6) 老李一句话也不说，眼睛看着窗外，很久很久。

9) 死 VP [crude] 别死不要脸，快放手吧！ (p. 23)

Used as an adverb, 死, like the adverbial 老, means "persistently," but 死 is stronger than 老 in that it implies the behavior is carried out with "dead" persistence. A variation of the adverbial 死 is 死也, meaning "..., even if (one) has to die for it." E.g. 我死也要把中文学会 "I must master Chinese even if it means dying for it." Both 死 and 死也 convey extreme persistence or perseverence.

例句： 1) 别死也不起来，老睡懒觉的！
2) 别死喊，我听得见！

改寫： 例：別老是說你自己對，你也有錯的時候。 別死說你自己對，你也有錯的時候。
1) 別緊緊地抓着我，快放手吧！
2) 我的妹妹真討厭，我走到哪兒她就跟到哪兒。她總是跟着我。
3) 他怎麼也不肯吃藥，病怎麼能好呢？
4) 別不斷地問呀問的，你先自己看看書不就知道爲什麼了？
5) 別老是說你不行，你應該先試試看。

10) 淨 (adv.) [uncommon] 小秦怎麼淨往蘇州跑哇？ (p. 24)

Like the adverbials 老 and 總是, the adverbial 淨 means "always, to keep on..., entirely, to be full of..."

例句： 1) 這座山淨是石頭。
2) 這些日子淨颳風。

改寫： 例：他的考試總是一百分。 他的考試淨是一百分。
1) 他的朋友都是從前和他一起插隊落戶的青年。
2) 這個學生上課的時候常常遲到。
3) 你到哪兒去幹活了？褲子上全是土。快換下來吧！
4) 你太粗心，所以常常寫錯字。
5) 你也該自己學學釘扣子了，不能總是交給你奶奶做。

11) 至少 一個月至少去兩趟。 (p. 24)

至少 is an adverb meaning "at least." As an adverb, it has the same grammatical function as 最多 (cf. Grammatical Note I.4.). 最少 and 至多 also exist, but are much less common than their synonyms 至少 and 最多.

例句： 1) 長城我至少去過三次了。
2) 你太忙，不能去醫院看他，也至少應該給他打個電話。

造句：

改寫： 例：這件衣裳要一個多星期才能做完。 這件衣裳至少要一個星期才能做完。
1) 這篇文章我寫完以後看過不只兩遍。
2) 我和我的朋友每個月通三次信。
3) 從這兒到天安門要走半個多鐘頭。
4) 他阿姨六十多歲了，怎麼還沒退休？
5) 他爸爸被隔離有六個多月，到現在那個疙瘩一直解不開。

改写： 例：别老是说你自己对，你也有错的时候。 别死说你自己对，你也有错的时候。
1) 别紧紧地抓着我，快放手吧！
2) 我的妹妹真讨厌，我走到哪儿她就跟到哪儿。她总是跟着我。
3) 他怎么也不肯吃药，病怎么能好呢？
4) 别不断地问呀问的，你先自己看看书不就知道为什么了？
5) 别老是说你不行，你应该先试试看。

10) 净 (adv.) [uncommon] 小秦怎么净往苏州跑哇？ (p. 25)

Like the adverbials 老 and 总是, the adverbial 净 means "always, to keep on..., entirely, to be full of..."

例句： 1) 这座山净是石头。
2) 这些日子净刮风。

改写： 例：他的考试总是一百分。 他的考试净是一百分。
1) 他的朋友都是从前和他一起插队落户的青年。
2) 这个学生上课的时候常常迟到。
3) 你到哪儿去干活了？裤子上全是土。快换下来吧！
4) 你太粗心，所以常常写错字。
5) 你也该自己学学钉扣子了，不能总是交给你奶奶做。

11) 至少 一个月至少去两趟。 (p. 25)

至少 is an adverb meaning "at least." As an adverb, it has the same grammatical function as 最多 (cf. Grammatical Note I.4.). 最少 and 至多 also exist, but are much less common than their synonyms 至少 and 最多.

例句： 1) 长城我至少去过三次了。
2) 你太忙，不能去医院看他，也至少应该给他打个电话。

造句：

改写： 例：这件衣裳要一个多星期才能做完。 这件衣裳至少要一个星期才能做完。
1) 这篇文章我写完以后看过不只两遍。
2) 我和我的朋友每个月通三次信。
3) 从这儿到天安门要走半个多钟头。
4) 他阿姨六十多岁了，怎么还没退休？
5) 他爸爸被隔离有六个多月，到现在那个疙瘩一直解不开。

12) 一…，不就…(嗎)？ 他一退休你不就可以頂替了嗎？ (p. 26)

In the above example, the familiar pattern "一…，就…," (meaning "as soon as..., then...") is combined with a negative rhetorical question in the second clause. The 嗎 in the rhetorical question may be omitted without changing the meaning, but the interrogative intonation is retained. To convey the rhetorical nature of the question, it is imperative that 不 precedes 就. Note the difference among these three sentences:

我們一上大學，就可以常在一起了。
Once we go to college, we'll be able to be together often.

我們一上大學，不就可以常在一起了嗎？
Once we go to college, we'll be able to be together often, won't we?

我們一上大學，就不可以常在一起了。
Once we go to college, we won't be able to be together often anymore.

例句：
1) 在外頭擺攤子，一颳風打雷，不就沒有顧客了嗎？
2) 一到中國，不就可以天天吃中國菜了嗎？

造句：

改寫：
例：他工作以後，就沒時間學習了。 他工作以後，不就沒時間學習了？
1) 他一被揭發，就一定會被隔離審查的。
2) 等你老伴也退休，你們倆就可以去美國看兒子了。
3) 那場誤會搞清，他心裡的那個疙瘩就能解開了。
4) 這種又好又便宜的衣裳，上市一會兒就會賣光的。

INCLUSIVE EXERCISES FOR SEGMENT II:

填充 (Translate the English words or short phrases into Chinese in the contexts provided. Then read the sentences for comprehension)：

1) (early in the morning) 這個商店就有很多 (customers).
2) 今天又 (has a wind storm) 又下雨，天氣不好，(another day) 我再去你那兒吧。
3) (bustle about) 了半天，幹得 (just about there) 了吧？快坐下休息一會兒吧。
4) 家裡就 (remain) 她一個人了，沒有人在她 (close by).
5) (at that time) 他要是不開車去舊金山就不會 (have accident) 了。
6) 我要 (rush, hurry) 在五點半以前把功課做完，然後把功課 (hand in to) 老師。

12) 一…，不就…(吗)? 他一退休你不就可以顶替了吗? (p. 27)

In the above example, the familiar pattern "一…，就…," (meaning "as soon as..., then...") is combined with a negative rhetorical question in the second clause. The 吗 in the rhetorical question may be omitted without changing the meaning, but the interrogative intonation is retained. To convey the rhetorical nature of the question, it is imperative that 不 precedes 就. Note the difference among these three sentences:

我们一上大学，就可以常在一起了。
Once we go to college, we'll be able to be together often.

我们一上大学，不就可以常在一起了吗?
Once we go to college, we'll be able to be together often, won't we?

我们一上大学，就不可以常在一起了。
Once we go to college, we won't be able to be together often anymore.

例句： 1) 在外头摆摊子，一刮风打雷，不就没有顾客了吗?
2) 一到中国，不就可以天天吃中国菜了吗?

造句：

改写： 例：他工作以后，就没时间学习了。 他工作以后，不就没时间学习了?
1) 他一被揭发，就一定会被隔离审查的。
2) 等你老伴也退休，你们俩就可以去美国看儿子了。
3) 那场误会搞清，他心里的那个疙瘩就能解开了。
4) 这种又好又便宜的衣裳，上市一会儿就会卖光的。

INCLUSIVE EXERCISES FOR SEGMENT II:

填充 (Translate the English words or short phrases into Chinese in the contexts provided. Then read the sentences for comprehension)：

1) (early in the morning) 这个商店就有很多 (customers).
2) 今天又 (has a wind storm) 又下雨，天气不好，(another day) 我再去你那儿吧。
3) (bustle about) 了半天，干得 (just about there) 了吧? 快坐下休息一会儿吧。
4) 家里就 (remain) 她一个人了，没有人在她 (close by).
5) (at that time) 他要是不开车去旧金山就不会 (have accident) 了。
6) 我要 (rush, hurry) 在五点半以前把功课做完，然后把功课 (hand in to) 老师。

7) 請你 (by all means) 別 (misunderstand) 我的意思。

8) (from) 小時候起，他就喜歡 (deceive) 人。

9) 今年 (at the end of the year) 有兩位先生要 (retire).

10) 這條褲子的 (measurements, size) 太小，不 (suitable).

翻譯：

1) No matter what, she was unwilling to expose her spouse.

2) She often goes to Suzhou, to see her uncle so they say. But I think there must be another reason.

3) Zhou Dama insisted that Zhihua eat that bowl of wonton, so Zhihua finally ate it.

4) Zhihua's sister writes at least one letter to her family each week.

5) Making these two dresses will keep her busy for a week.

6) It is only right that men learn to sew on buttons themselves.

7) (Colloquial) Qin Nan could use a sewing machine from the time she was eight years old.

8) Qin Nan keeps working all the time (does nothing but work), she never rests.

9) That book that you're writing, isn't it just about finished?

10) His health is not good, and moreover his wages are so meager, so he decided to retire.

11) Ever since Qin Nan went to Suzhou, Zhihua kept thinking of her.

12) As soon as you retire, won't your daughter be able to take over your job then?

7) 请你 (by all means) 别 (misunderstand) 我的意思。
8) (from) 小时侯起，他就喜欢 (deceive) 人。
9) 今年 (at the end of the year) 有两位先生要 (retire).
10) 这条裤子的 (measurements, size) 太小，不 (suitable).

翻译： See facing page.

SEGMENT III

1) Subj. 約-person (VP) 是他約我來的。 (p. 30)

"Subj. makes an appointment (or date) with so-and-so (to VP)." 約 can be the main verb in this pattern, with the object being the person with whom the appointment is made, e.g. 我約了他. But more commonly, 約 is a coverb, with a VP coming at the end. The persons doing the VP can be just the object of 約 (as in the above example), or they can also include the subject of the sentence, e.g.: 我約了他去看電影 "I made a date with him to go see a movie," implying that he and I will go together to see a movie.

例句： 1) 我從來沒有約過男朋友到家裡來。
2) 他們早就約好了一塊兒去長城，可是他們沒告訴我。
3) 我們跟父母約好了聖誕節到他們那裡吃晚飯。

造句：

改寫： 例：我沒有請他來，可是他自己來了。　我沒有約他來，可是他自己來了。
1) 昨天下午他說請我和我孫子去那個餐廳吃西餐。
2) 我已經告訴了張師傅下午來學校拿他的工錢。
3) 老師請我兩點鐘到他的辦公室去。
4) 你跟那位顧客說好了下午請他來取他的襯衫嗎？

2) 恐怕 我覺得這裡面恐怕有鬼。 (p. 32)

恐怕 "afraid that" is to be distinguished from 怕 "afraid, afraid of" in the following ways:

a. 恐怕 is a movable adverb and always applies to a specific instance, whereas 怕 is either a stative verb or a transitive verb with its object being a habitual fear.

恐怕會下雨。	I'm afraid it's going to rain (within a specific time period).
我一點兒都不怕。	I'm not the least bit afraid.
我怕下雨。	I dread rain.

b. 恐怕 is always followed by a clause, whereas the object of 怕 can be either a clause or a noun.

我恐怕考試考不好。	I'm afraid I won't do well on the exam.
我怕考試考不好。	I'm afraid of doing badly on exams. (clause-object)
我怕考試。	I'm afraid of exams. (noun-object).

SEGMENT III

1) Subj. 约-person (VP) 是他约我来的。 (p. 31)

"Subj. makes an appointment (or date) with so-and-so (to VP)." 约 can be the main verb in this pattern, with the object being the person with whom the appointment is made, e.g. 我约了他. But more commonly, 约 is a coverb, with a VP coming at the end. The persons doing the VP can be just the object of 约 (as in the above example), or they can also include the subject of the sentence, e.g.: 我约了他去看电影 "I made a date with him to go see a movie," implying that he and I will go together to see a movie.

例句： 1) 我从来沒有约过男朋友到家里来。
2) 他们早就约好了一块儿去长城，可是他们沒告诉我。
3) 我们跟父母约好了圣诞节到他们那里吃晚饭。

造句：

改写： 例：我沒有请他来，可是他自己来了。 我沒有约他来，可是他自己来了。
1) 昨天下午他说请我和我孙子去那个餐厅吃西餐。
2) 我已经告诉了张师傅下午来学校拿他的工钱。
3) 老师请我两点钟到他的办公室去。
4) 你跟那位顾客说好了下午请他来取他的衬衫吗？

2) 恐怕 我觉得这里面恐怕有鬼。 (p. 33)

恐怕 "afraid that" is to be distinguished from 怕 "afraid, afraid of" in the following ways:

a. 恐怕 is a movable adverb and always applies to a specific instance, whereas 怕 is either a stative verb or a transitive verb with its object being a habitual fear.

恐怕会下雨。	I'm afraid it's going to rain (within a specific time period).
我一点儿都不怕。	I'm not the least bit afraid.
我怕下雨。	I dread rain.

b. 恐怕 is always followed by a clause, whereas the object of 怕 can be either a clause or a noun.

我恐怕考试考不好。	I'm afraid I won't do well on the exam.
我怕考试考不好。	I'm afraid of doing badly on exams. (clause-object)
我怕考试。	I'm afraid of exams. (noun-object).

c. 恐怕 is often used in its derived meaning "perhaps," and does not necessarily imply fear. 怕 always implies fear. Used in the sense of "perhaps," 恐怕 indicates that the speaker - not the subject of the sentence - is of the opinion that the stated situation or event is likely.

他恐怕今天不會來。 Perhaps he won't be coming today.
我怕他來。 I dread his coming (every time he comes).

例句： 1) 你恐怕不知道他已經走了吧。
2) 早點兒走吧，要是晚了，恐怕趕不上火車了。
3) 這麼多菜，我們恐怕吃不完。

造句：

改寫： 例：我想也許他不來了。 恐怕他不來了。
1) 我孫子雖然能幹，可是也許不太懂事。
2) 他想也許他生病了，因爲他覺得很不舒服。
3) 今天可能要颳風。
4) 他好久沒給我來信了，大概是要和我一刀兩斷了。
5) 名牌腳踏車可能很難買到，我看你還是買些零件自己裝吧。

3) 一…，二…，… 我們一不偷，二不搶，… (p. 32)

"one, ...; two, ...; ..." This method of enumerating one's arguments in Chinese is very similar to English. However, in English, the numbers must come at the very beginning of clauses, whereas in Chinese, the numbers may come either at the beginning of clauses (before the subject, e.g. 一，今天天氣不好；二，我也沒有時間去。), or after the subject and before the VP as in the example from the film. Thus, the numbers in this Chinese sentence pattern can be treated as movable adverbs.

例句： 1) 他一不去讀書，二不去工作，天天在家裡，不知道幹什麼！
2) 我弟弟一不做功課，二不去上課，學習怎麼會好呢？
3) 他一有錢，二有個好工作，所以他對自己很滿意。

造句：

改寫： 例：這個孩子又不會念書，又不會幹活，長大了怎麼辦？
這個孩子一不會念書，二不會幹活，長大了怎麼辦？
1) 小張今天又不說話又不笑，一定有什麼心事。
2) 他又樂觀又挺文靜的，找個好對像一定不難。

c. 恐怕 is often used in its derived meaning "perhaps," and does not necessarily imply fear. 怕 always implies fear. Used in the sense of "perhaps," 恐怕 indicates that the speaker - not the subject of the sentence - is of the opinion that the stated situation or event is likely.

他恐怕今天不会来。	Perhaps he won't be coming today.
我怕他来。	I dread his coming (every time he comes).

例句： 1) 你恐怕不知道他已经走了吧。
2) 早点儿走吧，要是晚了，恐怕赶不上火车了。
3) 这么多菜，我们恐怕吃不完。

造句：

改写： 例：我想也许他不来了。 恐怕他不来了。
1) 我孙子虽然能干，可是也许不太懂事。
2) 他想也许他生病了，因为他觉得很不舒服。
3) 今天可能要刮风。
4) 他好久沒给我来信了，大概是要和我一刀两断了。
5) 名牌脚踏车可能很难买到，我看你还是买些零件自己装吧。

3) 一…，二…，… 我们一不偷，二不抢，… (p. 33)

"one, ...; two, ...; ..." This method of enumerating one's arguments in Chinese is very similar to English. However, in English, the numbers must come at the very beginning of clauses, whereas in Chinese, the numbers may come either at the beginning of clauses (before the subject, e.g. 一，今天天气不好；二，我也沒有时间去。), or after the subject and before the VP as in the example from the film. Thus, the numbers in this Chinese sentence pattern can be treated as movable adverbs.

例句： 1) 他一不去读书，二不去工作，天天在家里，不知道干什么！
2) 我弟弟一不做功课，二不去上课，学习怎么会好呢？
3) 他一有钱，二有个好工作，所以他对自己很满意。

造句：

改写： 例：这个孩子又不会念书，又不会干活，长大了怎么办？
这个孩子一不会念书，二不会干活，长大了怎么办？
1) 小张今天又不说话又不笑，一定有什么心事。
2) 他又乐观又挺文静的，找个好对象一定不难。

3) 這件衣裳又不合身，又那麼貴，你怎麼能只因爲是名牌就買了呢？
4) 他這個人又不會勞動，又不會和別人相處，所以常常和同事發生矛盾。

4) 越…越… 別人越是看不起你，你越是要看得起自己。(p. 32)

"The more..., the more..." 越, which functions as an adverb in this pattern, can be followed by either action verbs (as in the above example), or by stative verbs, e.g.:

越早越好 The earlier the better.

Even when only one action or situation is on the rise, it is essential that 越 is used in both parts of the sentence. In such cases, "越來越...," a variation of the above pattern, is used. In 越來越…, the 來 can be interpreted as a "dummy verb."

例句： 1) 別人越是不喜歡他來，他越是要來。
2) 媽媽越是討厭我穿那件襯衫，我越是要穿！

造句：

改寫： 例：別勸他了。你勸他，他哭得更厲害了。
別勸他了。你越勸他，他哭得越厲害了。
1) 我媽媽認爲要是孩子愛玩兒，就一定聰明。
2) 關於這個問題，他說了很多次，可是我一次比一次糊塗。
3) 冬冬跟男男要他的球，可是冬冬說了很多次，男男都不肯給。
4) 我跟他提了意見，可是他更不聽了。我看最省事就是跟他一刀兩斷了。
5) 他吃了三天的藥，可是病好像更厲害了。

5) …又來了 [very colloquial] 媽，您又來了。(p. 34)

"There (you or so-and-so) go again!" As in English, this idiomatic expression conveys irritation over someone getting into an annoying habit again. But note that the verb used in Chinese is 來, as opposed to "go" in English.

例句： 他老說這個故事，不知道說過幾遍了，現在他又來了。

填充 (Fill in the blanks with logical phrases. Then read for comprehension)：
例：媽媽：別看電視，先做完功課！
孩子：媽，你又來了！我知道了！

3) 这件衣裳又不合身，又那么贵，你怎么能只因为是名牌就买了呢？
4) 他这个人又不会劳动，又不会和别人相处，所以常常和同事发生矛盾。

4) 越…越… 别人越是看不起你，你越是要看得起自己。(p. 33)

"The more..., the more..." 越, which functions as an adverb in this pattern, can be followed by either action verbs (as in the above example), or by stative verbs, e.g.:

越早越好 The earlier the better.

Even when only one action or situation is on the rise, it is essential that 越 is used in both parts of the sentence. In such cases, "越来越...," a variation of the above pattern, is used. In 越来越…, the 来 can be interpreted as a "dummy verb."

例句： 1) 别人越是不喜欢他来，他越是要来。
2) 妈妈越是讨厌我穿那件衬衫，我越是要穿！

造句：

改写： 例：别劝他了。你劝他，他哭得更厉害了。
别劝他了。你越劝他，他哭得越厉害了。
1) 我妈妈认为要是孩子爱玩儿，就一定聪明。
2) 关于这个问题，他说了很多次，可是我一次比一次糊涂。
3) 冬冬跟男男要他的球，可是冬冬说了很多次，男男都不肯给。
4) 我跟他提了意见，可是他更不听了。我看最省事就是跟他一刀两断了。
5) 他吃了三天的药，可是病好像更厉害了。

5) …又来了 [very colloquial] 妈，您又来了。(p. 35)

"There (you or so-and-so) go again!" As in English, this idiomatic expression conveys irritation over someone getting into an annoying habit again. But note that the verb used in Chinese is 来, as opposed to "go" in English.

例句： 他老说这个故事，不知道说过几遍了，现在他又来了。

填充 (Fill in the blanks with logical phrases. Then read for comprehension)：
例：妈妈：别看电视，先做完功课！
孩子：妈，你又来了！我知道了！

1) 秦父：秦楠，你該找個對像了。
   秦楠：爸，__________！__________！
2) 奶奶：今天可能會颳風，你出門要穿大衣，戴上帽子。
   孫子：奶奶，__________！__________！
3) 張大媽：路上車子擠，你騎自行車可要當心啊！
   她老伴：__________！__________！

6) 到底　　媽，您到底要跟我說什麼？ (p. 34)

到底 (literally "reach bottom") is an adverb meaning "after all, after all is said and done."

例句：1) 你到底要我先做功課還是先吃飯？
　　　2) 到底是他說得對還是他老伴說得對？

造句：

填充 (Translate the English words or short phrases into Chinese in the contexts provided. Then read the sentences for comprehension)：

1) 秦楠又 (sensible) 又 (refined and quiet),可是高母不願意志華跟她結婚，爲什麼呢？
2) 他 (took over his father's job), 又有一個好的 ("intended"), 爲什麼那麼不 (optimistic) 呢？
3) 哪位老師 (capable) 呢？在這個問題上，學生們有不同的意見。

改寫 - Reword the three completed sentences in the preceding exercise, using pattern 6:

例：他總是跟他女朋友有矛盾, 爲什麼誰也不清楚。
　　他總是跟他女朋友有矛盾，到底爲什麼誰也不清楚。

7) 早 (就)…了　　他妹妹的衣服我早做好了。 (p. 36)

The 早 and the 了 work in tandem in this pattern, and 就 is almost always used after 早. The implication is that an event or action has taken place much earlier than the other person realizes. In translation, "早(就)…了" is best rendered as "...long ago" at the end of the sentence. E.g.:

我早就告訴過你了！　　I've told you this long ago!

例句：1) 那個問題早就解決了。
　　　2) 電影早就開演了，你來得太晚了。

1) 秦父：秦楠，你该找个对象了。
秦楠：爸，__________！__________！
2) 奶奶：今天可能会刮风，你出门要穿大衣，戴上帽子.
孙子：奶奶，__________！__________！
3) 张大妈：路上车子挤，你骑自行车可要当心啊！
她老伴：__________！__________！

6) 到底 妈，您到底要跟我说什么？ (p. 35)

到底 (literally "reach bottom") is an adverb meaning "after all, after all is said and done."

例句：1) 你到底要我先做功课还是先吃饭？
2) 到底是他说得对还是他老伴说得对？

造句：

填充 (Translate the English words or short phrases into Chinese in the contexts provided. Then read the sentences for comprehension)：

1) 秦楠又 (sensible) 又 (refined and quiet),可是高母不愿意志华跟她结婚，为什么呢？
2) 他 (took over his father's job), 又有一个好的 ("intended"), 为什么那么不 (optimistic) 呢？
3) 哪位老师 (capable) 呢？在这个问题上，学生们有不同的意见。

改写 - Reword the three completed sentences in the preceding exercise, using pattern 6:

例：他总是跟他女朋友有矛盾, 为什么谁也不清楚。
他总是跟他女朋友有矛盾，到底为什么谁也不清楚。

7) 早 (就)… 了 他妹妹的衣服我早做好了。 (p. 37)

The 早 and the 了 work in tandem in this pattern, and 就 is almost always used after 早. The implication is that an event or action has taken place much earlier than the other person realizes. In translation, "早(就)… 了" is best rendered as "...long ago" at the end of the sentence. E.g.:

我早就告诉过你了！ I've told you this long ago!

例句：1) 那个问题早就解决了。
2) 电影早就开演了，你来得太晚了。

造句：

填充： 1) 那件 (shirt) 兩個月前就做好了，可是 (customer) 怎麼還沒來取？
2) (boiled water) 擱了一個鐘頭，已經涼了，不能泡茶了。
3) 我父母好久以前就 (retired) 了，所以我現在沒法子 (take over their jobs) 了。
4) 我很久前就看出他這個 (self-employed person) 是一個又 (capable) 又有 (aspiration) 的人。

改寫 - Reword the four completed sentences in the preceding exercise, using pattern 7.

例：我上個月就把照片洗好了，今天才給我的朋友寄去。
我早就把照片洗好了，今天才給我的朋友寄去。

8) 笑/哭/氣/怕 - obj. 笑什麼？ (p. 38)

Certain verbs and adjectives in English, such as "laugh, cry, afraid, angry," cannot be followed immediately by objects, but are linked to objects by a preposition or relative pronoun. Their Chinese equivalents - 笑, 哭, 怕, 氣, etc. - can be followed immediately by objects (including the QW-objects 什麼 and 誰). The pattern 笑/哭/氣/怕 什麼？ also conveys the nuance that the speaker disdains the laughter, crying, anger, fear, etc., so the question is rhetorical. In contrast, a true question concerning the cause of the laughter, crying, etc. would be posed by the pattern 為什麼 笑/哭/etc.呢？

例句： 做錯就改嘛，哭什麼？
你認為你對就好好兒跟他說，喊什麼？

造句：

填充： 1) 你們以前是好朋友，有了 (conflict) 應該好好兒談一談，別生氣。
2) 你不必怕。這輛 (name brand bike) 又不是 (stolen) 的，儘管讓他們 (investigate) 吧。

改寫：例：孩子錯了應該告訴他什麼是對的，別大罵他。
孩子錯了應該告訴他什麼是對的，罵什麼？
1) 還有十五分鐘火車才開呢，別急！
2) 別叫，真難聽！我就在這兒，聽得見。
3) 這個笑話一點兒意思也沒有，有什麼好笑的？
4 - 5) Reword the two completed sentences from the preceding exercise.

造句：

填充：
1) 那件 (shirt) 两个月前就做好了，可是 (customer) 怎么还没来取？
2) (boiled water) 搁了一个钟头，已经凉了，不能泡茶了。
3) 我父母好久以前就 (retired) 了，所以我现在没法子 (take over their jobs) 了。
4) 我很久前就看出他这个 (self-employed person) 是一个又 (capable) 又有 (aspiration) 的人。

改写 - Reword the four completed sentences in the preceding exercise, using pattern 7.

例：我上个月就把照片洗好了，今天才给我的朋友寄去。
我早就把照片洗好了，今天才给我的朋友寄去。

8) 笑/哭/气/怕 - obj. 笑什么？ (p. 39)

Certain verbs and adjectives in English, such as "laugh, cry, afraid, angry," cannot be followed immediately by objects, but are linked to objects by a preposition or relative pronoun. Their Chinese equivalents - 笑, 哭, 怕, 气, etc. - can be followed immediately by objects (including the QW-objects 什么 and 谁). The pattern 笑/哭/气/怕 什么？ also conveys the nuance that the speaker disdains the laughter, crying, anger, fear, etc., so the question is rhetorical. In contrast, a true question concerning the cause of the laughter, crying, etc. would be posed by the pattern 为什么 笑/哭/etc.呢？

例句：
做错就改嘛，哭什么？
你认为你对就好好儿跟他说，喊什么？

造句：

填充：
1) 你们以前是好朋友，有了 (conflict) 应该好好儿谈一谈，别生气。
2) 你不必怕。这辆 (name brand bike) 又不是 (stolen) 的，尽管让他们 (investigate) 吧。

改写：例：孩子错了应该告诉他什么是对的，别大骂他。
孩子错了应该告诉他什么是对的，骂什么？

1) 还有十五分钟火车才开呢，别急！
2) 别叫，真难听！我就在这儿，听得见。
3) 这个笑话一点儿意思也没有，有什么好笑的？

4 - 5) Reword the two completed sentences from the preceding exercise.

9) 不是…，是… 媽這回不是想抱孫子了，媽是要你找個補褲子的。 (p. 40)

This pattern is used for clarification. It points out the contrast between what is and what isn't (despite what may seem to be). The two clauses in this pattern may be reversed for a slight shift in emphasis. E.g.:

我不是不想去，是沒有工夫去。

It's not that I don't want to go, it's because I have no time.

(emphasis on contradicting the other person's assumption or perception)

我是因爲沒有工夫，不是不想去。

It's because I have no time, not because I don't want to go.

(tone more conciliatory)

例句：
1) 我是不忍心看見你老是一個人，不是要逼你結婚。
2) 我不是要你把什麼都告訴我，我的意思是不要把什麼痛苦都悶在心裡。

造句：

填充：
1) 我不是說女孩子不可以 (be gregarious and jolly), 我是說女孩子 (refined and quiet) 一點兒好。
2) 他不是真的生氣了，他是 (misconstrued) 了你的意思。
3) 他的母親不是想 (retire), 是爲了讓兒子能早一點 (take over) 她的工作。
4) 我不是說不能 (make a suggestion), 是說要和人家 (get along together) 得好，不要老發生 (conflict).

改寫 - Reword the four completed sentences in the preceding exercise, using pattern 9.

INCLUSIVE 翻譯 EXERCISE FOR SEGMENT III:

1) That student comes to class today, doesn't come to class tomorrow (i.e., is frequently absent). After all, does he want to study Chinese or not?
2) The longer I lived in China, the more I felt that I didn't understand the Chinese people.
3) I made a date with her to go see a movie this Friday evening.
4) Maomao's girlfriend wants to break up with him, not because she doesn't like him, (but) because she looks down on self-employed people.

5 - 9) See bottom of facing page.

9) 不是…，是… 妈这回不是想抱孙子了，妈是要你找个补裤子的。(p. 41)

This pattern is used for clarification. It points out the contrast between what is and what isn't (despite what may seem to be). The two clauses in this pattern may be reversed for a slight shift in emphasis. E.g.:

我不是不想去，是沒有工夫去。

It's not that I don't want to go, it's because I have no time.

(emphasis on contradicting the other person's assumption or perception)

我是因为沒有工夫，不是不想去。

It's because I have no time, not because I don't want to go.

(tone more conciliatory)

例句： 1) 我是不忍心看见你老是一个人，不是要逼你结婚。

2) 我不是要你把什么都告诉我，我的意思是不要把什么痛苦都闷在心里。

造句：

填充： 1) 我不是说女孩子不可以 (be gregarious and jolly), 我是说女孩子 (refined and quiet) 一点儿好。

2) 他不是真的生气了，他是 (misconstrued) 了你的意思。

3) 他的母亲不是想 (retire), 是为了让儿子能早一点 (take over) 她的工作。

4) 我不是说不能 (make a suggestion), 是说要和人家 (get along together) 得好，不要老发生 (conflict).

改写 - Reword the four completed sentences in the preceding exercise, using pattern 9.

INCLUSIVE 翻译 EXERCISE FOR SEGMENT III:

1 - 4) See bottom of facing page.

5) His father died long ago, so he's been very sensible since he was small.

6) There you go again! Didn't I tell you just now not to bring up that matter anymore?

7) If Qin Nan doesn't solve this problem of hers, she'll probably be miserable (in pain) all her life.

8) I like her because: one, she's very capable; two, she is very optimistic; three, she is also very refined and quiet.

9) What's there to feel bad about? To rely on one's own labor for a living is fine too.

SEGMENT IV

1) Subj. 在 VP 你在騙我。 (p. 42)

在 is normally used to introduce a location or time element. But it can be used before a verb to indicate that the subject is in the midst of doing something. In English translation, this usage of 在 usually comes out as the progressive tense.

例句： 1) 我在猜那個電影後來怎麼樣了。
2) 他們在聊天。

填充： 1) 那位老師又 (is evading) 學生的問題。
2) 那位醫生 (is again saying that) 他的藥有 (special efficacy).
3) 秦楠 (is thinking) 要是社會不能 (treat her fairly) 她將來的 (situation) 會怎麼樣呢？
4) 媽媽 (is calculating) 我們家這個月的 (living allowance).

2) 究竟 [somewhat literary] 可你心裡究竟是怎麼想的？ (p. 42)

究竟 is a synonym of 到底 (cf. Grammatical Note III.6). Literally, 究竟 means "investigate thoroughly," so as an adverb, it implies that a situation has been murky or a person has been evasive, and the issue at hand is some decisive clarification. So in terms of meaning, there is a slight shade of difference between 究竟 and 到底. Moreover, 到底 is used a little more commonly than 究竟.

例句： 1) 你究竟去不去張老師的辦公室？
2) 這碗藥，你究竟喝不喝？

造句：

填充 (Translate the English words or short phrases into Chinese and fill in the blanks with logical phrases. Then read for comprehension)：

1) 我說了這麼半天，你 (after all) ___________?
2) 你 (after all) 是 _____________ 還是 _____________?
3) (coach)問他: 你 (after all) 要不要 (join) 我們這個球隊呢？
4) 你 (after all) 是把 (key) 放在家裡了，還是丟在路上了？
5) 因為他 (after all) 是不懂得怎麼 (assemble a bike) 所以他 (in vain) 花了半天工夫，車子還是壞的。

3) 有什麼…(的)？ 這樣獨立生活下去，有什麼不好？ (p. 42)

This is a rhetorical question in which the speaker contradicts or challenges an assumption or view.

SEGMENT IV

1) Subj. 在 VP 你在骗我。(p. 43)

在 is normally used to introduce a location or time element. But it can be used before a verb to indicate that the subject is in the midst of doing something. In English translation, this usage of 在 usually comes out as the progressive tense.

例句： 1) 我在猜那个电影后来怎么样了。
2) 他们在聊天。

填充： 1) 那位老师又 (is evading) 学生的问题。
2) 那位医生 (is again saying that) 他的药有 (special efficacy).
3) 秦楠 (is thinking) 要是社会不能 (treat her fairly) 她将来的 (situation) 会怎么样呢？
4) 妈妈 (is calculating) 我们家这个月的 (living allowance).

2) 究竟 [somewhat literary] 可你心里究竟是怎么想的？ (p. 43)

究竟 is a synonym of 到底 (cf. Grammatical Note III.6). Literally, 究竟 means "investigate thoroughly," so as an adverb, it implies that a situation has been murky or a person has been evasive, and the issue at hand is some decisive clarification. So in terms of meaning, there is a slight shade of difference between 究竟 and 到底. Moreover, 到底 is used a little more commonly than 究竟.

例句： 1) 你究竟去不去张老师的办公室？
2) 这碗药，你究竟喝不喝？

造句：

填充 (Translate the English words or short phrases into Chinese and fill in the blanks with logical phrases. Then read for comprehension)：

1) 我说了这么半天，你 (after all) ___________?
2) 你 (after all) 是 _____________ 还是 _____________?
3) (coach)问他: 你 (after all) 要不要 (join) 我们这个球队呢？
4) 你 (after all) 是把 (key) 放在家里了，还是丢在路上了？
5) 因为他 (after all) 是不懂得怎么 (assemble a bike) 所以他 (in vain) 花了半天工夫，车子还是坏的。

3) 有什么…(的)？ 这样独立生活下去，有什么不好？ (p. 43)

This is a rhetorical question in which the speaker contradicts or challenges an assumption or view.

例句： 1) 找不到工作就作個體戶，有什麼不好的？
2) 這件事跟你沒關係，所以才沒告訴你，這有什麼錯？

造句：

填充： 1) ______________, 有什麼不對的？
2) ____________, 有什麼不好意思的？
3) 我看這件衣服很 (fits), 那兒不合適呢？
4) (Coach) 一樣地 (treat) 所有的隊員，怎麼不公平呢？

改寫 - Rewrite the completed sentences 3) and 4) in the preceding exercise, using pattern 3.

4) 還 V 什麼 (O)？ [colloquial] 還結什麼婚？ (p. 42)

This is a rhetorical question implying that, given the situation at hand (usually negative), there is no point in doing V. E.g.: 他都病得快死了，還考什麼試？

例句： 1) 都這麼晚了，還看什麼電視？
2) 我的錢不夠，還念什麼大學？

填充： 1) 還有十分鐘就要上課了，你還 (sleep 什麼)?
2) 他已經 (resolved to...), 你還跟他 (make 什麼 suggestions) 呢？
3) 要是一個政府不能聽人民的意見，那麼這個國家還 (搞什麼 reform) 呢？
4) 一個從來都不學習的學生去 (participate in) 考試，他還能 (have what confidence)?
5) 你三個孩子都考上了大學，你還為他們 (worry 什麼)?

5) 並 沒(有)/不 VP 舊的習慣勢力並沒有統治所有的人。 (p. 44)

並 "actually (not)" is used only with a negative (不 or 沒). It conveys the sense that reality differs from an assumption or a prevalent view.

例句： 1) 我對那位新來的教練的印象並不怎麼好。
2) 她並不是你喜歡的那種天真的女孩子。

造句：

填充: 1) 我雖然不是個 (hero) 也並不是完全沒有 (courage).
2) 媽媽並沒有 (treat unfairly) 他的兩個孩子。
3) 校長並不是一個很 (influential/have force and influence) 的人。

例句： 1) 找不到工作就作个体户，有什么不好的？
2) 这件事跟你沒关系，所以才沒告诉你，这有什么错？

造句：

填充： 1) ______________, 有什么不对的？
2) ____________, 有什么不好意思的？
3) 我看这件衣服很 (fits), 那儿不合适呢？
4) (Coach) 一样地 (treat) 所有的队员，怎么不公平呢？

改写 - Rewrite the completed sentences 3) and 4) in the preceding exercise, using pattern 3.

4) 还 V 什么 (O)? [colloquial] 还结什么婚? (p. 43)

This is a rhetorical question implying that, given the situation at hand (usually negative), there is no point in doing V. E.g.: 他都病得快死了，还考什么试？

例句： 1) 都这么晚了，还看什么电视？
2) 我的钱不够，还念什么大学？

填充： 1) 还有十分钟就要上课了，你还 (sleep 什么)?
2) 他已经 (resolved to...), 你还跟他 (make 什么 suggestions) 呢？
3) 要是一个政府不能听人民的意见，那么这个国家还 (搞什么 reform) 呢？
4) 一个从来都不学习的学生去 (participate in) 考试，他还能 (have what confidence)?
5) 你三个孩子都考上了大學，你还为他们 (worry 什么)?

5) 并 沒(有)/不 VP 旧的习惯势力并沒有统治所有的人。 (p. 45)

并 "actually (not)" is used only with a negative (不 or 沒). It conveys the sense that reality differs from an assumption or a prevalent view.

例句： 1) 我对那位新来的教练的印象并不怎么好。
2) 她并不是你喜欢的那种天真的女孩子。

造句：

填充: 1) 我虽然不是个 (hero) 也并不是完全沒有 (courage).
2) 妈妈并沒有 (treat unfairly) 他的两个孩子。
3) 校长并不是一个很 (influential/have force and influence) 的人。

4) 別人都説那是一種特效藥，可是我並 ____________.
5) 他說他上個月給我寫過三封信，可是我並 ____________.

6) 別看…，… [colloquial] 你別看它樣子難看，… (p. 46)

"Don't just go on the appearance that..., (in reality)..." This is a more colloquial way of saying "(雖然)…好像…，可是…"

例句： 1) 別看你比我大兩歲，，可是我比你高。
2) 別看他才學了三年中文，他已經能看中文報了。

改寫 - Reword the following sentences, using pattern 6:
1) 你不要覺得你很聰明，有很多學生比你還聰明。
2) 不要覺得有很多人説秦楠的壞話就以為她不是個好人。

填充： 1) 你別看他平常那麼正經，____________.
2) 別看她外表那麼善良，____________.
3) 別看他説話的口氣那麼大，____________.

7) 完了 就/才 …，完了就去北京參加… (p. 46)

This pattern states a sequence of events. The adverb 就 in the second clause reinforces the idea that the event in this clause follows the event stated in the preceding clause, so 就 can be translated as "and then." If, instead of 就, the adverb 才 is used, then we have a very strong assertion that this event does not occur until the preceding one is completed. A slightly more formal way of conveying the same idea is the pattern "…，然後 就/才…"

例句： 1) 每天早上我起床以後先洗澡，完了就去吃早飯。
2) 你要先讀完大學，完了才去找工作。

改寫 - Reword the following sentences, using pattern 7:
1) 這個孩子每天老是先看電視，然後才做功課。
2) 中國人總是先吃飯，然後才喝湯；可是外國人總是先喝湯，然後才吃飯。

填充： 1) 你最好先 (solve) 了這個問題，(and when that's done, then) 想別的問題。
2) 你應當先 (understand his situation/plight)，完了才 ____________.
3) 我今天把你的襯衫做好，完了就 ____________.

8) 非…不可 我這次非把冠軍拿下來不可。 (p. 46)

4) 别人都说那是一种特效药，可是我并 ____________.
5) 他说他上个月给我写过三封信，可是我并 ____________.

6) 别看…，… [colloquial] 你别看它样子难看，… (p. 47)

"Don't just go on the appearance that..., (in reality)..." This is a more colloquial way of saying "(虽然)…好像…，可是…"

例句： 1) 别看你比我大两岁，，可是我比你高。
2) 别看他才学了三年中文，他已经能看中文报了。

改写 - Reword the following sentences, using pattern 6:
1) 你不要觉得你很聪明，有很多学生比你还聪明。
2) 不要觉得有很多人说秦楠的坏话就以为她不是个好人。

填充： 1) 你别看他平常那么正经，____________.
2) 别看她外表那么善良，____________.
3) 别看他说话的口气那么大，____________.

7) 完了 就/才 …，完了就去北京参加… (p. 47)

This pattern states a sequence of events. The adverb 就 in the second clause reinforces the idea that the event in this clause follows the event stated in the preceding clause, so 就 can be translated as "and then." If, instead of 就, the adverb 才 is used, then we have a very strong assertion that this event does not occur until the preceding one is completed. A slightly more formal way of conveying the same idea is the pattern "…，然后 就/才…"

例句： 1) 每天早上我起床以后先洗澡，完了就去吃早饭。
2) 你要先读完大学，完了才去找工作。

改写 - Reword the following sentences, using pattern 7:
1) 这个孩子每天老是先看电视，然后才做功课。
2) 中国人总是先吃饭，然后才喝汤；可是外国人总是先喝汤，然后才吃饭。

填充： 1) 你最好先 (solve) 了这个问题，(and when that's done, then) 想别的问题。
2) 你应当先 (understand his situation/plight), 完了才 ____________.
3) 我今天把你的衬衫做好，完了就 ____________.

8) 非…不可 我这次非把冠军拿下来不可。 (p. 47)

"非…不可" is a double-negative pattern literally meaning "(if) not..., then it is not permissible." It is a very strong statement or resolution (if the subject is 我) that something absolutely must be done. This pattern, if translated literally as a double negative, is very awkward in English. The idea is best conveyed in English by emphatic intonation on such words as "absolutely must."

例句： 1) 這個問題非解決不可。 2) 這次比賽，我非參加不可。

造句：

填充： 1) 我們一定要 (reform) 現在的體制。
2) 這次我們放三天假，我一定要學會使用電腦。
3) 你要是要和 (coach) 提意見，那就一定要有 (courage).
4) 劉先生已經該 (retire) 了，可是他一定要留下來工作。
5) 因爲婆婆很 (severe), 所以媳婦必得是一個 (capable) 的人。

改寫 - Rewrite the five completed sentences in the preceding exercise, using pattern 8.

9) …還 行/可以(嗎)？ [colloqial] …不拼搏還行？ (p. 46)

This is a rhetorical question literally meaning "is it (still) okay that...?" implying that it is not okay or it won't do. In this pattern, 行 and 可以 are synonymous and can be used interchangeably. In the above example, the optional particle 嗎 is omitted, but the interrogative intonation is retained.

例句： 1) 這裡太吵了，我不搬家還行？
2) 這是他自己的事，他不自己做還可以嗎？

填充： 1) 你已經不是一個小孩子了，不能那麼 (naive) 了！
2) 你說你愛她，那你就應當 (take initiative) 一點兒。
3) (painful) 的事已經過去了。你不能這樣 (torment) 自己一輩子。
4) 教練的這種做法很不 (fair), 我們不能不 (expose) 他。
5) 這些 (old, big, and difficult) 問題，不 (resolve) 是不行的。

改寫 - Rewrite the five completed sentences in the preceding exercise, using pattern 9.

10) 不(就)是…(嗎)？ [colloquial] 不就是拼搏出來的嗎？ (p. 46)

This is another rhetorical question, literally meaning "isn't it...?" implying that it is indeed so. The optional 就, literally meaning "precisely" here, gives the utterance extra punch. As in the last pattern, the particle 嗎 can be omitted, but the interrogative intonation must be retained.

"非…不可" is a double-negative pattern literally meaning "(if) not..., then it is not permissible." It is a very strong statement or resolution (if the subject is 我) that something absolutely must be done. This pattern, if translated literally as a double negative, is very awkward in English. The idea is best conveyed in English by emphatic intonation on such words as "absolutely must."

例句： 1) 这个问题非解决不可。 2) 这次比赛，我非参加不可。

造句：

填充： 1) 我们一定要 (reform) 现在的体制。
2) 这次我们放三天假，我一定要学会使用电脑。
3) 你要是要和 (coach) 提意见，那就一定要有 (courage).
4) 刘先生已经该 (retire) 了，可是他一定要留下来工作。
5) 因为婆婆很 (severe), 所以媳妇必得是一个 (capable) 的人。

改写 - Rewrite the five completed sentences in the preceding exercise, using pattern 8.

9) …还 行/可以(吗)？ [colloqial] …不拼搏还行？ (p. 47)

This is a rhetorical question literally meaning "is it (still) okay that...?" implying that it is not okay or it won't do. In this pattern, 行 and 可以 are synonymous and can be used interchangeably. In the above example, the optional particle 吗 is omitted, but the interrogative intonation is retained.

例句： 1) 这里太吵了，我不搬家还行？
2) 这是他自己的事，他不自己做还可以吗？

填充： 1) 你已经不是一个小孩子了，不能那么 (naive) 了！
2) 你说你爱她，那你就应当 (take initiative) 一点儿。
3) (painful) 的事已经过去了。你不能这样 (torment) 自己一辈子。
4) 教练的这种做法很不 (fair), 我们不能不 (expose) 他。
5) 这些 (old, big, and difficult) 问题，不 (resolve) 是不行的。

改写 - Rewrite the five completed sentences in the preceding exercise, using pattern 9.

10) 不(就)是…(吗)？ [colloquial] 不就是拼搏出来的吗？ (p. 47)

This is another rhetorical question, literally meaning "isn't it...?" implying that it is indeed so. The optional 就, literally meaning "precisely" here, gives the utterance extra punch. As in the last pattern, the particle 吗 can be omitted, but the interrogative intonation must be retained.

例句： 1) 你現在爲什麼那麼胖，不就是因爲你老吃巧克力糖嗎？
2) 媽媽那麼早就退休，不就是爲了讓女兒頂替她嗎？

填充： 1) 你爲什麼還沒做完功課，就是因爲你老 (chat with your friends)。
2) 你的病怎麼好的？就是因爲我送給你的那種 (special efficacy) 藥治好的。
3) 小王開車怎麼 (have an accident) 的？就是因爲他開得太快！
4) 我爸爸 (at that time) 怎麼會被 (investigate) 的？就是因爲他出過國！
5) (others) 都不相信小張，就是因爲他老 (deceive) 人。

改寫 - Rewrite the five completed sentences in the preceding exercise, using pattern 10.

11) SV (一)點兒 幹嘛不主動點兒？ (p. 48)

"SV (一)點兒," meaning "a little more SV," is used in three different ways: 1) suggestion or command, as in the above example; 2) description of something as being a little too SV, e.g. 這間屋子小一點兒 "This room is a little (too) small." 3) description of something as being SV in an implied comparison, e.g. 這間屋子小一點兒 "This room is a little smaller than..." (the comparative reference is implied).

例句： 1) 你可以不可以說得再慢一點兒？
2) 他應該再瘦一點兒就好了。

造句：

填充： 1) 今天的天氣比昨天 (hot) 一點兒。
2) 這件衣服請你幫我改得 (a little more fitting).
3) 這條 (pants) 的 (measurements) 應當再 (a little shorter).
4) 現在他給我們的 (impression) 比從前 (a little better) 了。
5) 我們希望秦楠 (treat) 生活要 (a little more optimistic).

INCLUSIVE 翻譯 EXERCISE FOR SEGMENT IV:

1) If all (we) comrades have courage, what is there that cannot be overcome (resolved)?
2) Don't be misled by his usually serious demeanor; actually he is quite mischievous at times.
3) Is it acceptable for a coach to treat athletes in such an unfair way? Will it do to leave this old, big and difficult problem unsolved?
4) Universities throughout the country (in the entire country) are in the midst of reform.
5) What is your impression of her after all? I feel that she is innocent and kind-hearted.
6 - 10) See bottom of facing page.

例句： 1) 你现在为什么那么胖，不就是因为你老吃巧克力糖吗？
2) 妈妈那么早就退休，不就是为了让女儿顶替她吗？

填充： 1) 你为什么还没做完功课，就是因为你老 (chat with your friends)。
2) 你的病怎么好的？就是因为我送给你的那种 (special efficacy) 药治好的。
3) 小王开车怎么 (have an accident) 的？就是因为他开得太快！
4) 我爸爸 (at that time) 怎么会被 (investigate) 的？就是因为他出过国！
5) (others) 都不相信小张，就是因为他老 (deceive) 人。

改写 - Rewrite the five completed sentences in the preceding exercise, using pattern 10.

11) SV (一)点儿 干嘛不主动点儿？ (p. 49)

"SV (一)点儿," meaning "a little more SV," is used in three different ways: 1) suggestion or command, as in the above example; 2) description of something as being a little too SV, e.g. 这间屋子小一点儿 "This room is a little (too) small." 3) description of something as being SV in an implied comparison, e.g. 这间屋子小一点儿 "This room is a little smaller than..." (the comparative reference is implied).

例句： 1) 你可以不可以说得再慢一点儿？
2) 他应该再瘦一点儿就好了。

造句：

填充： 1) 今天的天气比昨天 (hot) 一点儿。
2) 这件衣服请你帮我改得 (a little more fitting).
3) 这条 (pants) 的 (measurements) 应当再 (a little shorter).
4) 现在他给我们的 (impression) 比从前 (a little better) 了。
5) 我们希望秦楠 (treat) 生活要 (a little more optimistic).

INCLUSIVE 翻译 EXERCISE FOR SEGMENT IV:

1 - 5) See bottom of facing page.

6) Zhihua, if you want to attain success, then you absolutely must take a little more initiative.

7) I must first finish making this shirt. When that's done, I'll then be able to mend your pants.

8) I'm returning to China next year, (so) what's the point of buying a house?

9) This famous precious medicine doesn't have any special efficacy (contrary to one's hopes).

10) Aren't you just torturing yourself for the rest of your life?

SEGMENT V

1) 趁…，…　　　　　　　　　　　　　　　趁冬冬沒醒，我得趕緊走。(p. 54)

This pattern is best translated as "While..., ..." - meaning one should take advantage of the circumstances described in the "while" clause to do the thing stated in the following clause. 趁 can also be followed by a single word, in which case it means "to avail oneself of, to take advantage of." E.g.: 趁便 "taking advantage of the convenience"; 趁早 "while it is early"; 趁機 "seizing the opportunity."

例句： 1) 趁老師不注意，他偷偷看了考題。
2) 趁着放假，我一定要學會開車。

造句：

填充： 1) 現在媽媽還沒有回來，我們 (quickly, hurry to) 把屋子整理好吧。
2) 我們要在 (Party branch secretary) 不在的時候做出一些 (reforms).
3) 你 ("auntie") 這個星期 (on vacation)，你可以請她幫你做一件 (sweater).
4) 最好在 (early in the morning) 天氣還不太 (hot) 的時候把外頭的 (labor) 做完，要不然就太 (hot) 了。
5) 她爸爸希望她能在還年輕的時候找個好的 ("intended"), 因爲過了三十歲，這個 (old, big, and difficult) 問題就不容易 (solve) 了。

改寫 - Reword the five completed sentences from the preceding exercise, using pattern 1.

2) V 起 (O) 來　　　　　　　　　　　　　　接電話的工夫就下起雨來。(p. 54)

The 起來 in this pattern functions as the postverb attached to the preceding verb. If the verb has an object, the object would be placed between 起 and 來, e.g. 下起雪來, 唱起歌來. As postverb, 起來 has two meanings: 1) "to begin to," e.g. 你怎麼抽起煙來了? "How come you've taken up smoking?" (cf. p. 55). A variation of this is SV-起來, meaning "to begin to become SV," e.g. 他好起來了 "He has begun to get well." 2) "when it comes to," e.g.: 踏板松了，看你蹬起來好吃力. "The pedal is loose, (I) see that it's quite a strain when you come to pedalling it." (cf. p. 133).

例句： 他們邊走邊唱起歌來。
這麼大熱天，跑起步來，夠吃力的！

造句：

填充： 1) 他們常常發生 (conflict). 你看，現在又開始 (quarrel) 了。

SEGMENT V

1) 趁…，… 趁冬冬沒醒，我得赶紧走。(p. 55)

This pattern is best translated as "While..., ..." - meaning one should take advantage of the circumstances described in the "while" clause to do the thing stated in the following clause. 趁 can also be followed by a single word, in which case it means "to avail oneself of, to take advantage of." E.g.: 趁便 "taking advantage of the convenience"; 趁早 "while it is early"; 趁机 "seizing the opportunity."

例句： 1) 趁老师不注意，他偷偷看了考题。
2) 趁着放假，我一定要学会开车。

造句：

填充： 1) 现在妈妈还沒有回来，我们 (quickly, hurry to) 把屋子整理好吧。
2) 我们要在 (Party branch secretary) 不在的时候做出一些 (reforms).
3) 你 ("auntie") 这个星期 (on vacation)，你可以请她帮你做一件 (sweater).
4) 最好在 (early in the morning) 天气还不太 (hot) 的时候把外头的 (labor) 做完，要不然就太 (hot) 了。
5) 她爸爸希望她能在还年轻的时候找个好的 ("intended"), 因为过了三十岁，这个 (old, big, and difficult) 问题就不容易 (solve) 了。

改写 - Reword the five completed sentences from the preceding exercise, using pattern 1.

2) V 起 (O) 来 接电话的工夫就下起雨来。(p. 55)

The 起来 in this pattern functions as the postverb attached to the preceding verb. If the verb has an object, the object would be placed between 起 and 来, e.g. 下起雪来, 唱起歌来. As postverb, 起来 has two meanings: 1) "to begin to," e.g. 你怎么抽起烟来了? "How come you've taken up smoking?" (cf. p. 55). A variation of this is SV-起来, meaning "to begin to become SV," e.g. 他好起来了 "He has begun to get well." 2) "when it comes to," e.g.: 踏板松了，看你蹬起来好吃力. "The pedal is loose, (I) see that it's quite a strain when you come to pedalling it." (cf. p. 133).

例句： 他们边走边唱起歌来。
这么大热天，跑起步来，够吃力的！

造句：

填充： 1) 他们常常发生 (conflict). 你看，现在又开始 (quarrel) 了。

2) 我真不喜歡我的同屋，他一開始 (make a phone call) 就講個沒完。
3) 那個小孩子 (start to speak) 好像一個大人。

改寫 - Reword the following sentences and the completed sentences from the preceding exercise, using pattern 2.

1) 從前他是學生，現在開始教書了。
2) 他上個月答應他愛人不再喝酒了，可是他上星期又開始喝了。

3) (person) 來 電話/信 誰來電話？ (p. 56)

This is an idiomatic expression signifying that a phone call or a letter has arrived. The subject of this expression is the originator of the phone call or letter, which may be unknown and/or left unstated. E.g. 來電話了 "A phone call has come." can be said even before a ringing phone is answered.

例句： 1) 他去紐約已經快一個月了，可是沒來過一封信。
2) 他很少來信，可是經常來電話。

填充： 1) 我們的 (neighbor) 說今天下午 (someone tried to call us on the phone).
2) 那兒的 (Party branch secretary) (wrote a letter) 通知我說我的老伴正在被 (investigate).
3) 奶奶很 (concerned with) 我，所以 (often) (calls) 問我的 (situation) 怎麼樣。

4) …，免得… 就在屋裡做，免得在外面風吹日曬的。 (p. 56)

This is a two-clause construction in which the first clause states the action taken, and the second clause - introduced by 免得 - states the undesirable situation avoided by taking that action. Translating 免得 literally as "to avoid, to be spared (doing something or having something happen)" is awkward, so it is better to paraphrase it as "..., so as not to..."

例句： 1) 天冷，多穿些衣服吧，免得生病。
2) 咱們問一問路吧，免得走錯了。

造句：

填充： 1) 你一定要在家裡等我，免得我 (come for nothing) 一趟。
2) 你應當先給朋友打一個電話，免得 ______________.
3) 出門的時候最好看一看是不是帶了 (key), 免得 ________________.
4) ______________, 免得以後 (regret).
5) 你得好好兒地 (educate and nurture) 他，免得 ________________.

2) 我真不喜欢我的同屋，他一开始 (make a phone call) 就讲个没完。
3) 那个小孩子 (start to speak) 好象一个大人。

改写 - Reword the following sentences and the completed sentences from the preceding exercise, using pattern 2.

1) 从前他是学生，现在开始教书了。
2) 他上个月答应他爱人不再喝酒了，可是他上星期又开始喝了。

3) (person) 来 电话/信 谁来电话？ (p. 57)

This is an idiomatic expression signifying that a phone call or a letter has arrived. The subject of this expression is the originator of the phone call or letter, which may be unknown and/or left unstated. E.g. 来电话了 "A phone call has come." can be said even before a ringing phone is answered.

例句： 1) 他去纽约已经快一个月了，可是没来过一封信。
2) 他很少来信，可是经常来电话。

填充： 1) 我们的 (neighbor) 说今天下午 (someone tried to call us on the phone).
2) 那儿的 (Party branch secretary) (wrote a letter) 通知我说我的老伴正在被 (investigate).
3) 奶奶很 (concerned with) 我，所以 (often) (calls) 问我的 (situation) 怎么样。

4) …，免得… 就在屋里做，免得在外面风吹日晒的。 (p. 57)

This is a two-clause construction in which the first clause states the action taken, and the second clause - introduced by 免得 - states the undesirable situation avoided by taking that action. Translating 免得 literally as "to avoid, to be spared (doing something or having something happen)" is awkward, so it is better to paraphrase it as "..., so as not to..."

例句： 1) 天冷，多穿些衣服吧，免得生病。
2) 咱们问一问路吧，免得走错了。

造句：

填充： 1) 你一定要在家里等我，免得我 (come for nothing) 一趟。
2) 你应当先给朋友打一个电话，免得 ______________.
3) 出门的时候最好看一看是不是带了 (key), 免得 _________________.
4) _________________, 免得以后 (regret).
5) 你得好好儿地 (educate and nurture) 他，免得 _________________.

5) 唯一　　我唯一不放心的是我妹妹蕭雲。(p, 58)

唯一 ("the sole..., the only...") is followed by a noun phrase, which may be a simple noun (e.g. 他唯一的親人 "his only relative"), a noun modified by a phrase (e.g. 他唯一還在世的親人 "his only relative who is still alive"), or a modified noun phrase (ending in 的) in which the head noun is understood and therefore unstated, as in the example above.

例句： 1) 現在我唯一的辦法就是找個工作。
2) 我唯一希望的就是考上大學。

造句：

填充： 1) 我只有一樣東西想要，就是 ________________.
2) 只有一件事讓我感到生氣，就是他 (lied to me).
3) 這個孩子的功課很好。只有一門功課讓他感到 (strenuous)，就是 ______________.
4) 我只有一種 (situation) 不能 (forgive), 就是 ________________.

改寫 - Rewrite the completed sentences from the preceding exercise, using pattern 5.

例：我只有一個要求，就是請你別在晚上十二點以後來電話。
我唯一的要求就是請你別在晚上十二點以後來電話。

6) 包括…(在內)　　我不希望其他朋友知道我的醜事，包括秦楠在內。(p. 58)

In this pattern, the 在內 ("within") at the end reinforces 包括 and is optional. This phrase usually follows the main clause, as in the above example. But when stating a sum total, it normally precedes the main clause, e.g.: 包括今天，秦楠已經有三天沒來了。"Including today, it's been three days already that Qin Nan has not come."

例句： 1) 我們家包括我在內有四口人。
2) 這二十塊錢已經包括小費在內了。

造句：

填充： 1) 租這個房子，每個月要 (250) 元，但是水電的錢不在裡頭。
2) 加上這個週末，你們一共 (on vacation) 一個月。
3) 我們已經 (notified) 四個朋友來我家談一談，加上你跟我，一共有六個人了。
4) 真不 (fortuitous), 上個星期我已經買了這本書，前天我的男朋友又送給我一本，加上今天你送給我的，我現在有三本同樣的書了。

5) 唯一 我唯一不放心的是我妹妹肖云。(p, 59)

唯一 ("the sole..., the only...") is followed by a noun phrase, which may be a simple noun (e.g. 他唯一的亲人 "his only relative"), a noun modified by a phrase (e.g. 他唯一还在世的亲人 "his only relative who is still alive"), or a modified noun phrase (ending in 的) in which the head noun is understood and therefore unstated, as in the example above.

例句： 1) 现在我唯一的办法就是找个工作。
2) 我唯一希望的就是考上大学。

造句：

填充： 1) 我只有一样东西想要，就是 ________________.
2) 只有一件事让我感到生气，就是他 (lied to me).
3) 这个孩子的功课很好。只有一门功课让他感到 (strenuous)，就是 ______________.
4) 我只有一种 (situation) 不能 (forgive), 就是 ________________.

改写 - Rewrite the completed sentences from the preceding exercise, using pattern 5.
例：我只有一个要求，就是请你别在晚上十二点以后来电话。
我唯一的要求就是请你别在晚上十二点以后来电话。

6) 包括…(在内) 我不希望其他朋友知道我的丑事，包括秦楠在内。(p. 59)

In this pattern, the 在内 ("within") at the end reinforces 包括 and is optional. This phrase usually follows the main clause, as in the above example. But when stating a sum total, it normally precedes the main clause, e.g.: 包括今天，秦楠已经有三天没来了。"Including today, it's been three days already that Qin Nan has not come."

例句： 1) 我们家包括我在内有四口人。
2) 这二十块钱已经包括小费在内了。

造句：

填充： 1) 租这个房子，每个月要 (250) 元，但是水电的钱不在里头。
2) 加上这个周末，你们一共 (on vacation) 一个月。
3) 我们已经 (notified) 四个朋友来我家谈一谈，加上你跟我，一共有六个人了。
4) 真不 (fortuitous), 上个星期我已经买了这本书，前天我的男朋友又送给我一本，加上今天你送给我的，我现在有三本同样的书了。

改寫 - Rewrite the completed sentences from the preceding exercise, using pattern 6.

例：我們的學費裡面沒有書錢。 我們的學費不包括書錢(在內)。

7) 反倒 [uncommon] 我們的情況比過去好了，他反倒不珍惜自己了。 (p. 60)

反倒 is synonymous with the more widely used 反而. Both are adverbs meaning "on the contrary." In some contexts, a direct translation of 反倒 or 反而 is awkward, and the idea is best conveyed by a paraphrase, e.g., 他終於能頂替他母親了，可他反倒寧願繼續作個體戶了。"Finally he can take his mother's place (in a state job), but now - as it turns out - he'd rather remain self-employed."

例句： 1) 他說沒有錢買自行車，可是反倒買了汽車，真奇怪！
2) 昨天天氣那麼熱，你不想去游泳；今天天氣冷，你反倒想去了！

造句：

填充： 1) 這次考試 (ordinarily) 不努力的學生考得好，可是努力學習的學生考得不好。
2) 我們學校的 (organization, system) 這十年來不但沒有 (reform), 而且比從前更壞了。
3) 在紐約，有的時候開車很慢，____比較快。
4) 對他的太太跟孩子，他從來都不 (concerned), 可是對他女朋友，他很 ____.
5) 中文課本他都看不懂，可是中國電影他 ____________.

Add 反倒 or 反而 into the completed sentences from the preceding exercise, deleting or replacing existing words if necessary.

例：洗衣服他沒時間，看小說他就有時間了。
洗衣服他沒時間，看小說他反而有時間了。

8) 只要…，(…) 就… 只要有勇氣站起來，他就會活得更好。 (p. 60)

"If only..., then..." In Chinese, the tandem relationship between the two clauses in this construction requires the use of both 只要 and 就, even though leaving 就 untranslated would result in a smoother English translation.

例句： 1) 只要楊梅一上市，他就叫他的媽媽去買。
2) 只要她的媽媽退休，她就可以得到她媽媽的工作了。

造句：

填充： 1) 只要你把你的 (situation, plight) 告訴別人，別人就一定會 (forgive) 你的。
2) 只要你 (notify) 了他，他就一定 ____________.

改写 - Rewrite the completed sentences from the preceding exercise, using pattern 6.

例：我们的学费里面沒有书钱。　　　我们的学费不包括书钱(在内)。

7) 反倒 [uncommon]　　　我们的情况比过去好了，他反倒不珍惜自己了。(p. 61)

反倒 is synonymous with the more widely used 反而. Both are adverbs meaning "on the contrary." In some contexts, a direct translation of 反倒 or 反而 is awkward, and the idea is best conveyed by a paraphrase, e.g., 他终于能顶替他母亲了，可他反倒宁愿继续作个体户了。"Finally he can take his mother's place (in a state job), but now - as it turns out - he'd rather remain self-employed."

例句：1) 他说沒有钱买自行车，可是反倒买了汽车，真奇怪！

2) 昨天天气那么热，你不想去游泳；今天天气冷，你反倒想去了！

造句：

填充：1) 这次考试 (ordinarily) 不努力的学生考得好，可是努力学习的学生考得不好。

2) 我们学校的 (organization, system) 这十年来不但沒有 (reform), 而且比从前更坏了。

3) 在纽约，有的时候开车很慢，____比较快。

4) 对他的太太跟孩子，他从来都不 (concerned), 可是对他女朋友，他很 _____.

5) 中文课本他都看不懂，可是中国电影他 _____________.

Add 反倒 or 反而 into the completed sentences from the preceding exercise, deleting or replacing existing words if necessary.

例：洗衣服他沒时间，看小说他就有时间了。

洗衣服他沒时间，看小说他反而有时间了。

8) 只要…，(…) 就…　　　只要有勇气站起来，他就会活得更好。(p. 61)

"If only..., then..." In Chinese, the tandem relationship between the two clauses in this construction requires the use of both 只要 and 就, even though leaving 就 untranslated would result in a smoother English translation.

例句：1) 只要杨梅一上市，他就叫他的妈妈去买。

2) 只要她的妈妈退休，她就可以得到她妈妈的工作了。

造句：

填充：1) 只要你把你的 (situation, plight) 告诉别人，别人就一定会 (forgive) 你的。

2) 只要你 (notify) 了他，他就一定 _____________.

3) ______________, 這個問題就一定能解決了。

4) 只要你找到一個好工作, ______________.

5) 只要你跟他 (make a clean break), 你就 ______________.

INCLUSIVE 翻譯 EXERCISE FOR SEGMENT V:

1) Aiya! It's started to rain. Hurry up and take the things in. Otherwise, everything will get wet!

2) You had best come to an agreement with him beforehand, so as to avoid having a misunderstanding later.

3) Everyone, including Gao Zhihua, was very surprised upon discovering that Xiao Jian had committed a crime.

4) As long as you are willing to accept reform, (and) turn over a new leaf ("to be a decent person anew"), then we will certainly forgive you.

5) My neighbor is an old lady who cannot stand noisiness (is very fearful of noisiness), therefore, I want to take advantage of her being out of town to have a party (invite guests over).

6) The Party branch secretary just called (on the phone) to notify me that Xiao Jian has committed a crime.

7) Because she is handicapped, it is very inconvenient when it comes to walking.

8) After she knew of his difficult situation, not only was she not concerned, on the contrary she felt that it served him right (use 是…的 pattern).

3) ______________, 这个问题就一定能解决了。

4) 只要你找到一个好工作, ________________.

5) 只要你跟他 (make a clean break), 你就 _______________.

INCLUSIVE 翻译 EXERCISE FOR SEGMENT V: See facing page.

SEGMENT VI

1) 使 + clause [somewhat literary] …批準我篆刻私章的執照，使我的生活有了保障。 (p. 66)

使 "to cause..., to give rise to...," can be the main verb in a sentence (e.g. 他使我非常生氣 "He made me very angry.") But more frequently, it introduces a clause which follows the main clause of a sentence. In this context, the main clause states an action or situation which gives rise to the situation in the following 使-clause. The above excerpt from the film script exemplifies this usage.

例句： 1) 秦楠又來看望冬冬了，這使他很高興。
2) 那個小孩兒每天晚上哭哭啼啼，使鄰居們很生氣。

造句：

填充： 1) 那個孩子不聽父母的 (advice), 使父母 ___________.
2) 他們被 (approved) (to divorce) 了，這件事使他的父母很痛苦。
3) 知道了蕭雲是一個 (handicapped person), 使秦楠很 (surprised).
4) 醫生把他的病 (thoroughly) 治好了，使他 ___________.
5) 他 (usually) 把他的衣裳 (everywhere) 亂放，這使他的太太 _____________.

2) 能 VP, (subj.) (不) 就 VP (嗎?) 能帶回去不早就帶回去了！ (p. 70)

In the basic pattern "...能 VP, (subj.) 就 VP," meaning "(if)...can..., then...," an "if" is implied in the first clause, and the two VP's may be, but need not be, the same, e.g.:

我能頂替我母親就不當個體戶了。
If I could take my mother's place, I would not be self-employed anymore.
秦楠能把冬冬帶回上海，她就一定帶回去了。
If Qin Nan could take Dongdong back to Shanghai, she would certainly do it.

We can superimpose the rhetorical question pattern "不…(嗎)?" (cf. Grammatical Note IV.10) onto the above basic pattern and derive the pattern "...能 VP, (subj.) 不就 VP (嗎)?" which conveys the same "facts" as the basic pattern (in positive form), but is more emphatic. Note that the 嗎 at the end can be omitted.

例句： 1) 能解決不早就解決了！
2) 能告訴他不早就告訴他了！

SEGMENT VI

1) 使 + clause [somewhat literary] …批准我篆刻私章的执照，使我的生活有了保障。 (p. 67)
使 "to cause..., to give rise to...," can be the main verb in a sentence (e.g. 他使我非常生气 "He made me very angry.") But more frequently, it introduces a clause which follows the main clause of a sentence. In this context, the main clause states an action or situation which gives rise to the situation in the following 使-clause. The above excerpt from the film script exemplifies this usage.

例句： 1) 秦楠又来看望冬冬了，这使他很高兴。
2) 那个小孩儿每天晚上哭哭啼啼，使邻居们很生气。

造句：

填充： 1) 那个孩子不听父母的 (advice), 使父母 ___________.
2) 他们被 (approved) (to divorce) 了，这件事使他的父母很痛苦。
3) 知道了肖云是一个 (handicapped person), 使秦楠很 (surprised).
4) 医生把他的病 (thoroughly) 治好了，使他 ____________.
5) 他 (usually) 把他的衣裳 (everywhere) 乱放，这使他的太太 _____________.

2) 能 VP, (subj.) (不) 就 VP (吗?) 能带回去不早就带回去了！ (p. 71)
In the basic pattern "...能 VP, (subj.) 就 VP," meaning "(if)...can..., then...," an "if" is implied in the first clause, and the two VP's may be, but need not be, the same, e.g.:

我能顶替我母亲就不当个体户了。
If I could take my mother's place, I would not be self-employed anymore.
秦楠能把冬冬带回上海，她就一定带回去了。
If Qin Nan could take Dongdong back to Shanghai, she would certainly do it.

We can superimpose the rhetorical question pattern "不…(吗)?" (cf. Grammatical Note IV.10) onto the above basic pattern and derive the pattern "...能 VP, (subj.) 不就 VP (吗)?" which conveys the same "facts" as the basic pattern (in positive form), but is more emphatic. Note that the 吗 at the end can be omitted.

例句： 1) 能解决不早就解决了！
2) 能告诉他不早就告诉他了！

填充： 1) A: 他病得很利害，你應當 (at least) 去看看他。
B: 我能_____就_____! 可是我真是太忙了。
2) A: 既然小陳和他愛人在一起那麼 (painful), 他們為什麼不 (divorce) 呢？
B: 能____________! 可是他們的兩個孩子怎麼辦？
3) A: 我真不敢 (imagine), 他去了那麼多次 (hospital), 他的病還沒好。醫生就沒有辦法嗎？
B: 咳！能____________!
4) A: 你為什麼還不把你的報告交給老師？
B: 能____________! 可是我沒有時間寫呀！
5) A: 這些 (shirt) 已經過時了，你應該快點把它們賣出去才好。
B: 能____________! 可是沒有人願意買呀！

3) 偏偏 [colloquial] 偏偏下午有課。(p. 72)

The two related meanings of this adverb are given in the glossary (cf. Part I, p. 72), but it has no literal translation in English. To allow this term to "sink in," the instructor should provide many examples and opportunities for students to make up examples. 偏 can be used without reduplication, especially if combined with an auxiliary verb (cf. 我偏要玩兒 on p. 84 of Part I.)

例句： 1) 我們說好今天去長城，可是今天偏偏下雨了。
2) 今天忘了帶執照，公安局可偏偏派人來查了。

造句：

填充： 1) 從前叫你去，你__________, 現在 (regret) 有什麼用？！
2) 她父親想把她 (marry) 給 (Party branch secretary), 可是她_____愛上了一個 (rightist).
3) 小高 (advise) 過蕭健別作那樣的事，可是蕭健_____不聽，結果 (committed a crime).
4) 小李又 (capable) 又 (kind-hearted), (the sole) 的缺點就是他很有自己的 (own ideas), 不大願意 (accept) 別人的意見。
(insist on) 他自己的 (subjective views).

4) 從來 沒/不… 真怪，從來沒聽說她嫁過人。(p. 74)

The adverb 從來 is always used with a negative - 沒 or 不. 從來不 implies that one has not done that something in the past and would not do so in the present or future. 從來沒 implies only that one has not done something in the past, but makes no assumptions about the present or future.

填充： 1) A: 他病得很利害，你应当 (at least) 去看看他。
B: 我能_____就_____! 可是我真是太忙了。
2) A: 既然小陈和他爱人在一起那么 (painful), 他们为什么不 (divorce) 呢？
B: 能______________! 可是他们的两个孩子怎么办？
3) A: 我真不敢 (imagine), 他去了那么多次 (hospital), 他的病还没好。医生就没有办法吗？
B: 咳！能______________!
4) A: 你为什么还不把你的报告交给老师？
B: 能_____________! 可是我没有时间写呀！
5) A: 这些 (shirt) 已经过时了，你应该快点把它们卖出去才好。
B: 能_____________! 可是没有人愿意买呀！

3) 偏偏 [colloquial] 偏偏下午有课。(p. 73)

The two related meanings of this adverb are given in the glossary (cf. Part I, p. 72), but it has no literal translation in English. To allow this term to "sink in," the instructor should provide many examples and opportunities for students to make up examples. 偏 can be used without reduplication, especially if combined with an auxiliary verb (cf. 我偏要玩儿 on p. 85 of Part I.)

例句： 1) 我们说好今天去长城，可是今天偏偏下雨了。
2) 今天忘了带执照，公安局可偏偏派人来查了。

造句：

填充： 1) 从前叫你去，你____________, 现在 (regret) 有什么用？！
2) 她父亲想把她 (marry) 給 (Party branch secretary), 可是她_____爱上了一个 (rightist).
3) 小高 (advise) 过肖健别作那样的事，可是肖健_____不听，结果 (committed a crime).
4) 小李又 (capable) 又 (kind-hearted), (the sole) 的缺点就是他很有自己的 (own ideas), 不大愿意 (accept) 别人的意见。
(insist on) 他自己的 (subjective views).

4) 从来 没/不… 真怪，从来没听说她嫁过人。(p. 75)

The adverb 从来 is always used with a negative - 沒 or 不. 从来不 implies that one has not done that something in the past and would not do so in the present or future. 从来沒 implies only that one has not done something in the past, but makes no assumptions about the present or future.

例句： 1) 我從來沒去過英國。
2) 爸爸晚上從來不看電視，他太忙了。

造句： 1) 從來不：
2) 從來沒：

填充： 1) 這是我第一次去 (commune hospital), 我從來 _________.
2) 我的個子高，(coach) 希望我 (join) 籃球隊。可是我從來 _________, 因爲我不喜歡運動。
3) 他已經四十歲了，連一個女朋友都 ___ 交過，他怎麼能找到 (potential spouse) 呢？
4) 當然我喜歡 (everywhere) 去走走，可是我 (never go out), 因爲自從那年 (stumbled and fell) 以後，我就變成個 (handicapped person) 了。

5) 一下子 怎麼一下子會有這麼大孩子啦！ (p. 74)

This is an adverbial time phrase meaning "suddenly, in an instant, in a short time." It is related to the 一下 in the pattern "V-一下," meaning "to V briefly."

例句： 1) 他昨天還好好的，怎麼今天一下子就住醫院啦？
2) 才六個月沒看見這孩子，怎麼一下子長得這麼大了？

造句：

填充： 1) 去年她告訴我她和她先生的 (conflict) 都 (resolved), 怎麼 (suddenly got divorced)?
2) 他從前老是 (gregarious and jolly), 現在 (suddenly) 變得那麼不愛說話了，到底是出了什麼事？
3) 從前這個地方有很多人沒有工作，可是自從經濟 (reform) 以來，他們 (suddenly) 都變成了 (self-employed entrepreneurs) 了。
4) 我 (maternal grandfather) (whole life) 都是個很 (kind-hearted) 的醫生，可是在文化大革命的時候 (suddenly) 被打成 (rightist).

INCLUSIVE 翻譯 EXERCISE FOR SEGMENT VI:

1) I knew that they sometimes fought, but I never imagined that they would get a divorce.
2) You cannot suddenly leave this job. You must notify us at least two weeks in advance.
3) Setting up communes was originally intended to make ("to cause") the people's livelihood secure.
4) The weather is usually very good here, but it just so happened that on the day we had off it rained.

5 - 6) See bottom of facing page.

例句： 1) 我从来沒去过英国。
2) 爸爸晚上从来不看电视，他太忙了。

造句： 1) 从来不：
2) 从来沒：

填充： 1) 这是我第一次去 (commune hospital), 我从来 ________.
2) 我的个子高，(coach) 希望我 (join) 篮球队。可是我从来 ________, 因为我不喜欢运动。
3) 他已经四十岁了，连一个女朋友都 ___ 交过，他怎么能找到 (potential spouse) 呢？
4) 当然我喜欢 (everywhere) 去走走，可是我 (never go out), 因为自从那年 (stumbled and fell) 以后，我就变成个 (handicapped person) 了。

5) 一下子 怎么一下子会有这么大孩子啦！ (p. 75)

This is an adverbial time phrase meaning "suddenly, in an instant, in a short time." It is related to the 一下 in the pattern "V-一下," meaning "to V briefly."

例句： 1) 他昨天还好好的，怎么今天一下子就住医院啦？
2) 才六个月沒看见这孩子，怎么一下子长得这么大了？

造句：

填充： 1) 去年她告诉我她和她先生的 (conflict) 都 (resolved), 怎么 (suddenly got divorced)?
2) 他从前老是 (gregarious and jolly), 现在 (suddenly) 变得那么不爱说话了，到底是出了什么事？
3) 从前这个地方有很多人沒有工作，可是自从经济 (reform) 以来，他们 (suddenly) 都变成了 (self-employed entrepreneurs) 了。
4) 我 (maternal grandfather) (whole life) 都是个很 (kind-hearted) 的医生，可是在文化大革命的时候 (suddenly) 被打成 (rightist).

INCLUSIVE 翻译 EXERCISE FOR SEGMENT VI:

1 - 4) See bottom of facing page.

5) If Mrs. Gao can understand and forgive Qin Nan, wouldn't Zhihua and Qin Nan be able to get married then?

6) She went to the commune hospital to see Dongdong (and) will be back shortly. Why don't you just wait a little while here?

SEGMENT VII

1) V-死 [uncommon] and SV-死了 [colloquial] 你不要把人看死了。(p. 76)

As postverb, 死 does not carry its primary meaning of "die," but conveys the notion of "fixity," inflexibility, rigidity, and persistence. Thus 封死 means "to seal tight," 看死 means "to have a rigid view." This usage of 死 is to be distinguished from its usage following a SV (i.e. SV + 死了), in which case it means "extremely SV" (e.g.: 熱死了 "it's extremely hot!" 我餓死了 "I'm famished!").

例句： 1) 你有什意見現在就提吧。以後説死了就不能改了。
2) 這箱子封死了，怎麼也開不開了。
3) 這人沈默死了，我從來沒看見過他有説有笑的。
4) 他意想不到地考上了北京大學，所以高興死了。

造句： SV 死了：

填充： 1) 我 (husband) 非常 (muddle-headed), 常常把我 ("anger to death") 了。
2) 你對一個人的第一個 (impression) 不一定是可靠的，所以不能 (have a rigid view of a person).
3) 上海的公共汽車 (are extremely crowded), 所以我多半是 (ride a bike to work).
4) 我們鄰居家裡一天到晚 (quarrel), 孩子們也鬧得很, (it's extremely noisy).

2) …而… 秦楠是個沒有丈夫而有個五歲孩子的母親！(p. 80)

而 links two verbs, stative verbs, verb phrases, or clauses. It can mean either "but" (as in the above example) or "and" (e.g. 他殘廢而有病 "He is handicapped and is moreover ill.").

例句： 1) 蕭雲是個處境困難而樂觀的人。
2) 他昨天提醒了我們而今天自己就忘了。真糊塗！
3) 中國男人都喜歡找善良而文靜的對像嗎？
4) 你提出的計劃，公社已經考慮而批準了。

造句：

填充： 1) 冬冬不願意離開他母親，使他母親感到又 (conflicted) 又 (melancholy).
2) 他 (advise) 別人要 (love and protect) 小孩子，可是他常常打自己的兒子。
3) 通過那次 (test/trial) 以後，他更堅強，更 (sensible) 了。
4) 雖然他 (uncle) 家每天都有 (chocolates) 吃，可是他不要跟他 (uncle) 住，要跟他 (auntie) 住。

SEGMENT VII

1) V-死 [uncommon] and SV-死了 [colloquial] 你不要把人看死了。 (p. 77)

As postverb, 死 does not carry its primary meaning of "die," but conveys the notion of "fixity," inflexibility, rigidity, and persistence. Thus 封死 means "to seal tight," 看死 means "to have a rigid view." This usage of 死 is to be distinguished from its usage following a SV (i.e. SV + 死了), in which case it means "extremely SV" (e.g.: 热死了 "it's extremely hot!" 我饿死了 "I'm famished!").

例句： 1) 你有什意见现在就提吧。以后说死了就不能改了。
2) 这箱子封死了，怎么也开不开了。
3) 这人沈默死了，我从来沒看见过他有说有笑的。
4) 他意想不到地考上了北京大学，所以高兴死了。

造句： SV 死了：

填充： 1) 我 (husband) 非常 (muddle-headed), 常常把我 ("anger to death") 了。
2) 你对一个人的第一个 (impression) 不一定是可靠的，所以不能 (have a rigid view of a person).
3) 上海的公共汽车 (are extremely crowded), 所以我多半是 (ride a bike to work).
4) 我们邻居家里一天到晚 (quarrel), 孩子们也闹得很, (it's extremely noisy).

2) …而… 秦楠是个沒有丈夫而有个五岁孩子的母亲！ (p. 81)

而 links two verbs, stative verbs, verb phrases, or clauses. It can mean either "but" (as in the above example) or "and" (e.g. 他残废而有病 "He is handicapped and is moreover ill.").

例句： 1) 肖云是个处境困难而乐观的人。
2) 他昨天提醒了我们而今天自己就忘了。真糊涂！
3) 中国男人都喜欢找善良而文静的对象吗？
4) 你提出的计划，公社已经考虑而批准了。

造句：

填充： 1) 冬冬不愿意离开他母亲，使他母亲感到又 (conflicted) 又 (melancholy).
2) 他 (advise) 别人要 (love and protect) 小孩子，可是他常常打自己的儿子。
3) 通过那次 (test/trial) 以后，他更坚强，更 (sensible) 了。
4) 虽然他 (uncle) 家每天都有 (chocolates) 吃，可是他不要跟他 (uncle) 住，要跟他 (auntie) 住。

改寫 - Reword the completed sentences from the preceding exercise, using pattern 2.

3) 不能不… 媽不能不提醒你一聲兒。 (p. 82)

不能不 "cannot but" is a double negative pattern which conveys the same meaning as 必得, but is more emphatic than 必得. 不可不 and 不得不 are two other synonymous patterns.

例句： 1) 雖然我不是冬冬的爸爸，可是我不能不愛護他。
2) 在一個傳統的中國社會裡，一個女人不能不結婚。

造句：

填充： 1) 他是你的 (husband), 他做錯事你必須 (forgive) 他，因爲你們還要在 (together) 過 (a whole lifetime) 呢。
2) (Comrades) 都已經看出來這個 (system) 一定得 (reform) 了。
3) 他這個人那麼 (muddle-headed), 重要的事你只好 (remind) 他。
4) 因爲她的 (heart and soul) 有過 (wound), 所以很 (reticent). 你必得同情她。
5) 你 (in a short time, soon) 就二十五歲了，結婚這件事你必須 (consider) 了。

改寫 - Reword the completed sentences from the preceding exercise, using pattern 3.

4) 千萬… 千萬不能糊塗哇！ (p. 82)

千萬, literally "a thousand and ten thousand," is an adverb meaning "by all means." It is a strong warning or alert that one must or mustn't do something. When it is used with a negative (別, 不能, 不可, etc.) it is an injunction against something. This pattern does not have a good direct English translation, and the sense of it is best conveyed by using emphatic intonation and such words as "must," e.g. 你千萬別告訴冬冬 "You must not tell Dongdong!"

例句： 1) 你千萬得在放假以前解決這個問題。
2) 你千萬別再犯罪了。你再犯罪公安局就不會再原諒你了。

造句：

填充： 1) 黨支部書記的 (power) 很大，你怎麼也不能跟他 (quarrel).
2) 這孩子的 (heart has been wounded), 所以你必須 (love and protect) 他。
3) 你不能隨便 (divorce), 這事一定要好好兒地 (consider).
4) 你 (absolutely mustn't) 以爲她是個 (handicapped person) 就什麼也不能作，她才 (capable) 呢！

改写 - Reword the completed sentences from the preceding exercise, using pattern 2.

3) 不能不… 妈不能不提醒你一声儿。 (p. 83)

不能不 "cannot but" is a double negative pattern which conveys the same meaning as 必得, but is more emphatic than 必得. 不可不 and 不得不 are two other synonymous patterns.

例句： 1) 虽然我不是冬冬的爸爸，可是我不能不爱护他。
2) 在一个传统的中国社会里，一个女人不能不结婚。

造句：

填充： 1) 他是你的 (husband), 他做错事你必须 (forgive) 他，因为你们还要在 (together) 过 (a whole lifetime) 呢。
2) (Comrades) 都已经看出来这个 (system) 一定得 (reform) 了。
3) 他这个人那么 (muddle-headed), 重要的事你只好 (remind) 他。
4) 因为她的 (heart and soul) 有过 (wound), 所以很 (reticent). 你必得同情她。
5) 你 (in a short time, soon) 就二十五岁了，结婚这件事你必须 (consider) 了。

改写 - Reword the completed sentences from the preceding exercise, using pattern 3.

4) 千万… 千万不能糊涂哇！ (p. 83)

千万, literally "a thousand and ten thousand," is an adverb meaning "by all means." It is a strong warning or alert that one must or mustn't do something. When it is used with a negative (别, 不能, 不可, etc.) it is an injunction against something. This pattern does not have a good direct English translation, and the sense of it is best conveyed by using emphatic intonation and such words as "must," e.g. 你千万别告诉冬冬 "You must not tell Dongdong!"

例句： 1) 你千万得在放假以前解决这个问题。
2) 你千万别再犯罪了。你再犯罪公安局就不会再原谅你了。

造句：

填充： 1) 党支部书记的 (power) 很大，你怎么也不能跟他 (quarrel).
2) 这孩子的 (heart has been wounded), 所以你必须 (love and protect) 他。
3) 你不能随便 (divorce), 这事一定要好好儿地 (consider).
4) 你 (absolutely mustn't) 以为她是个 (handicapped person) 就什么也不能作，她才 (capable) 呢！

改寫 - Reword the first three completed sentences from the preceding exercise, using pattern 4.

5) 自從 自從冬冬回來以後，這兩天外面有些流言蜚語吧？ (p. 82)

自從, usually translated as "ever since..., from the time..., after...," is used to introduce a time phrase that precedes the main clause of a sentence, and is usually (but not necessarily) coupled with 以來 or 以後 at the end of the time phrase. 以來 at the end of the time phrase refers to the period from that past event up to and including the present. 以後 at the end of the time phrase is a little more ambiguous. It refers to a period that began from that past event, but may or may not have ended before the present. E.g.:

自從她媽去世以來，她就不再有說有笑了。
Ever since her mother died, she has never been gregarious and jolly anymore.
(This state persists through the present.)

自從她媽去世以後，她就不再有說有笑了。
After her mother died, she did not chatter happily anymore.
(It's unclear whether this state persisted to the present.)

自從她媽去世以後，她頭五年都沒再有說有笑了。
After her mother died, she did not chatter happily for the first five years.
(This state no longer holds.)

例句：
1) 自從她母親自殺以後，他父親就瘋了。
2) 自從她丈夫死了以來，她一直沒考慮過重新找對像。

造句：

填充：
1) 自從我們上次 (quarreled) 以來，_______________.
2) 自從 (Public Security Bureau) (approved) 他擺攤以後，_______________.
3) 自從 _______________, 他對社會主義就失去了信心。
4) 自從 _______________, 她就不像從前那麼天真了。
5) 自從 (commune) 的黨支部書記被 (exposed) 以後，_______________.

6) 既然…，(就)… 現在既然把他帶回來了，…也好，…也好，我都不怕。 (p. 84)

The adverb 既然, meaning "given the fact that..., since...," marks the first clause in a two- or multiple-clause sentence in which the 既然 clause states the given situation and the following clause(s) gives the thrust of the sentence. The main clause can be either a statement or a question. When it is a statement, it often contains the adverb 就 to reinforce the linkage between the two clauses. Examples:

改写 - Reword the first three completed sentences from the preceding exercise, using pattern 4.

5) 自从 自从冬冬回来以后，这两天外面有些流言蜚语吧？ (p. 83)

自从, usually translated as "ever since..., from the time..., after...," is used to introduce a time phrase that precedes the main clause of a sentence, and is usually (but not necessarily) coupled with 以来 or 以后 at the end of the time phrase. 以来 at the end of the time phrase refers to the period from that past event up to and including the present. 以后 at the end of the time phrase is a little more ambiguous. It refers to a period that began from that past event, but may or may not have ended before the present. E.g.:

自从她妈去世以来，她就不再有说有笑了。
Ever since her mother died, she has never been gregarious and jolly anymore.
(This state persists through the present.)

自从她妈去世以后，她就不再有说有笑了。
After her mother died, she did not chatter happily anymore.
(It's unclear whether this state persisted to the present.)

自从她妈去世以后，她头五年都没再有说有笑了。
After her mother died, she did not chatter happily for the first five years.
(This state no longer holds.)

例句： 1) 自从她母亲自杀以后，他父亲就疯了。
2) 自从她丈夫死了以来，她一直没考虑过重新找对象。

造句：

填充： 1) 自从我们上次 (quarreled) 以来，______________.
2) 自从 (Public Security Bureau) (approved) 他摆摊以后，______________.
3) 自从 ______________, 他对社会主义就失去了信心。
4) 自从 ______________, 她就不象从前那么天真了。
5) 自从 (commune) 的党支部书记被 (exposed) 以后，______________.

6) 既然…，(就)… 现在既然把他带回来了，…也好，…也好，我都不怕。 (p. 85)

The adverb 既然, meaning "given the fact that..., since...," marks the first clause in a two- or multiple-clause sentence in which the 既然 clause states the given situation and the following clause(s) gives the thrust of the sentence. The main clause can be either a statement or a question. When it is a statement, it often contains the adverb 就 to reinforce the linkage between the two clauses. Examples:

冬冬既然是我的孩子，他就有權利和我在一起。

Given the fact that Dongdong is my child, he has the right to be with me.

志華既然愛秦楠，他怎麼受得了別人的流言蜚語呢？

Since Zhihua loves Qin Nan, how can he endure other people's malicious gossip?

例句： 1) 她既然怕別人的流言，那何必把冬冬帶來上海呢？
2) 你既然吃飽了飯沒事幹就應該多幫幫你老伴的忙。

造句：

填充： 1) 他 (committed a crime), 可是現在他 (regret) 了，你就應該 (forgive) 他。
2) 你愛秦楠，要和她 (get married), 那就也應該 (love and protect) 冬冬。
3) 你們不能 (get along together)，那就應該 (consider getting a divorce)，(why must you) 痛苦 (your) (whole life)？
4) 他不 (accept the suggestion I made), 那我就不想再跟他合作了。

改寫 - Rewrite the completed sentences from the preceding exercise, using pattern 6.

7) …也好，…也好，…都… [colloquial] 流言蜚語也好，造謠中傷也好，我都不怕。(p. 84)

In this construction, 也好 does not mean literally "also good," but rather something like "okay, alright," conveying reluctant acceptance of an undesirable situation. The 都 in the last phrase reinforces the idea that the resolve or situation holds under all the above circumstances.

例句： 颳風也好，打雷也好，我今天晚上一定要趕到那兒去。
她哭也好，罵也好，我已經下了決心跟她一刀兩斷了。

造句：

填充： 1) 不管是不是 (vacation), 也不管 (retired) 沒有，他每天照樣 (labor).
2) 不管他母親怎麼 (advise) 他，怎麼 (warn) 他，他還是要和秦楠結婚。
3) 雖然他吃了 (special efficacy medicine), 看了最 (capable) 的醫生，可是他的病還是治不好。
4) 雖然加了 (wages), (reform) 了 (system), 這個工廠還是沒有什麼進步。

改寫 - Rewrite the completed sentences from the preceding exercise, using pattern 7.

8) …才 是…/VP/SV [colloquial] 你們家的孩子才是真正的野種哪！ (p. 86)

冬冬既然是我的孩子，他就有权利和我在一起。
Given the fact that Dongdong is my child, he has the right to be with me.
志华既然爱秦楠，他怎么受得了别人的流言蜚语呢？
Since Zhihua loves Qin Nan, how can he endure other people's malicious gossip?

例句： 1) 她既然怕别人的流言，那何必把冬冬带来上海呢？
2) 你既然吃饱了饭没事干就应该多帮帮你老伴的忙。

造句：

填充： 1) 他 (committed a crime), 可是现在他 (regret) 了，你就应该 (forgive) 他。
2) 你爱秦楠，要和她 (get married), 那就也应该 (love and protect) 冬冬。
3) 你们不能 (get along together)，那就应该 (consider getting a divorce)，(why must you) 痛苦 (your) (whole life)？
4) 他不 (accept the suggestion I made), 那我就不想再跟他合作了。

改写 - Rewrite the completed sentences from the preceding exercise, using pattern 6.

7) …也好，…也好，…都… [colloquial] 流言蜚语也好，造谣中伤也好，我都不怕。(p. 85)
In this construction, 也好 does not mean literally "also good," but rather something like "okay, alright," conveying reluctant acceptance of an undesirable situation. The 都 in the last phrase reinforces the idea that the resolve or situation holds under all the above circumstances.

例句： 刮风也好，打雷也好，我今天晚上一定要赶到那儿去。
她哭也好，骂也好，我已经下了决心跟她一刀两断了。

造句：

填充： 1) 不管是不是 (vacation), 也不管 (retired) 沒有，他每天照样 (labor).
2) 不管他母亲怎么 (advise) 他，怎么 (warn) 他，他还是要和秦楠结婚。
3) 虽然他吃了 (special efficacy medicine), 看了最 (capable) 的医生，可是他的病还是治不好。
4) 虽然加了 (wages), (reform) 了 (system), 这个工厂还是沒有什么进步。

改写 - Rewrite the completed sentences from the preceding exercise, using pattern 7.

8) …才 是…/VP/SV [colloquial] 你们家的孩子才是真正的野种哪！(p. 87)

The usage of 才 in this pattern differs from its usual adverbial meaning of "only then (temporal or conditional)." In this usage, the speaker is lending emphasis to the statement, and at the same time contradicting a previous statement or assumption of another person. In this context, Dongdong has just called Nannan a bastard. In this sentence, Granny You is calling Dongdong a bastard, and at the same time contradicting what Dongdong said. This meaning of 才 can also be used with a stative verb or a verb phrase other than 是; and whichever kind of verb is used, it may be in the positive or negative. E.g.:

我沒錢，他才有錢呢。
我早就明白了，你才不明白呢！
高母才不會讓志華和秦楠結婚呢。
Mrs. Gao would certainly not agree to let Zhihua marry Qin Nan.
(implying: contrary to Zhihua's assumption or hope.)

This usage of 才 defies direct translation, and is best conveyed by the use of stress and emphatic words such as "certainly" (as in the above example).

例句： 1) 我才不相信你們說的流言呢！
2) 高母偏要小高和秦楠一刀兩斷，他才不肯呢！

造句：

填充： 1) 你說我 (muddle-headed), 你自己是真的 (muddle-headed) 呢！
2) 別以爲美國的 (chocolates) 貴就好吃，其實並不好吃呢！
3) 人家說她的 (husband) 很 (fierce), 其實她是真正的 (fierce) 呢！
4) 從前在我 (imagination) 中，他是一個理想的 (potential spouse). 後來我發現我從小的 (neighbor) 朋友是真正的理想的 (potential spouse).

改寫 - Rewrite the completed sentences from the preceding exercise, using pattern 8.

9) 何必…(呢)? 大人何必跟着慪氣呢？ (p. 86)

"Why must...?" This is a rhetorical question implying that there is no need to do that certain thing. The 呢 at the end is optional, but the question intonation is always retained.

例句： 不理他就是了，何必跟他吵架呢？
你要是剛才叫我一聲兒我就會來幫你了，你何必一個人搬那麼重的縫紉機？

造句：

The usage of 才 in this pattern differs from its usual adverbial meaning of "only then (temporal or conditional)." In this usage, the speaker is lending emphasis to the statement, and at the same time contradicting a previous statement or assumption of another person. In this context, Dongdong has just called Nannan a bastard. In this sentence, Granny You is calling Dongdong a bastard, and at the same time contradicting what Dongdong said. This meaning of 才 can also be used with a stative verb or a verb phrase other than 是; and whichever kind of verb is used, it may be in the positive or negative. E.g.:

我沒钱，他才有钱呢。
我早就明白了，你才不明白呢！
高母才不会让志华和秦楠结婚呢。
Mrs. Gao would certainly not agree to let Zhihua marry Qin Nan.
(implying: contrary to Zhihua's assumption or hope.)

This usage of 才 defies direct translation, and is best conveyed by the use of stress and emphatic words such as "certainly" (as in the above example).

例句： 1) 我才不相信你们说的流言呢！
2) 高母偏要小高和秦楠一刀两断，他才不肯呢！

造句：

填充： 1) 你说我 (muddle-headed), 你自己是真的 (muddle-headed) 呢！
2) 别以为美国的 (chocolates) 贵就好吃，其实并不好吃呢！
3) 人家说她的 (husband) 很 (fierce), 其实她是真正的 (fierce) 呢！
4) 从前在我 (imagination) 中，他是一个理想的 (potential spouse). 后来我发现我从小的 (neighbor) 朋友是真正的理想的 (potential spouse).

改写 - Rewrite the completed sentences from the preceding exercise, using pattern 8.

9) 何必…(呢)? 大人何必跟着怄气呢？ (p. 87)

"Why must...?" This is a rhetorical question implying that there is no need to do that certain thing. The 呢 at the end is optional, but the question intonation is always retained.

例句： 不理他就是了，何必跟他吵架呢？
你要是刚才叫我一声儿我就会来帮你了，你何必一个人搬那么重的缝纫机？

造句：

填充： 1) 你爲什麼一定要用那麼多錢買一輛 (name brand bike) 呢？
2) 冬冬的病不 (severe), 吃吃藥就好了，不必把他送去 (hospital).
3) 這種 (matches) (everywhere) 都有，你爲什麼一定要從廣西帶來呢？
4) 你不必一天到晚那麼 (melancholy). 你雖然這次做錯了，你的朋友 (for sure) 會 (forgive) 你的。

改寫 - Rewrite the completed sentences from the preceding exercise, using pattern 9.

INCLUSIVE 翻譯 EXERCISE FOR SEGMENT VII:

1) Ever since she brought Dongdong to Shanghai, she has encountered many unexpected difficulties.
2) She may be self-employed, and she may be never-married yet has a child, I don't care. I still love her.
3) This child is very ill-behaved. He obstinately wants to eat chocolates before dinner.
4) Why must you view this matter so rigidly? You should give it a little more consideration (consider it a little more).
5) Since you are so muddle-headed, I have no choice but to remind you that you must not fall in love with a woman who already has a husband.
6) Just because you heard the neighbors' malicious gossip, you no longer like Qin Nan. It's you who's muddle-headed.
7) Qin Nan has never been married but has a five-year-old child. This is a very big test of ("with regards to") Zhihua's love.
8) If you love and care about Qin Nan, then you must not (under any circumstances) listen to the words of those idlers (who have nothing to do after their bellies are filled).

填充： 1) 你为什么一定要用那么多钱买一辆 (name brand bike) 呢？
2) 冬冬的病不 (severe), 吃吃药就好了，不必把他送去 (hospital).
3) 这种 (matches) (everywhere) 都有，你为什么一定要从广西带来呢？
4) 你不必一天到晚那么 (melancholy). 你虽然这次做错了，你的朋友 (for sure) 会 (forgive) 你的。

改写 - Rewrite the completed sentences from the preceding exercise, using pattern 9.

INCLUSIVE 翻译 EXERCISE FOR SEGMENT VII: See facing page.

SEGMENT VIII

1) 又沒/不… [colloquial] 我又沒跟他玩。(p. 88)

Here, 又 is used with a negative for emphasis, and does not mean literally "again." In translation, the sense can best be conveyed by putting extra stress on the key word, e.g.: 我又沒跟他玩 "I didn't play with him."

例句： 1) 我又沒跟他吵架。
2) 她又沒作什麼虧心的事，只是太天真了。你應該原諒她。

填充： 1) 小高實在沒 (bully) 你，你怎麼 ________?
2) 我實在沒 (commit a crime), (Public Security Bureau) 來找我, ________?
3) 其實爸爸不是不 (understand) 你，你何必 (hide the truth from him) 呢？
4) (Street Party committee) 只是 (advise) 你，實在不是 (criticize) 你，你 (why must) 那麼難過？

改寫 - Rewrite the completed sentences from the preceding exercise, using pattern 1.

2) 上…的當 你是不是上了男人的當了？(p. 90)

上當 is a V-O compound meaning "to be taken advantage of." When the person taking the advantage is added to this V-O compound, it becomes the modifier of the O, e.g. 別上他們的當 "Don't be taken in by them." This pattern applies to other V-O compounds as well, e.g. 生氣: 生誰的氣；隨便: 隨他的便.

例句： 1) 這位老太婆很糊塗，所以常上他孫子的當。
2) 這並不是真的名牌車，你別上他的當。

造句：

填充： 1) 他 (young) 的時候很 (naive), 常被別人騙。
2) (Party branch secretary) 老說要 (reform), 已經說了十幾年了，都沒什麼結果。我們不要再被他騙了。
3) 那家 (self-employed entrepreneur) 商店 (treats people kindly), 又 (honest), 你在他們那兒買 (bicycle), 一定不會被騙。
4) 她在鄉下 (joined a rural production team) 的時候被一個男人騙過，(no wonder) 以後她都不信任男人了。

SEGMENT VIII

1) 又 沒/不… [colloquial] 我又沒跟他玩。(p. 89)

Here, 又 is used with a negative for emphasis, and does not mean literally "again." In translation, the sense can best be conveyed by putting extra stress on the key word, e.g.: 我又沒跟他玩 "I didn't play with him."

例句： 1) 我又沒跟他吵架。
2) 她又沒作什么亏心的事，只是太天真了。你应该原谅她。

填充： 1) 小高实在沒 (bully) 你，你怎么 ____________?
2) 我实在沒 (commit a crime), (Public Security Bureau) 来找我, ______________?
3) 其实爸爸不是不 (understand) 你，你何必 (hide the truth from him) 呢？
4) (Street Party committee) 只是 (advise) 你，实在不是 (criticize) 你，你 (why must) 那么难过？

改写 - Rewrite the completed sentences from the preceding exercise, using pattern 1.

2) 上…的当 你是不是上了男人的当了？ (p. 91)

上当 is a V-O compound meaning "to be taken advantage of." When the person taking the advantage is added to this V-O compound, it becomes the modifier of the O, e.g. 别上他们的当 "Don't be taken in by them." This pattern applies to other V-O compounds as well, e.g. 生气: 生谁的气；随便: 随他的便.

例句： 1) 这位老太婆很糊涂，所以常上他孙子的当。
2) 这并不是真的名牌车，你别上他的当。

造句：

填充： 1) 他 (young) 的时候很 (naive), 常被别人骗。
2) (Party branch secretary) 老说要 (reform), 已经说了十几年了，都沒什么结果。我们不要再被他骗了。
3) 那家 (self-employed entrepreneur) 商店 (treats people kindly), 又 (honest), 你在他们那儿买 (bicycle), 一定不会被骗。
4) 她在乡下 (joined a rural production team) 的时候被一个男人骗过，(no wonder) 以后她都不信任男人了。

5) 我 (advised) 她別和那個男的交朋友，她 (obstinately) 要和他交朋友，結果被他騙了，(serve her right)!

改寫 - Rewrite the completed sentences from the preceding exercise, using pattern 2.

3) 一時 (也)… [somewhat formal] 那都是過去的事了，一時也說不清楚。(p. 90)

This adverbial phrase means "in an instant, on the spot." The 也 emphasizes the "on the spot" nature of the situation; its sense can be conveyed only through intonation in English.

例句：
1) 她發現自己有了孩子，一時不知道怎麼辦，就隨隨便便地結婚了。
2) 這個難題，你叫我一時怎麼去解決？

填充：
1) 小高知道了冬冬的事，不能馬上 (understand and forgive)，也 (difficult to blame) 他，可是 (by and by/after a while) 他會 (forgive) 你的。
2) 他自己心裡很亂，一下子沒 (consider) 到要 (love and protect) 冬冬，你應該 (forgive) 他，他 (after all) 是愛你的。
3) 秦楠不舒服，(for the moment) (can't take off/walk away)，你去 (hospital) (take care of) 冬冬吧。
4) 我一時不 (sensible)，(committed a crime)，你能 (forgive) 我，使我非常 (moved). 今後我們的 (friendship) 更 (strong/firm)了。

改寫 - Rewrite the first two completed sentences from the preceding exercise, using pattern 3.

4) 再說… 再說，外面七嘴八舌的。(p. 90)

再說 "furthermore, ..." introduces further argument to support the speaker's view.

例句：
1) 像小高這麼老實的人實在難找。再說，你年紀也不小了，結婚的事不能再拖了。
2) 你不該打冬冬，他畢竟是個聽話的孩子。再說，這次和男男吵架也不是他的錯。

造句：

填充：
1) 孩子這麼大了，已經 (sensible) 了，你可以放心讓他一個人 (go out of town)了。而且到了那邊，他 (uncle) 會 (take care of) 他的。
2) 你別把這事 (hold/suppress in your heart) 了， (street Party committee) 已經 (criticized) 尤奶奶了。而且別的 (neighbors) 也都覺得尤奶奶太沒道理了。
3) 你不必因爲她是個 (handicapped person) 而爲她難過。(Public Security Bureau) (approved) 了她刻圖章，使她生活有 (security). 而且有很多朋友和鄰居都很 (concerned for) 她。

5) 我 (advised) 她别和那個男的交朋友，她 (obstinately) 要和他交朋友，结果被他骗了, (serve her right)!

改写 - Rewrite the completed sentences from the preceding exercise, using pattern 2.

3) 一时 (也)⋯ [somewhat formal] 那都是过去的事了，一时也说不清楚。 (p. 91)

This adverbial phrase means "in an instant, on the spot." The 也 emphasizes the "on the spot" nature of the situation; its sense can be conveyed only through intonation in English.

例句： 1) 她发现自己有了孩子，一时不知道怎么办，就随随便便地结婚了。
2) 这个难题，你叫我一时怎么去解决？

填充： 1) 小高知道了冬冬的事，不能马上 (understand and forgive)，也 (difficult to blame) 他，可是 (by and by/after a while) 他会 (forgive) 你的。
2) 他自己心里很乱，一下子沒 (consider) 到要 (love and protect) 冬冬，你应该 (forgive) 他，他 (after all) 是爱你的。
3) 秦楠不舒服, (for the moment) (can't take off/walk away), 你去 (hospital) (take care of) 冬冬吧。
4) 我一時不 (sensible), (committed a crime), 你能 (forgive) 我，使我非常 (moved). 今后我们的 (friendship) 更 (strong/firm)了。

改写 - Rewrite the first two completed sentences from the preceding exercise, using pattern 3.

4) 再说⋯ 再说，外面七嘴八舌的。 (p. 91)

再说 "furthermore, ..." introduces further argument to support the speaker's view.

例句： 1) 象小高这么老实的人实在难找。再说，你年纪也不小了，结婚的事不能再拖了。
2) 你不该打冬冬，他毕竟是个听话的孩子。再说，这次和男男吵架也不是他的错。

造句：

填充： 1) 孩子这么大了，已经 (sensible) 了，你可以放心让他一个人 (go out of town)了。而且到了那边，他 (uncle) 会 (take care of) 他的。
2) 你别把这事 (hold/suppress in your heart) 了， (street Party committee) 已经 (criticized) 尤奶奶了。而且别的 (neighbors) 也都觉得尤奶奶太沒道理了。
3) 你不必因为她是个 (handicapped person) 而为她难过。(Public Security Bureau) (approved) 了她刻图章，使她生活有 (security). 而且有很多朋友和邻居都很 (concerned for) 她。

4) 高母很怕別人説他們家的 (malicious gossip), 而且她只有志華這個 (precious son), (no wonder) 她不同意小高和秦楠結婚。

改寫 - Rewrite the completed sentences from the preceding exercise, using pattern 4.

5) 也就…了 [colloquial] 他們說膩了，也就不説了。(p. 90)

也就…了 usually appears in the second clause of a two-clause sentence, in which the event or situation stated in the first clause leads to a changed event or situation in the second clause. The adverb 也 may be added for emphasis, as in the above example; its sense can best be conveyed through intonation in English.

例句： 1) 日子長了，他也就會慢慢地理解你了。
2) 你別看她那麼憂鬱，你開導開導她，她也就會樂觀點兒了。

填充： 1) 我看如果你多給她些 (encouragement) 她一定會有 (courage) 把冬冬帶回上海的。
2) 你好好兒地跟他説，他一定會 (accept) 你的 (advice).
3) 如果尤奶奶能好好兒地管教她的 (grandson), 他就一定不會 (bully) 別的孩子了。
4) 等他長大了，不那麼 (naive) 了，就一定不會那樣常常 (be taken advantage of) 了。

改寫 - Rewrite the completed sentences from the preceding exercise, using pattern 5.

6) A 叫 B VP 她叫我不要告訴他。(p. 96)

In this pattern, A and B both refer to persons. If what follows "A 叫 B" is a verb phrase, as in the above example, the expression means "A tells B to (do something)." If what follows "A 叫 B" is a noun, then the expression means "A calls B (by the name or title of)..."

例句： 1) 小高叫冬冬走開是因爲他怕冬冬動他的小零件。
2) 他今天已經夠忙的了，你別再叫他幫你搬東西了。

造句：

填充： 1) 我已經 (tired to death), 你還 (ask me) 去送貨，真 (outrageous)!
2) 高母 (asked her son to resolve to) 跟秦楠 (make a clean break), 小高怎麼會願意呢？
3) 小高這幾天 ("busy to death"), 所以 (he asked me) 替他把這件做好的 (shirt) (deliver) 來給你。
4) 我 (clearly) 叫你別 (bully) 冬冬，怎麼我一 (walked away) 你就又 (bully) 他了？！

4) 高母很怕别人说他们家的 (malicious gossip), 而且她只有志华这个 (precious son), (no wonder) 她不同意小高和秦楠结婚。

改写 - Rewrite the completed sentences from the preceding exercise, using pattern 4.

5) 也就…了 [colloquial] 他们说腻了，也就不说了。 (p. 91)

也就…了 usually appears in the second clause of a two-clause sentence, in which the event or situation stated in the first clause leads to a changed event or situation in the second clause. The adverb 也 may be added for emphasis, as in the above example; its sense can best be conveyed through intonation in English.

例句： 1) 日子长了，他也就会慢慢地理解你了。
2) 你别看她那么忧郁，你开导开导她，她也就会乐观点儿了。

填充： 1) 我看如果你多给她些 (encouragement) 她一定会有 (courage) 把冬冬带回上海的。
2) 你好好儿地跟他说，他一定会 (accept) 你的 (advice).
3) 如果尤奶奶能好好儿地管教她的 (grandson), 他就一定不会 (bully) 别的孩子了。
4) 等他长大了，不那么 (naive) 了，就一定不会那样常常 (be taken advantage of) 了。

改写 - Rewrite the completed sentences from the preceding exercise, using pattern 5.

6) A 叫 B VP 她叫我不要告诉他。 (p. 97)

In this pattern, A and B both refer to persons. If what follows "A 叫 B" is a verb phrase, as in the above example, the expression means "A tells B to (do something)." If what follows "A 叫 B" is a noun, then the expression means "A calls B (by the name or title of)..."

例句： 1) 小高叫冬冬走开是因为他怕冬冬动他的小零件。
2) 他今天已经够忙的了，你别再叫他帮你搬东西了。

造句：

填充： 1) 我已经 (tired to death), 你还 (ask me) 去送货，真 (outrageous)!
2) 高母 (asked her son to resolve to) 跟秦楠 (make a clean break), 小高怎么会愿意呢？
3) 小高这几天 ("busy to death"), 所以 (he asked me) 替他把这件做好的 (shirt) (deliver) 来给你。
4) 我 (clearly) 叫你别 (bully) 冬冬，怎么我一 (walked away) 你就又 (bully) 他了？！

7) 讓-A VP 本來蕭健來信是讓我去… (p. 98)

The primary meaning of 讓 is "to permit." But in colloquial Chinese, it often means "to ask/make (someone to do something)." Whether 讓 means "to permit" or "to ask/make" can only be determined from context.

例句： 1) 他讓我放假的時候去他那兒休息幾天。
2) 他讓我把這些腳踏車當作名牌車賣，我才不幹呢！

造句：

填充： 1) 醫生說我 (husband) 的病 (is almost well). 他 (asked me) 明天 (in the early morning) 到 (commune hospital) 去接他回家。
2) 秦楠的 (uncle) (would not have) 秦楠把冬冬帶去上海，可是秦楠已經 (made up her mind).
3) 文化大革命的時候，紅衛兵 (made) 秦楠的媽 (expose) 她的 (old "companion").
4) 高母怎麼能 (have the heart to) (while/taking advantage of an opportune moment) 小高不在家的時候 (make) 秦楠 (move her sewing stall away) 呢？這不是一件 (unconscionable) 的事嗎？

8) SV 得要命 [colloquial] 我說蕭健的事真把我氣得要命。 (p. 98)

"SV 得要命," literally "SV to the point of demanding one's life," is synonymous with "SV 死了" (cf. Grammatical Note VII.1.). Both convey an extreme degree, and are more colloquial than "SV 極了."

例句： 1) 今年夏天全世界到處都熱得要命。
2) 你別再批評他了，他已經難過得要命了。

造句：

填充： 1) 這個人 (is terribly honest), 他 (has never) 做過一件 (unconscionable) 的事。
2) 我剛下鄉的時候覺得農村的 (labor) (was terribly strenuous), 後來 (by and by) 也就習慣了。
3) 冬冬這孩子 (is terribly well-behaved). 高母給他 (chocolates), 他都帶回家給 (grandpa) 吃。
4) 我的 (aunt) 又 (kind-hearted) 又 (optimistic), 可是她 (is terribly muddle-headed), 常常 (is taken advantage of by others).

7) 让-A VP 本来肖健来信是让我去… (p. 99)

The primary meaning of 让 is "to permit." But in colloquial Chinese, it often means "to ask/make (someone to do something)." Whether 让 means "to permit" or "to ask/make" can only be determined from context.

例句： 1) 他让我放假的时候去他那儿休息几天。
2) 他让我把这些脚踏车当作名牌车卖，我才不干呢！

造句：

填充： 1) 医生说我 (husband) 的病 (is almost well). 他 (asked me) 明天 (in the early morning) 到 (commune hospital) 去接他回家。
2) 秦楠的 (uncle) (would not have) 秦楠把冬冬带去上海，可是秦楠已经 (made up her mind).
3) 文化大革命的时候，红卫兵 (made) 秦楠的妈 (expose) 她的 (old "companion").
4) 高母怎么能 (have the heart to) (while/taking advantage of an opportune moment) 小高不在家的时候 (make) 秦楠 (move her sewing stall away) 呢？这不是一件 (unconscionable) 的事吗？

8) SV 得要命 [colloquial] 我说肖健的事真把我气得要命。 (p. 99)

"SV 得要命," literally "SV to the point of demanding one's life," is synonymous with "SV 死了" (cf. Grammatical Note VII.1.). Both convey an extreme degree, and are more colloquial than "SV 极了."

例句： 1) 今年夏天全世界到处都热得要命。
2) 你别再批评他了，他已经难过得要命了。

造句：

填充： 1) 这个人 (is terribly honest), 他 (has never) 做过一件 (unconscionable) 的事。
2) 我刚下乡的时候觉得农村的 (labor) (was terribly strenuous), 后来 (by and by) 也就习惯了。
3) 冬冬这孩子 (is terribly well-behaved). 高母给他 (chocolates), 他都带回家给 (grandpa) 吃。
4) 我的 (aunt) 又 (kind-hearted) 又 (optimistic), 可是她 (is terribly muddle-headed), 常常 (is taken advantage of by others).

9) 根本 (就) 我根本不知道這件事。 (p. 98)

根本 "fundamentally" is an adverb which adds emphasis to an assertion. It is commonly, but not necessarily, used in combination with 不 or 沒. 根本 most commonly occurs in sentences with negative connotations. 就 "precisely, indeed" may also be added for extra emphasis.

例句： 1) 他們兩個人根本就是很矛盾，怎麼能在一起生活呢？
2) 黨支部書記老說這說那，其實根本什麼也沒改革。

造句：

填充： 1) 別 (hide the truth from) 我了，我知道你本來就沒 (consider) 和我結婚。
2) 別以爲在一個 (socialist) 國家裡人民都有 (guarantee/security), 其實不是那麼回事。
3) 你 (deceived) 我說你今天 (at the crack of dawn) 就出去 (labor) 了，我知道你其實就是在家 (sleeping in).
4) 上次他說他已經 (reformed), 其實他一點兒也沒 (reform). 你看，他不是上個星期又 (committed a crime)?

改寫 - Rewrite the completed sentences from the preceding exercise, using pattern 9.

10) 却 [somewhat formal] 可你却告訴她是我在… (p. 100)

却 is an adverb indicating that an action or situation is contrary to what is expected or reasonable. It is usually translatable as "but." In fact, to reinforce the idea of "but," 可 or 可是 may be added before the subject. As an adverb (and not a movable adverb), 却 is always positioned within the verb phrase. It is similar in meaning to 倒, but is a bit more formal, and it cannot be used in conjunction with 也 as 倒 can. (Cf. Grammatical Note I.12.)

例句： 1) 你自己忘了，却怪別人沒提醒你。
2) 男男欺負了冬冬，却說是冬冬先打他的。

造句：

填充： 1) 她很會 (take care of) 別人，可是不怎麼會 (love and protect) 自己。
2) 你只會 (criticize) 別人，而不會看看自己多麼 (ugly).
3) 她自己是個 (self-employed entrepreneur), 可是不願意 (to be married to) 一個 (self-employed entrepreneur).

9) 根本 (就) 我根本不知道这件事。 (p. 99)

根本 "fundamentally" is an adverb which adds emphasis to an assertion. It is commonly, but not necessarily, used in combination with 不 or 沒. 根本 most commonly occurs in sentences with negative connotations. 就 "precisely, indeed" may also be added for extra emphasis.

例句： 1) 他们两个人根本就是很矛盾，怎么能在一起生活呢？
2) 党支部书记老说这说那，其实根本什么也沒改革。

造句：

填充： 1) 别 (hide the truth from) 我了，我知道你本来就沒 (consider) 和我结婚。
2) 别以为在一个 (socialist) 国家里人民都有 (guarantee/security), 其实不是那么回事。
3) 你 (deceived) 我说你今天 (at the crack of dawn) 就出去 (labor) 了，我知道你其实就是在家 (sleeping in).
4) 上次他说他已经 (reformed), 其实他一点儿也沒 (reform). 你看，他不是上个星期又 (committed a crime)?

改写 - Rewrite the completed sentences from the preceding exercise, using pattern 9.

10) 却 [somewhat formal] 可你却告诉她是我在… (p. 101)

却 is an adverb indicating that an action or situation is contrary to what is expected or reasonable. It is usually translatable as "but." In fact, to reinforce the idea of "but," 可 or 可是 may be added before the subject. As an adverb (and not a movable adverb), 却 is always positioned within the verb phrase. It is similar in meaning to 倒, but is a bit more formal, and it cannot be used in conjunction with 也 as 倒 can. (Cf. Grammatical Note I.12.)

例句： 1) 你自己忘了，却怪别人沒提醒你。
2) 男男欺负了冬冬，却说是冬冬先打他的。

造句：

填充： 1) 她很会 (take care of) 别人，可是不怎么会 (love and protect) 自己。
2) 你只会 (criticize) 别人，而不会看看自己多么 (ugly).
3) 她自己是个 (self-employed entrepreneur), 可是不愿意 (to be married to) 一个 (self-employed entrepreneur).

4) 他的朋友作了一件對他 (unconscionable) 的事，可是他對這朋友的 (friendship) 更 (firm) 了。

改寫 - Rewrite the completed sentences from the preceding exercise, using pattern 10.

INCLUSIVE 翻譯 EXERCISE FOR SEGMENT VIII:

1) Xiao Yun has had many difficulties in her life, and yet she is very optimistic.
2) Zhihua did not finish reading Xiao Jian's letter at all, that's why he didn't know about Xiao Yun.
3) The street Party committee has already criticized her (and) told her not to call Dongdong a bastard anymore.
4) Dongdong didn't want to play with Nannan. Clearly it was Nannan who first bullied him.
5) That day, you gave me so much encouragement, I was very moved, but I didn't know how to thank you on the spot.
6) Even the world's most delicious food should not be eaten every day. If one eats too much of it, one will also grow tired of (eating) it.
7) That young man is very kind-hearted and honest, but he doesn't know how to take care of himself, so he is often duped by others.
8) Mrs. Gao should understand Zhihua (and) let him marry Qin Nan. What's more, Zhihua has already made up his mind, so even if Mrs. Gao objects, it's useless.
9) As soon as she heard that Dongdong had taken ill, she was beside herself with anxiety (so anxious that she could die). So she immediately took a train to Suzhou.

4) 他的朋友作了一件对他 (unconscionable) 的事，可是他对这朋友的 (friendship) 更 (firm) 了。

改写 - Rewrite the completed sentences from the preceding exercise, using pattern 10.

INCLUSIVE 翻译 EXERCISE FOR SEGMENT VIII: See facing page.

SEGMENT IX

1) 絶沒有… 我絶沒有這個意思。(p. 102)

絶 "absolutely" is an adverb that adds stress to what follows. The single syllable 絶 can only be used with a negative (不, 沒有, 沒, 無), while its bisyllabic synonym 絶對 can occur with either a positive or a negative verb. Translating 絶 or 絶對 literally as "absolutely" is sometimes awkward, and the sense is sometimes better conveyed in English by proper use of stress and intonation.

例句： 1) 你絶對不能再帶孩子去坐飛船了，太危險了！
2) 你對我這麼好，我絶對忘不了你的友情。

造句：

填充： 1) (Individual enterprise) 修 (bicycle) 的 (skill) 一定會比 (state-operated unit) 的高，我勸你讓他們修。
2) 我知道你 (object to) 志華和秦楠 (get married/"form a family"), 可是你一定 (unable to best him in an argument). 我看你算了吧！
3) 雖然我們不能説下鄉這個 (policy) 一定是錯的，可是實在給不少 (young people) 帶來了 (bitterness).
4) 如果你肯 (resolve to) (thoroughly) (reform), 你的妹妹蕭雲一定會 (forgive) 你的。

改寫 - Rewrite the completed sentences from the preceding exercise, using pattern 1.

2) Subj. 就是 VP [colloquial] 我就是不去！ (p. 106)

就是 preceding a VP indicates that the subject is obstinately set on doing something or being a certain way, and there are no two ways about it.

例句： 1) 國營商店就是亂，怎麼也改革不了。
2) 我就是要玩你的球，你不給我我就打你了。

造句：

填充： 1) 這個人實在 (naive), 不管他 (to be taken advantage of) 幾次 (__) 還是一樣。
2) 我 (old "companion") 總是那麼 (disgusting), 我常常 (advise) 他，(criticize) 他，他還是老樣子。
3) 他這個人老是喜歡跟人 (quarrel), 其實他對你並沒什麼壞意，你可別把這件事 (beset your heart).

SEGMENT IX

1) 绝沒有… 我绝沒有这个意思。(p. 103)

绝 "absolutely" is an adverb that adds stress to what follows. The single syllable 绝 can only be used with a negative (不, 沒有, 沒, 无), while its bisyllabic synonym 绝对 can occur with either a positive or a negative verb. Translating 绝 or 绝对 literally as "absolutely" is sometimes awkward, and the sense is sometimes better conveyed in English by proper use of stress and intonation.

例句： 1) 你绝对不能再带孩子去坐飞船了，太危险了！
2) 你对我这么好，我绝对忘不了你的友情。

造句：

填充： 1) (Individual enterprise) 修 (bicycle) 的 (skill) 一定会比 (state-operated unit) 的高，我劝你让他们修。
2) 我知道你 (object to) 志华和秦楠 (get married/"form a family"), 可是你一定 (unable to best him in an argument). 我看你算了吧！
3) 虽然我们不能说下乡这个 (policy) 一定是错的，可是实在给不少 (young people) 带来了 (bitterness).
4) 如果你肯 (resolve to) (thoroughly) (reform), 你的妹妹肖云一定会 (forgive) 你的。

改写 - Rewrite the completed sentences from the preceding exercise, using pattern 1.

2) Subj. 就是 VP [colloquial] 我就是不去！(p. 107)

就是 preceding a VP indicates that the subject is obstinately set on doing something or being a certain way, and there are no two ways about it.

例句： 1) 国营商店就是乱，怎么也改革不了。
2) 我就是要玩你的球，你不给我我就打你了。

造句：

填充： 1) 这个人实在 (naive), 不管他 (to be taken advantage of) 几次 (__) 还是一样。
2) 我 (old "companion") 总是那么 (disgusting), 我常常 (advise) 他，(criticize) 他，他还是老样子。
3) 他这个人老是喜欢跟人 (quarrel), 其实他对你并沒什么坏意，你可别把这件事 (beset your heart).

4) 我怎麼也不同意你和秦楠 ("form a family"), 你 (while it's still early) (give up hope) 吧!

改寫 - Rewrite the completed sentences from the preceding exercise, using pattern 2.

3) 萬一… 那萬一要是變… (p. 106)

This is an adverb that literally means "one chance out of ten thousand." It is used in an "if" clause that precedes the main clause of a sentence. In the "if" clause, 萬一 means "in case," indicating that the chance of that "if" circumstance occurring is very small. 萬一 can be used only in a clause that refers to an unfortunate or undesirable circumstance or event. 萬一 can usually be translated as "if by any chance."

例句： 1) 這件毛衣我這星期還不需要，所以你萬一織不完也不要緊。
2) 我只有這一個親人，萬一他死了，誰來關心我呢？

造句：

填充： 1) 你寫這樣的文章太不 (safe/secure) 了，如果 (policy) 變，那你就肯定完了。
2) 我能 (guarantee) 明天做好，如果明天作不好，後天 (absolutely) 能做好。
3) 這個 (season) 天氣很容易變，你最好多帶件大衣，如果忽然 (have a wind storm), 你就不會着涼了。
4) 這個孩子那麼喜歡 (move), 你千萬別讓他坐 (spaceship). 如果他摔下來，肯定會 (smashed to bits).

改寫 - Rewrite the completed sentences from the preceding exercise, using pattern 3.

4) Subj. V 得/不 過 A [somewhat uncommon] 我說不過你。 (p. 106)

V-得過 is an RV, meaning "able to pass or get by at V-ing." When the RV is followed by a person-object (A), it can also mean "able to best so-and-so at V-ing." V-不過 literally means "unable to pass/surpass at V-ing." When followed by a person-object, the expression indicates that the subject is not as good at doing V as A is. A wordier but more standard way of expressing the same thing is "subj. 沒有 A 那麼會 V."

例句： 1) 別以爲可以把這部車當名牌車賣，才騙不過人哪！
2) 我們是多年的朋友了，你心裡痛苦瞞得過我嗎？

造句：

4) 我怎么也不同意你和秦楠 ("form a family"), 你 (while it's still early) (give up hope) 吧！

改写 - Rewrite the completed sentences from the preceding exercise, using pattern 2.

3) 万一… 那万一要是变… (p. 107)

This is an adverb that literally means "one chance out of ten thousand." It is used in an "if" clause that precedes the main clause of a sentence. In the "if" clause, 万一 means "in case," indicating that the chance of that "if" circumstance occurring is very small. 万一 can be used only in a clause that refers to an unfortunate or undesirable circumstance or event. 万一 can usually be translated as "if by any chance."

例句： 1) 这件毛衣我这星期还不需要，所以你万一织不完也不要紧。
2) 我只有这一个亲人，万一他死了，谁来关心我呢？

造句：

填充： 1) 你写这样的文章太不 (safe/secure) 了，如果 (policy) 变，那你就肯定完了。
2) 我能 (guarantee) 明天做好，如果明天作不好，后天 (absolutely) 能做好。
3) 这个 (season) 天气很容易变，你最好多带件大衣，如果忽然 (have a wind storm), 你就不会着凉了。
4) 这个孩子那么喜欢 (move), 你千万别让他坐 (spaceship). 如果他摔下来，肯定会 (smashed to bits).

改写 - Rewrite the completed sentences from the preceding exercise, using pattern 3.

4) Subj. V 得/不 过 A [somewhat uncommon] 我说不过你。 (p. 107)

V-得过 is an RV, meaning "able to pass or get by at V-ing." When the RV is followed by a person-object (A), it can also mean "able to best so-and-so at V-ing." V-不过 literally means "unable to pass/surpass at V-ing." When followed by a person-object, the expression indicates that the subject is not as good at doing V as A is. A wordier but more standard way of expressing the same thing is "subj. 沒有 A 那么会 V."

例句： 1) 别以为可以把这部车当名牌车卖，才骗不过人哪！
2) 我们是多年的朋友了，你心里痛苦瞒得过我吗？

造句：

填充： 1) 我愛人比我 (fierce) 得多，我知道我 (clearly cannot win in a quarrel with her), 所以我從來不跟她 (fight/argue).
2) 冬冬當然 (cannot win in a fight with) 男男，可是他跑_______男男，所以每次男男要 (bully) 他的時候，他就跑_______.
3) 他比我聰明好幾倍。不管我多麼 (diligently) 學習，我都 (cannot beat him in an exam).
4) 做買賣還是 (honest) 一點兒好，因爲剛開始的時候也許 (can deceive) 人家，可是 (by and by) 就會沒有 (customers) 了。

5) Subj. 跟-X 有什麼相干? [somewhat colloquial] 跟外人有什麼相干？ (p. 108)

"What is the relevance of X for the subj.?" This is a rhetorical question which really means that X is irrelevant to the subj. A more standard way of saying the same thing is to replace 相干 with 關係. In the example above, the unstated subject is the relationship between Zhihua and Qin Nan.

例句： 1) 平常街道黨委和公安局沒有什麼相干。
2) 在中國的米的價錢和我們這個問題有什麼相干?

造句：

填充： 1) 國家的 (policy) 跟我們 (whether or not to "form a family") 有什麼關係?
2) 我和 (husband) (quarrel) 跟你有什麼關係? 你 (why must) 管?
3) 這個問題和 (neighbors) 沒什麼關係? (street Party committee) 不會管的。
4) 冬冬和你有什麼關係? 他又不是你的兒子，你爲什麼那麼 (concerned for) 他?

改寫 - Rewrite the completed sentences from the preceding exercise, using pattern 5.

6) X 這麼一個 N [colloquial] 只有志華這麼一個兒子，… (p. 110)

This is an appositive construction in which X is elaborated by 這麼一個 N "such a N as X." 這麼一個 is a convenient way of referring to some special quality about X without stating that quality explicitly. Whatever that quality is, it is already implicit in the context. This construction can be modified by adding the quality after 這麼 to make that quality explicit.

例句： 1) 像高志華這麼一個有志氣的男人實在難得。
2) 像男男這麼一個孩子真討厭!

填充： 1) (Ever since) 他妻子自殺以後，家裡只 (remain) 他女兒了。
2) 上海是一個非常 (crowded) 的城，怎麼會有那麼多人要住在那兒?

填充： 1) 我爱人比我 (fierce) 得多，我知道我 (clearly cannot win in a quarrel with her), 所以我从来不跟她 (fight/argue).
2) 冬冬当然 (cannot win in a fight with) 男男，可是他跑______男男，所以每次男男要 (bully) 他的时候，他就跑______.
3) 他比我聪明好几倍。不管我多么 (diligently) 学习，我都 (cannot beat him in an exam).
4) 做买卖还是 (honest) 一点儿好，因为刚开始的时候也许 (can deceive) 人家，可是 (by and by) 就会沒有 (customers) 了。

5) Subj. 跟-X 有什么相干? [somewhat colloquial] 跟外人有什么相干？ (p. 109)
"What is the relevance of X for the subj.?" This is a rhetorical question which really means that X is irrelevant to the subj. A more standard way of saying the same thing is to replace 相干 with 关系. In the example above, the unstated subject is the relationship between Zhihua and Qin Nan.

例句： 1) 平常街道党委和公安局沒有什么相干。
2) 在中国的米的价钱和我们这个问题有什么相干？

造句：

填充： 1) 国家的 (policy) 跟我们 (whether or not to "form a family") 有什么关系？
2) 我和 (husband) (quarrel) 跟你有什么关系？你 (why must) 管？
3) 这个问题和 (neighbors) 沒什么关系？(street Party committee) 不会管的。
4) 冬冬和你有什么关系？他又不是你的儿子，你为什么那么 (concerned for) 他？

改写 - Rewrite the completed sentences from the preceding exercise, using pattern 5.

6) X 这么一个 N [colloquial] 只有志华这么一个儿子，… (p. 111)
This is an appositive construction in which X is elaborated by 这么一个 N "such a N as X." 这么一个 is a convenient way of referring to some special quality about X without stating that quality explicitly. Whatever that quality is, it is already implicit in the context. This construction can be modified by adding the quality after 这么 to make that quality explicit.

例句： 1) 象高志华这么一个有志气的男人实在难得。
2) 象男男这么一个孩子真讨厌！

填充： 1) (Ever since) 他妻子自杀以后，家里只 (remain) 他女儿了。
2) 上海是一个非常 (crowded) 的城，怎么会有那么多人要住在那儿？

3) 這個 (self-employed enterprise) 很好，比 (state-operated units) 都好得多。
4) 下鄉這個 (policy) (after all) 有沒有一點好的結果？

改寫 - Rewrite the completed sentences from the preceding exercise, using pattern 6.

7) 另外　　　　我一定另外找個地方。 (p. 112)

另外 "in addition, besides, another," can function as either an adverb or a noun-modifier. The best translation into English does not necessarily retain the same part of speech as in the Chinese original. In the above example, 另外 is an adverb, but in translation, its meaning is conveyed by an adjective ("I'll certainly find another place."). 另外 can mean either in addition to, or instead of, what is already there. E.g., 我另外買了一個大西瓜 "In addition, I bought a big watermelon;" 他另外找到了一所房子 "He found another house."

例句： 1) 除了這個國營商店以外，這兒另外有些個體戶攤子。 (另外 as adv.)
2) 真意想不到他在鄉下還有一個另外的家。 (另外 as noun-modifier)

造句：

填充： 1) 管理員說在弄堂口 (set up a stall) 礙事，所以秦楠 (had no choice but) 找一個別的地方。
2) 周大媽不但 (criticized) 那些 (bully) 秦楠的 (neighbors), 並且還請秦楠到她家去談心。
3) 我的這 (heart) 都是你的了，我 (absolutely) 沒有別的女朋友了。
4) 當然你有責任 (love and protect) 冬冬，可是你也要 (consider) 你自己的前途。

改寫 - Rewrite the completed sentences from the preceding exercise, using pattern 7.

8) 生 X (的) 氣　　　　你千萬別生我的氣呀！ (p. 112)

By logic the object of 生氣 "to get angry" is the person with whom the subject is angry, but grammatically, this "logical object" does not follow 生氣, but is inserted between 生 and 氣, just as other modifiers of 氣. (Cf. Grammatical Note VIII.2.)

例句： 1) 那不是冬冬的錯，你別生他的氣。
2) 這只是一場小誤會，用不着生那麼大的氣。

造句：

3) 这个 (self-employed enterprise) 很好，比 (state-operated units) 都好得多。
4) 下乡这个 (policy) (after all) 有没有一点好的结果？

改写 - Rewrite the completed sentences from the preceding exercise, using pattern 6.

7) 另外 我一定另外找个地方。 (p. 113)

另外 "in addition, besides, another," can function as either an adverb or a noun-modifier. The best translation into English does not necessarily retain the same part of speech as in the Chinese original. In the above example, 另外 is an adverb, but in translation, its meaning is conveyed by an adjective ("I'll certainly find another place."). 另外 can mean either in addition to, or instead of, what is already there. E.g., 我另外买了一个大西瓜 "In addition, I bought a big watermelon;" 他另外找到了一所房子 "He found another house."

例句： 1) 除了这个国营商店以外，这儿另外有些个体户摊子。 (另外 as adv.)
2) 真意想不到他在乡下还有一个另外的家。 (另外 as noun-modifier)

造句：

填充： 1) 管理员说在弄堂口 (set up a stall) 碍事，所以秦楠 (had no choice but) 找一个别的地方。
2) 周大妈不但 (criticized) 那些 (bully) 秦楠的 (neighbors), 并且还请秦楠到她家去谈心。
3) 我的这 (heart) 都是你的了，我 (absolutely) 没有别的女朋友了。
4) 当然你有责任 (love and protect) 冬冬，可是你也要 (consider) 你自己的前途。

改写 - Rewrite the completed sentences from the preceding exercise, using pattern 7.

8) 生 X (的) 气 你千万别生我的气呀！ (p. 113)

By logic the object of 生气 "to get angry" is the person with whom the subject is angry, but grammatically, this "logical object" does not follow 生气, but is inserted between 生 and 气, just as other modifiers of 气. (Cf. Grammatical Note VIII.2.)

例句： 1) 那不是冬冬的错，你别生他的气。
2) 这只是一场小误会，用不着生那么大的气。

造句：

填充： 1) 我已經 (regret) 了，(forgive) 我吧，別 (be angry with me anymore).
2) 志華這個人 (treats others with sincerity and kindness), 從來不 (get angry with others).
3) 你沒聽別人的 (advice), 結果 (had an accident). 你不能怪別人，只能 (get angry with yourself).
4) 連最 (kind-hearted) 的母親也免不了有時候會 (get angry with their own children).

INCLUSIVE 翻譯 EXERCISE FOR SEGMENT IX:

1) You had best not provoke him. He is tall and heavy. You certainly will not be able to best him in a fight.
2) Please believe me, I have absolutely never done anything unconscionable.
3) Before you marry her, you must clarify this matter (with her). What if by some chance her husband is still alive? Then what?
4) Although Xiao Yun's situation (plight) is none of her business, Qin Nan is very concerned with her. This caused Zhihua to be very moved.
5) I will not listen to you! I will marry Qin Nan! You might as well give up (your idea) while you're ahead (while it is still early).
6) The next day, Zhihua was no longer angry with Dongdong. He recognized that Dongdong was not a despicable child but a lovable one.
7) Mrs. Gao has only this one son Zhihua, so (you) cannot blame her for wanting Zhihua to "form a family" (and) to have a son.
8) Now even state-run units are no longer secure, therefore you had best learn another skill. Relying on one's own labor is the truly secure way (contrary to preconceptions).

填充： 1) 我已经 (regret) 了，(forgive) 我吧，别 (be angry with me anymore).

2) 志华这个人 (treats others with sincerity and kindness), 从来不 (get angry with others).

3) 你没听别人的 (advice), 结果 (had an accident). 你不能怪别人，只能 (get angry with yourself).

4) 连最 (kind-hearted) 的母亲也免不了有时候会 (get angry with their own children).

INCLUSIVE 翻译 EXERCISE FOR SEGMENT IX: See facing page.

SEGMENT X

1) 乾脆　　　　我就乾脆不回家了。(p. 114)

Although 乾脆 means "straight forward, clear-cut, in a decisive snappy way," it is not easy to translate into English. It implies that one does not dawdle in considering the pros and cons nor agonize over the negative repercussions or implications (even though the decision does entail some of these), that one gets straight to the point without hemming and hawing. In the above example, 乾脆 can be rendered by "just," as in "I'll just not go home." But in another context, a different translation would work better, e.g.: 你乾脆別回家了 "You might as well not go home."

例句： 1) 我乾脆說穿了，你就是討厭秦楠沒有丈夫而有個孩子。
2) 你一天到晚淨跑蘇州，又費時間又費錢，你乾脆把冬冬接來上海算了。

造句：

填充： 1) 她 (absolutely) 不會聽你的，你 (might as well give up hope) 吧。
2) 要是你那麼 (afraid), 你 (might as well) 別去了。
3) 看樣子你是 (cannot win in a quarrel against) 他的，你 (might as well surrender before it's too late).
4) 我 (hold the opinion that) 你們倆的 (conflict) 是 (cannot be resolved) 的，你們 (might as well divorce) 吧。

2) 為了…，…　　　　為了自己的幸福，就是要和媽的封建思想鬥到底。(p. 114)

為了 "for the sake of" is a conjunction that introduces the purpose or cause for the action or situation stated in the following main clause of the sentence. While 為了 and 為 both mean "for, for the sake of," they function differently grammatically. 為 is a coverb. It occurs in the pattern "為-obj. V," meaning "to V for the sake of the obj.," where the obj. is a noun, pronoun, or verb functioning as a noun. 為了, on the other hand, introduces a phrase or clause that is separated from the main clause of the sentence by a comma. In some cases, both 為了 and 為 can be used, but the comma at the end of the 為了 phrase gives weight to the phrase, as if the pause gives one a bit more time to ponder that phrase. Thus, 為了孩子，他整天做事 and 他為孩子整天做事 convey the same information, but the first sentence lends greater weight to 孩子. As a variation, the order of the 為了 phrase and the clause to which it relates can be reversed, as exemplified in the second example below.

例句： 1) 為了要獲得冠軍，英華必須努力訓練，所以連回家的時間都沒有。
2) 志華把冬冬抱緊，是為了不讓冬冬害怕。

SEGMENT X

1) 干脆 我就干脆不回家了。(p. 115)

Although 干脆 means "straight forward, clear-cut, in a decisive snappy way," it is not easy to translate into English. It implies that one does not dawdle in considering the pros and cons nor agonize over the negative repercussions or implications (even though the decision does entail some of these), that one gets straight to the point without hemming and hawing. In the above example, 干脆 can be rendered by "just," as in "I'll just not go home." But in another context, a different translation would work better, e.g.: 你干脆别回家了 "You might as well not go home."

例句： 1) 我干脆说穿了，你就是讨厌秦楠没有丈夫而有个孩子。
2) 你一天到晚净跑苏州，又费时间又费钱，你干脆把冬冬接来上海算了。

造句：

填充： 1) 她 (absolutely) 不会听你的，你 (might as well give up hope) 吧。
2) 要是你那么 (afraid), 你 (might as well) 别去了。
3) 看样子你是 (cannot win in a quarrel against) 他的，你 (might as well surrender before it's too late).
4) 我 (hold the opinion that) 你们俩的 (conflict) 是 (cannot be resolved) 的，你们 (might as well divorce) 吧。

2) 为了…，… 为了自己的幸福，就是要和妈的封建思想斗到底。(p. 115)

为了 "for the sake of" is a conjunction that introduces the purpose or cause for the action or situation stated in the following main clause of the sentence. While 为了 and 为 both mean "for, for the sake of," they function differently grammatically. 为 is a coverb. It occurs in the pattern "为-obj. V," meaning "to V for the sake of the obj.," where the obj. is a noun, pronoun, or verb functioning as a noun. 为了, on the other hand, introduces a phrase or clause that is separated from the main clause of the sentence by a comma. In some cases, both 为了 and 为 can be used, but the comma at the end of the 为了 phrase gives weight to the phrase, as if the pause gives one a bit more time to ponder that phrase. Thus, 为了孩子，他整天做事 and 他为孩子整天做事 convey the same information, but the first sentence lends greater weight to 孩子. As a variation, the order of the 为了 phrase and the clause to which it relates can be reversed, as exemplified in the second example below.

例句： 1) 为了要获得冠军，英华必须努力训练，所以连回家的时间都没有。
2) 志华把冬冬抱紧，是为了不让冬冬害怕。

造句：

填充： 1) _ _ 去 (countryside) 看他，我 (asked for three day off).
2) _ _ (reform) 國家的 (policies), 我們非 (smash the Gang of Four) 不可。
3) _ _ 你 (whole life) 的 (happiness), 你不能 (lightly) 找 (potential spouse).
4) 他剛 (came out of the hospital), _ _ 不讓他 (become worried), 我沒告訴他住 (hospital) 的費用多少。

3) V 到底 爲了自己的幸福，就是要和媽的封建思想鬥到底。 (p. 114)
"To V to the end" implies that one will not give up until one has reached the very end. 到底 can also function as an adverb (cf. Grammatical Note III.6.).

例句： 1) 如果你真心愛一個人，你就應該愛他愛到底。
2) 秦楠的事他雖然知道一些，但是還沒了解到底。

造句：

填充： 1) 他這個人很少跟別人 (vie), 可是他一 (resolve to) 和別人 (vie), 就要 (vie to the end).
2) (Others) 錯了，你可以 (criticize) 他們，可是不必 (criticize to the end), 要不然會 (give rise to) 他們的反感。
3) 這是個 (old big difficult) 問題，看樣子 (unless) (work hard to the end), 要不然是不可能 (succeed) 的。
4) 志華對蕭健的 (friendship) 是很 (firm) 的，我 (hold the opinion that) 他會幫他 (help to the end) 的。

4) 除非…，(要不然)… 除非再把秦楠請回來，不然，你不要回家。 (p. 114)
除非 "unless" is a movable adverb usually used in the first clause of a two-clause sentence. The second clause may, but need not, contain the adverb (要)不然 "otherwise" to reinforce the linkage between the two clauses. Sometimes the 除非 clause follows the main clause, but when it does, it is an afterthought, e.g. 我明天一定來，除非下雨 "I'll certainly come tomorrow - unless it rains."

例句： 1) 除非他媽的封建思想能改革，你和她成家是不會幸福的。
2) 她回上海只好當個體戶，除非她媽退休，讓她頂替。

造句：

造句：

填充： 1) __ __ 去 (countryside) 看他，我 (asked for three day off).
2) __ __ (reform) 国家的 (policies), 我们非 (smash the Gang of Four) 不可。
3) __ __ 你 (whole life) 的 (happiness), 你不能 (lightly) 找 (potential spouse).
4) 他刚 (came out of the hospital), __ __ 不让他 (become worried), 我没告诉他住 (hospital) 的费用多少。

3) V 到底 为了自己的幸福，就是要和妈的封建思想斗到底。 (p. 115)

"To V to the end" implies that one will not give up until one has reached the very end. 到底 can also function as an adverb (cf. Grammatical Note III.6.).

例句： 1) 如果你真心爱一个人，你就应该爱他爱到底。
2) 秦楠的事他虽然知道一些，但是还没了解到底。

造句：

填充： 1) 他这个人很少跟别人 (vie), 可是他一 (resolve to) 和别人 (vie), 就要 (vie to the end).
2) (Others) 错了，你可以 (criticize) 他们，可是不必 (criticize to the end), 要不然会 (give rise to) 他们的反感。
3) 这是个 (old big difficult) 问题，看样子 (unless) (work hard to the end), 要不然是不可能 (succeed) 的。
4) 志华对肖健的 (friendship) 是很 (firm) 的，我 (hold the opinion that) 他会帮他 (help to the end) 的。

4) 除非…，(要不然)… 除非再把秦楠请回来，不然，你不要回家。 (p. 115)

除非 "unless" is a movable adverb usually used in the first clause of a two-clause sentence. The second clause may, but need not, contain the adverb (要)不然 "otherwise" to reinforce the linkage between the two clauses. Sometimes the 除非 clause follows the main clause, but when it does, it is an afterthought, e.g. 我明天一定来，除非下雨 "I'll certainly come tomorrow - unless it rains."

例句： 1) 除非他妈的封建思想能改革，你和她成家是不会幸福的。
2) 她回上海只好当个体户，除非她妈退休，让她顶替。

造句：

填充： 1) (Unless) 國家的 (policies) (thoroughly reform), 要不然 ____________.
2) __________, 要不然媽不會那麼 (lightly) (be in favor of) 你和秦楠結婚的。
3) (Unless) 你 (at the crack of dawn) 來 (hospital) (register), ____________.
4) 現在去已經 (not enough time/too late) 了，除非 ______________.

5) SV 成 這樣/那樣 [colloquial] 人都瘦成這樣了。 (p. 116)

"SV to such a point as this/that." This pattern is similar to, but a bit more colloquial than, "SV 得..." We may also have a descriptive phrase instead of 這樣/那樣 in this pattern, e.g. 瘦成像一把骨頭 "skinny to the point of resembling a pack of bones." 成 also occurs in the compound V-成, meaning "V into...," e.g. 把這塊布做成衣服 "make this cloth into a garment."

例句： 1) 男男常欺負他，讓他害怕成連門都不敢出了。
2) 你的房子亂成這樣，誰願意和你成家呢？

造句：

填充，include the use of "SV 得…" or "SV 成…" in each of the following sentences:
1) 她 (is so feudal that) 連最 (filial)、 最 (kind-hearted) 的姑娘也不願意當她的媳婦。
2) 她生了冬冬以後就變得 (have such an inferiority complex that) 不敢 (consider finding a potential spouse).
3) 你 (have gotten so tired), 我看最好 (ask for a few days off) 休息休息。
4) 在過去幾十年中，這地方人口增加了一倍，(no wonder) (main roads) (are crowded to such a point).

6) V-遍 (了) 弄堂前前後後我都找遍了。 (p. 118)

遍 is a postverb meaning "all over, all through, thoroughly." It may be translated differently depending on the context. Some other verbs that occur with 遍 are 走 ("travel all through"), 看 ("look all through"), and 查 ("examine thoroughly").

例句： 1) 我在單位裡找遍了也沒找到一個合適的人。
2) 他沒犯罪，公安局審查遍了也不會審查出什麼結果來。

造句：

填充： 1) 你別看秦楠沒有 (husband) 而有孩子, (search all through) 上海也 (cannot find) 一個那麼好的 (potential spouse).

填充： 1) (Unless) 国家的 (policies) (thoroughly reform), 要不然 ____________.
2) __________, 要不然妈不会那么 (lightly) (be in favor of) 你和秦楠结婚的。
3) (Unless) 你 (at the crack of dawn) 来 (hospital) (register), ____________.
4) 现在去已经 (not enough time/too late) 了，除非 ______________.

5) SV 成 这样/那样 [colloquial] 人都瘦成这样了。(p. 117)

"SV to such a point as this/that." This pattern is similar to, but a bit more colloquial than, "SV 得..." We may also have a descriptive phrase instead of 这样/那样 in this pattern, e.g. 瘦成象一把骨头 "skinny to the point of resembling a pack of bones." 成 also occurs in the compound V-成, meaning "V into...," e.g. 把这块布做成衣服 "make this cloth into a garment."

例句： 1) 男男常欺负他，让他害怕成连门都不敢出了。
2) 你的房子乱成这样，谁愿意和你成家呢？

造句：

填充，include the use of "SV 得···" or "SV 成···" in each of the following sentences:
1) 她 (is so feudal that) 连最 (filial)、 最 (kind-hearted) 的姑娘也不愿意当她的媳妇。
2) 她生了冬冬以后就变得 (have such an inferiority complex that) 不敢 (consider finding a potential spouse).
3) 你 (have gotten so tired), 我看最好 (ask for a few days off) 休息休息。
4) 在过去几十年中，这地方人口增加了一倍，(no wonder) (main roads) (are crowded to such a point).

6) V-遍 (了) 弄堂前前后后我都找遍了。(p. 119)

遍 is a postverb meaning "all over, all through, thoroughly." It may be translated differently depending on the context. Some other verbs that occur with 遍 are 走 ("travel all through"), 看 ("look all through"), and 查 ("examine thoroughly").

例句： 1) 我在单位里找遍了也没找到一个合适的人。
2) 他没犯罪，公安局审查遍了也不会审查出什么结果来。

造句：

填充： 1) 你别看秦楠没有 (husband) 而有孩子, (search all through) 上海也 (cannot find) 一个那么好的 (potential spouse).

2) 那麼小的一根 (needle) (disappeared), 房子裡 (search all through) 也 (cannot find), 再買一根吧。
3) 秦楠把冬冬這個問題 (thought through thoroughly) 了以後，就 (made up her mind) 把他帶回上海了。
4) 他去年 (retired) 以後，預備去中國一年，要 (have fun all through) 全中國才回來。可是 (unexpectedly) 他就在中國病死了。

7) 有沒有 VP [colloquial and regional] 同志，有沒有見到一個五歲的小男孩兒？ (p. 118)

"Have (you)...?" This is a more colloquial way of saying "V 了沒有?"

例句： 1) 你們有沒有看出來她最近很沈默？
2) 志華今天帶冬冬去玩兒，沒去上班，他有沒有請假？

造句：

填充： 1) 今天早上你到 (hospital) 去的時候, (registered) 了嗎？
2) 冬冬前天 (under the weather), 你帶他去看 (doctor) 了嗎？
3) 你訂的新車子明天就能來 (pick up) 了，可是你買了 (insurance) 沒有？
4) 你和你 (spouse) 在一塊兒已經三十年了, (have you ever had a quarrel)?

改寫 - Rewrite the completed sentences from the preceding exercise, using pattern 7.

8) Subj. 被(-X) VP 了 在馬路上被腳踏車撞傷了。 (p. 118)

This is a passive pattern in which the subject is the "receiver" of the action, and the object of the coverb 被, if it is stated, is the person or thing doing the V.

例句： 1) 冬冬的蘋果又被男男搶去了。
2) 秦楠的事被鄰居們知道以後肯定會有不少流言蜚語的。

造句：

填充： 1) 在文化大革命的時候，她父親 (was isolated and investigated).
2) 自從她 __ 她男朋友 (deceived) 以後就再也不那麼 (naive) 了。
3) 雖然他常 __ 他 (spouse) (criticize), 他一點兒也不 (have an inferiority complex).
4) 蕭健 (committed a crime), __ (Public Security Bureau) 送到一個農場去 (to be reformed) 了。

2) 那么小的一根 (needle) (disappeared), 房子里 (search all through) 也 (cannot find), 再买一根吧。

3) 秦楠把冬冬这个问题 (thought through thoroughly) 了以后，就 (made up her mind) 把他带回上海了。

4) 他去年 (retired) 以后，预备去中国一年，要 (have fun all through) 全中国才回来。可是 (unexpectedly) 他就在中国病死了。

7) 有沒有 VP [colloquial and regional] 同志，有沒有见到一个五岁的小男孩儿？ (p. 119)

"Have (you)...?" This is a more colloquial way of saying "V 了沒有?"

例句： 1) 你们有沒有看出来她最近很沈默？

2) 志华今天带冬冬去玩儿，沒去上班，他有沒有请假？

造句：

填充： 1) 今天早上你到 (hospital) 去的时候, (registered) 了吗？

2) 冬冬前天 (under the weather), 你带他去看 (doctor) 了吗？

3) 你订的新车子明天就能来 (pick up) 了，可是你买了 (insurance) 沒有？

4) 你和你 (spouse) 在一块儿已经三十年了, (have you ever had a quarrel)?

改写 - Rewrite the completed sentences from the preceding exercise, using pattern 7.

8) Subj. 被(-X) VP 了 在马路上被脚踏车撞伤了。 (p. 119)

This is a passive pattern in which the subject is the "receiver" of the action, and the object of the coverb 被, if it is stated, is the person or thing doing the V.

例句： 1) 冬冬的苹果又被男男抢去了。

2) 秦楠的事被邻居们知道以后肯定会有不少流言蜚语的。

造句：

填充： 1) 在文化大革命的时候，她父亲 (was isolated and investigated).

2) 自从她 __ 她男朋友 (deceived) 以后就再也不那么 (naive) 了。

3) 虽然他常 __ 他 (spouse) (criticize), 他一点儿也不 (have an inferiority complex).

4) 肖健 (committed a crime), __ (Public Security Bureau) 送到一个农场去 (to be reformed) 了。

9) …又怎麼樣？ [colloquial] 是我的爸爸又怎麼樣？ (p. 122)

This is an idiomatic expression meaning "so what if...?" The phrase that precedes the 又怎麼樣 may be hypothetical (as in the above example) or actual (e.g. 我搶了他的球又怎麼樣？ "Yeah, I grabbed his ball, so what about it?").

例句： 1) 沒有丈夫而有孩子又怎麼樣？
2) 考不上大學又怎麼樣？

造句：

填充： 1) (Self-employed) 有什麼關係？我們不也是爲人民服務？
2) 志華已經 (made up his mind), 他母親 (object) 又有什麼關係呢？
3) 尤奶奶 (curse) 他是 (bastard) 又有什麼關係呢？別人 (absolutely) 不會相信的。
4) 她現在 (regret) 也沒什麼用了，我已經 (decided to make a clean break with her).

改寫 - Rewrite the completed sentences from the preceding exercise, using pattern 8.

10) 從來 (也) 不/沒 V 過 他呀，從來也不給我削蘋果。 (p. 122)

This pattern is discussed in Grammatical Note VI.4. In this pattern, the "experiential marker" 過 usually occurs in conjunction with 沒. The adverb 也 may be added to reinforce the negative 不/沒 and is best conveyed in English translation by stressing the word "never" (e.g., in the above example, "He never peels apples for me.").

例句： 1) 我試過好多次，可從來也沒成功過。
2) 這個教練從來不發脾氣，難怪運動員都喜歡他。

造句：

填充： 1) 他 (has never before asked for a leave), 今天是他頭一次。
2) 我 (grandmother has never ridden on a spaceship before), 所以她很 (afraid).
3) 他説他和他的 (old "companion") 結婚四十年， (have never had a quarrel), 這可能嗎？
4) 我今天才 (understand) 爲什麼蕭雲 (never goes out), 原來她是個 (handicapped person).

INCLUSIVE 翻譯 EXERCISE FOR SEGMENT X:

1) Have you registered yet? If not (not yet registered), then come with me.
2) I have looked through all the dresses in this store, but I cannot find even one that I like.

9) …又怎么样？ [colloquial] 是我的爸爸又怎么样？ (p. 123)

This is an idiomatic expression meaning "so what if...?" The phrase that precedes the 又怎么样 may be hypothetical (as in the above example) or actual (e.g. 我抢了他的球又怎么样？ "Yeah, I grabbed his ball, so what about it?").

例句： 1) 沒有丈夫而有孩子又怎么样？
2) 考不上大学又怎么样？

造句：

填充： 1) (Self-employed) 有什么关系？我们不也是为人民服务？
2) 志华已经 (made up his mind), 他母亲 (object) 又有什么关系呢？
3) 尤奶奶 (curse) 他是 (bastard) 又有什么关系呢？别人 (absolutely) 不会相信的。
4) 她现在 (regret) 也沒什么用了，我已经 (decided to make a clean break with her).

改写 - Rewrite the completed sentences from the preceding exercise, using pattern 8.

10) 从来 (也) 不/沒 V 过 他呀，从来也不给我削苹果。 (p. 123)

This pattern is discussed in Grammatical Note VI.4. In this pattern, the "experiential marker" 过 usually occurs in conjunction with 沒. The adverb 也 may be added to reinforce the negative 不/沒 and is best conveyed in English translation by stressing the word "never" (e.g., in the above example, "He <u>never</u> peels apples for me.").

例句： 1) 我试过好多次，可从来也沒成功过。
2) 这个教练从来不发脾气，难怪运动员都喜欢他。

造句：

填充： 1) 他 (has never before asked for a leave), 今天是他头一次。
2) 我 (grandmother has never ridden on a spaceship before), 所以她很 (afraid).
3) 他说他和他的 (old "companion") 结婚四十年， (have never had a quarrel), 这可能吗？
4) 我今天才 (understand) 为什么肖云 (never goes out), 原来她是个 (handicapped person).

INCLUSIVE 翻译 EXERCISE FOR SEGMENT X: See facing page.

3) So what if you object to my way of doing things? Anyway, there are plenty of people who are in favor of it.
4) If one wants to succeed, then one must strive hard to the end, (and) not (cannot) surrender lightly.
5) Because Zhihua has never been unfilial toward his mother before, Mrs. Gao was especially hurt this time.
6) The reason why Qin Nan is in such a state of anxiety is because Dongdong has disappeared.
7) Unless Zhihua can love Dongdong (and) not consider him a bastard, (otherwise) Qin Nan would absolutely not marry him.
8) After Granny You was criticized by the street Party committee, she never again dared to call Dongdong a bastard anymore.
9) The train is leaving in half an hour. It's too late (for you to catch it), you might as well (in a decisive snappy way) take the next train.
10) For the sake of Zhihua's future happiness, Yinghua asked for a leave of absence to go home and persuade their mother to allow Zhihua to marry Qin Nan.

SEGMENT XI

1) 等…再… 　　　　　　　　　　等你了解了再… (p. 128)

"Wait until...(and) then..." The meaning of 再 in this pattern is the same as in "先…，再… (first..., then...)." Remember that 再 has nothing to do with "again" in this context.

例句： 1) 你最好等冬冬出了院再和秦楠提結婚的事吧。
　　　2) 你不能等到冬冬長大了再考慮你自己的前途。

造句：

填充： 1) 你應該一有了汽車就買 (insurance), 別 (wait until you have an accident and then buy it).
　　　2) 她希望先結了婚再 (immigrate) 到美國去，可是他 (holds the view that) 應該 (wait until he is settled in the U.S. and then) 回來和她結婚。
　　　3) 孩子從小就應該好好兒地 (educate and nurture), 不能 (wait until they commit a crime and then educate and nurture).
　　　4) 出國必須先 (wait until your unit approved and then) 去辦 (passport procedures).

2) 在…的第 Nu M (N) 　　　　　　　　　在爸爸被關進牛棚的第三天，… (p. 130)

The M in this construction refers to a measure of time (day, month, year, etc.) and the "..." following 在 refers to an event or time period. The whole phrase is a time-when expression which states a time in reference to a particular event or time period, and can be translated as "on/in the ordinal-Nu... after (event) / of (time period)..." Thus, the above example means "on the third day after Dad was incarcerated." A variation of this pattern is "在…的頭 Nu M (N)" (第 is replaced by 頭), which means "on/in the first Nu ...." Other examples:

在開學的第二個星期 　　in the second week after school began
在開學的頭兩個星期 　　in the first two weeks after school began
(note the distinction between 第二 "the second" and 頭兩 "the first two.")
在那年的第三個月 　　in the third month of that year
我懷孕(後)的第三個月 　　the third month after I became pregnant (cf. Scene 73)

例句： 1) 在冬冬出生以後的第三個月秦楠就自己回上海了。
　　　2) 在她擺縫紉攤的第二天就認識了高志華。

填充： 1) (In the first year of the Cultural Revolution), 蕭雲的媽就被打成 (rightist) 了。

SEGMENT XI

1) 等…再… 等你了解了再… (p. 129)

"Wait until...(and) then..." The meaning of 再 in this pattern is the same as in "先…，再… (first..., then...)." Remember that 再 has nothing to do with "again" in this context.

例句： 1) 你最好等冬冬出了院再和秦楠提结婚的事吧。
2) 你不能等到冬冬长大了再考虑你自己的前途。

造句：

填充： 1) 你应该一有了汽车就买 (insurance), 别 (wait until you have an accident and then buy it).
2) 她希望先结了婚再 (immigrate) 到美国去，可是他 (holds the view that) 应该 (wait until he is settled in the U.S. and then) 回来和她结婚。
3) 孩子从小就应该好好儿地 (educate and nurture), 不能 (wait until they commit a crime and then educate and nurture).
4) 出国必须先 (wait until your unit approved and then) 去办 (passport procedures).

2) 在…的第 Nu M (N) 在爸爸被关进牛棚的第三天，… (p. 131)

The M in this construction refers to a measure of time (day, month, year, etc.) and the "..." following 在 refers to an event or time period. The whole phrase is a time-when expression which states a time in reference to a particular event or time period, and can be translated as "on/in the ordinal-Nu... after (event) / of (time period)..." Thus, the above example means "on the third day after Dad was incarcerated." A variation of this pattern is "在…的头 Nu M (N)" (第 is replaced by 头), which means "on/in the first Nu ...." Other examples:

在开学的第二个星期 in the second week after school began
在开学的头两个星期 in the first two weeks after school began
(note the distinction between 第二 "the second" and 头两 "the first two.")
在那年的第三个月 in the third month of that year
我怀孕(后)的第三个月 the third month after I became pregnant (cf. Scene 73)

例句： 1) 在冬冬出生以后的第三个月秦楠就自己回上海了。
2) 在她摆缝纫摊的第二天就认识了高志华。

填充： 1) (In the first year of the Cultural Revolution), 肖云的妈就被打成 (rightist) 了。

2) (In the first month after her daughter went down to the countryside), 她每天都 (weep bitterly and shed tears).
3) (In the first year after her boyfriend went to the U.S.), 她每天都 (wait) 着他的信，可是後來她就 (gave up hope).
4) (In the first three years of their marriage), 他們的 (feelings for each other) 非常好，可是後來就發生 (conflict) 了。

3) …。因此，… [formal] 文化大革命剛開始，他的祖父…。因此，我和他都屬於… (p. 132)

因此 links what precedes with what follows in a cause-effect relationship. The preceding sentence is initially just a factual statement. The 因此 at the beginning of the following sentence shifts the focus from the factual aspect to its being the cause of something. The 因爲…, (所以)… pattern conveys the same cause-effect relationship, but differs from this pattern in that one is aware from the outset that the first clause is the cause for the second clause. Thus, these two patterns differ in focus.

例句：
1) 秦楠要志華了解她過去的一切，又不知道怎麼跟他説，因此她決定讓志華看她的筆記本。
2) 他從小就死了父親，母親身體也一直不好，因此他從小就學會了照顧自己。

造句：

填充：
1) 那兒的生活非常 (monotonous), 因此 ________________.
2) ________________, 因此別的 ("educated youths") 都 (discriminate against) 他們，不願意 (get close to) 他們。
3) 她經歷過不少 (bitter circumstances), 因此, ________________.
4) (New Year's Eve) 那晚, (production team) 只 (remained) 他們兩個，天氣又特別 (cold), 因此, ________________.

4) Clause 1, 而 clause 2 [formal] 他相信人生的遭遇…，而命運是不可抗拒的。 (p. 132)

As a link between two clauses, 而 can mean "and" or "but"; and when the two clauses are in a cause-effect relationship (with 因 or 因爲 in the first clause), it can mean "therefore." Cf. Grammatical Note VII.2. for explication of this pattern. Another example of this usage is 艱難而遲緩 in Scene 71, line 2. In some contexts, as in the above example,而 can be interpreted as both "and" and "but." But in English translation, one must make a choice between the two and relinquish the marvelous ambiguity that 而 provides in Chinese.

例句：
1) 秦楠是個會關心別人而不會照顧自己的人。
2) 你不會只因爲他抽起煙來而要和他一刀兩斷吧。

2) (In the first month after her daughter went down to the countryside), 她每天都 (weep bitterly and shed tears).
3) (In the first year after her boyfriend went to the U.S.), 她每天都 (wait) 着他的信，可是后来她就 (gave up hope).
4) (In the first three years of their marriage), 他们的 (feelings for each other) 非常好，可是后来就发生 (conflict) 了。

3) …。因此，… [formal] 文化大革命刚开始，他的祖父…。因此，我和他都属于… (p. 133)
因此 links what precedes with what follows in a cause-effect relationship. The preceding sentence is initially just a factual statement. The 因此 at the beginning of the following sentence shifts the focus from the factual aspect to its being the cause of something. The 因为…, (所以)… pattern conveys the same cause-effect relationship, but differs from this pattern in that one is aware from the outset that the first clause is the cause for the second clause. Thus, these two patterns differ in focus.

例句： 1) 秦楠要志华了解她过去的一切，又不知道怎么跟他说，因此她决定让志华看她的笔记本。
2) 他从小就死了父亲，母亲身体也一直不好，因此他从小就学会了照顾自己。

造句：

填充： 1) 那儿的生活非常 (monotonous), 因此 ________________.
2) ________________, 因此别的 ("educated youths") 都 (discriminate against) 他们，不愿意 (get close to) 他们。
3) 她经历过不少 (bitter circumstances), 因此, ________________.
4) (New Year's Eve) 那晚, (production team) 只 (remained) 他们两个，天气又特别 (cold), 因此, ________________.

4) Clause 1, 而 clause 2 [formal] 他相信人生的遭遇…，而命运是不可抗拒的。 (p. 133)
As a link between two clauses, 而 can mean "and" or "but"; and when the two clauses are in a cause-effect relationship (with 因 or 因为 in the first clause), it can mean "therefore." Cf. Grammatical Note VII.2. for explication of this pattern. Another example of this usage is 艰难而迟缓 in Scene 71, line 2. In some contexts, as in the above example, 而 can be interpreted as both "and" and "but." But in English translation, one must make a choice between the two and relinquish the marvelous ambiguity that 而 provides in Chinese.

例句： 1) 秦楠是个会关心别人而不会照顾自己的人。
2) 你不会只因为他抽起烟来而要和他一刀两断吧。

造句：

填充： 1) 他在 (Cultural Revolution) 的時候吃了不少苦，可是他一點兒也不 (pessimistic).
2) 其他的 ("educated youths") 都回家過 (Spring Festival) 了，我一個人在那兒過了個又 (monotonous) 又寂寞的 (Spring Festival).
3) 英華 (opposes) 她媽的 (feudal) 思想，並且 (encourages) 她哥哥向秦楠表示他的 (feelings).
4) 志華對他媽很 (filial), 並且對秦楠也很 (sincere and kind), 所以他爲他媽不喜歡秦楠而感到很 (hurt).

改寫 - Rewrite the first three completed sentences from the preceding exercise, using pattern 4.

5) 才不… [colloquial] 我才不作這樣的夢。 (p. 132)

The usage of 才 for emphasis is discussed in Grammatical Note VII.8. It implies contradiction to or defiance of the other person's assumption, suggestion, or view. Here it is used with a negative verb.

例句： 1) 一個知青才不會輕易和一個農民成家呢。
2) 護照才不那麼容易能申請到。

造句：

填充： 1) 像英華那麼有 (aspiration) 的人一定不會 (surrender) 的。
2) (Unless) 那兒的待遇特別好，要不然，我絕對不會 (immigrate) 到那兒去。
3) 他連自己的孩子都不懂得 (love and protect), 怎麼會 (concerned for) 別人的孩子呢？
4) 上次 (taken advantage of by him) 以後，我再也不信任他了。以後我絕對不會像上次那麼 (muddle-headed) 了。

改寫 - Rewrite the completed sentences from the preceding exercise, using pattern 5.

6) …，也就是… 七七年五月，也就是我懷孕後的第三個月，… (p. 136)

This is an appositive construction, in which the phrase introduced by 也就是 gets closer to the heart of the matter.

例句： 1) 我那時的男朋友，也就是冬冬的爸爸，去了加拿大就再也沒他的消息了。
2) 上星期五，也就是男男欺負冬冬的那天，周大媽主動請了秦楠去她家談心。

造句：

填充：1) 他在 (Cultural Revolution) 的时候吃了不少苦，可是他一点儿也不 (pessimistic).
2) 其他的 ("educated youths") 都回家过 (Spring Festival) 了，我一个人在那儿过了个又 (monotonous) 又寂寞的 (Spring Festival).
3) 英华 (opposes) 她妈的 (feudal) 思想，并且 (encourages) 她哥哥向秦楠表示他的 (feelings).
4) 志华对他妈很 (filial), 并且对秦楠也很 (sincere and kind), 所以他为他妈不喜欢秦楠而感到很 (hurt).

改写 - Rewrite the first three completed sentences from the preceding exercise, using pattern 4.

5) 才不… [colloquial] 我才不作这样的梦。(p. 133)

The usage of 才 for emphasis is discussed in Grammatical Note VII.8. It implies contradiction to or defiance of the other person's assumption, suggestion, or view. Here it is used with a negative verb.

例句：1) 一个知青才不会轻易和一个农民成家呢。
2) 护照才不那么容易能申请到。

造句：

填充：1) 象英华那么有 (aspiration) 的人一定不会 (surrender) 的。
2) (Unless) 那儿的待遇特别好，要不然，我绝对不会 (immigrate) 到那儿去。
3) 他连自己的孩子都不懂得 (love and protect), 怎么会 (concerned for) 别人的孩子呢？
4) 上次 (taken advantage of by him) 以后，我再也不信任他了。以后我绝对不会象上次那么 (muddle-headed) 了。

改写 - Rewrite the completed sentences from the preceding exercise, using pattern 5.

6) …，也就是… 七七年五月，也就是我怀孕后的第三个月，… (p. 137)

This is an appositive construction, in which the phrase introduced by 也就是 gets closer to the heart of the matter.

例句：1) 我那时的男朋友，也就是冬冬的爸爸，去了加拿大就再也没他的消息了。
2) 上星期五，也就是男男欺负冬冬的那天，周大妈主动请了秦楠去她家谈心。

填充： 1) (Spring Festival) 後的第三天, ＿＿＿ 孟彬拿到 (passport) 的那天，我發現我 (pregnant) 了。
2) 志華家前頭, ＿＿＿ 他們 (set up stall) 的那個地方，是在一條大街旁邊，所以生意很好。
3) 1976 年, ＿＿＿ 毛澤東去世的那年, (Gang of Four) 被 (overthrown) 了。
4) 秦楠的爸爸, ＿＿＿ 冬冬的 (maternal grandfather), 原來是志華的小學老師, (no wonder) 志華那麼 (concerned for) 秦楠。

7) 只好… 我實在沒臉…，只好遷居到蘇州鄉下我舅舅家裡。 (p. 136)

只好 is an adverb meaning "can only..., have no choice but..." Note that the meaning of 好 in this pattern is far removed from the primary meaning of this word.

例句： 1) 爲了要留在加拿大經商，我只好同意和一個加拿大人結婚了。
2) 英華忙得沒時間回家，所以志華只好把媽給她織的毛衣送去。

造句：

填充： 1) 爲了讓他 (gone down to the countryside) 的兒子回上海，他提早 (retired), 讓他兒子 (take over his job), 沒別的辦法。
2) 雖然我不愛她，可是她 (got pregnant), 我就必得和她結婚了。
3) 蕭雲沒辦法自己 (go out), 要買東西就得請 (street Party committee) 幫忙，沒別的法子。
4) 我的 (work unit) 要把我 (transfer) 到那兒去，我沒法子 (resist/protest), 就必得去了。

改寫 - Rewrite the completed sentences from the preceding exercise, using pattern 7.

8) time-span 來/以來 那年冬天是我二十多年來感到最寒冷的冬天。 (p. 136)

This is an adverbial time expression indicating a span of time up to the present, and is translatable as "for the past..." 來 and 以來 are interchangeable in this context, but "...來" is somewhat colloquial. The "time-span" preceding 來/以來 can be replaced by a past event which marks the beginning of a span of time up to the present, in which case, the expression is translatable as "(ever) since..." This latter pattern is synonymous with "自從…以來" (cf. Grammatical Note VII.5.).

例句： 1) 他一個月來都沒抽煙了，我看他這次戒煙是真的成功了。
2) 自從四人幫打倒以來，我們的生活就越來越改進了。

造句：

填充： 1) (Spring Festival) 后的第三天, ____ 孟彬拿到 (passport) 的那天，我发现我 (pregnant) 了。
2) 志华家前头, ____ 他们 (set up stall) 的那个地方，是在一条大街旁边，所以生意很好。
3) 1976 年, ____ 毛泽东去世的那年, (Gang of Four) 被 (overthrown) 了。
4) 秦楠的爸爸, ____ 冬冬的 (maternal grandfather), 原来是志华的小学老师, (no wonder) 志华那么 (concerned for) 秦楠。

7) 只好… 我实在沒脸…，只好迁居到苏州乡下我舅舅家里。 (p. 137)

只好 is an adverb meaning "can only..., have no choice but..." Note that the meaning of 好 in this pattern is far removed from the primary meaning of this word.

例句： 1) 为了要留在加拿大经商，我只好同意和一个加拿大人结婚了。
2) 英华忙得沒时间回家，所以志华只好把妈给她织的毛衣送去。

造句：

填充： 1) 为了让他 (gone down to the countryside) 的儿子回上海，他提早 (retired), 让他儿子 (take over his job), 沒别的办法。
2) 虽然我不爱她，可是她 (got pregnant), 我就必得和她结婚了。
3) 肖云沒办法自己 (go out), 要买东西就得请 (street Party committee) 帮忙，沒别的法子。
4) 我的 (work unit) 要把我 (transfer) 到那儿去，我沒法子 (resist/protest), 就必得去了。

改写 - Rewrite the completed sentences from the preceding exercise, using pattern 7.

8) time-span 来/以来 那年冬天是我二十多年来感到最寒冷的冬天。 (p. 137)

This is an adverbial time expression indicating a span of time up to the present, and is translatable as "for the past..." 来 and 以来 are interchangeable in this context, but "...来" is somewhat colloquial. The "time-span" preceding 来/以来 can be replaced by a past event which marks the beginning of a span of time up to the present, in which case, the expression is translatable as "(ever) since..." This latter pattern is synonymous with "自从…以来" (cf. Grammatical Note VII.5.).

例句： 1) 他一个月来都沒抽烟了，我看他这次戒烟是真的成功了。
2) 自从四人帮打倒以来，我们的生活就越来越改进了。

造句：

填充： 1) (In the past fifteen years), 中國的 (policies) 有了不少 (reforms).
2) (In the past six months), 這兒的很多 ("educated youths") 都 (transferred) 回城了，只 (remain) 我們幾個。
3) (Ever since) 冬冬 (had an accident), 志華比從前更 (love and protect) 他了。
4) (Ever since) 她母親被 (investigated), 她的同學們都不敢 (get close to her any more).

INCLUSIVE 翻譯 EXERCISE FOR SEGMENT XI:

1) I certainly don't believe that Meng Bin would come back to get Qin Nan after he has settled in Canada.
2) When did you start having a sewing stall on the street?
From the time I was transferred back to Shanghai.
3) Although he doesn't have much feeling for her, (but) because she is already pregnant, he has no choice but to marry her.
4) Both my parents were rightists. Therefore, others all discriminated against me, even my friends dared not get close to me.
5) His health is still not too good. Wait until he gets out of the hospital before bringing up this matter with him.
6) Meng Bin of course wanted very much to emigrate to Canada, and yet was unwilling to leave Qin Nan. Therefore, he felt very conflicted.
7) In the second year after the Cultural Revolution began, I was sent to a commune in the countryside to be re-educated (to receive re-education).
8) In the last twelve years, that is, since the Gang of Four was smashed, there came to be more and more individual enterprises in China. Perhaps in the future they will be even more numerous than state-managed ones.

填充： 1) (In the past fifteen years), 中国的 (policies) 有了不少 (reforms).

2) (In the past six months), 这儿的很多 ("educated youths") 都 (transferred) 回城了，只 (remain) 我们几个。

3) (Ever since) 冬冬 (had an accident), 志华比从前更 (love and protect) 他了。

4) (Ever since) 她母亲被 (investigated), 她的同学们都不敢 (get close to her any more).

INCLUSIVE 翻译 EXERCISE FOR SEGMENT XI: See facing page.

SEGMENT XII

1) 再也不/沒 VP 了　　　　以後就再也沒有音信了嗎？ (p. 140)

An emphatic and colloquial way of saying "never VP again/anymore." A more standard way of saying the same thing is "不/沒 再 VP 了." In both these patterns, 不 implies that the act will never be done again from now on, and 沒 implies that the act has never again been done since a certain time in the past.

例句： 1) 我下了決心以後再也不抽煙了。
2) 那年他考大學沒考上，以後再也沒試了。

造句：

填充： 1) 經過那場 (test/trial) 以後，我覺得人生 (never again) 會有什麼 (unsolvable problems).
2) 聽了你的 (advice) 以後，他 (never again discriminated against orphans and widowed mothers).
3) 自從他和我 (cousin) (divorced) 以後，我 ________________.
4) 噢，原來她是上過男人的當, (no wonder) 從那以後她再也沒 ________________.

2) 快…的時候　　　　在冬冬快滿兩週歲的時候，… (p. 140)

"When (subj.) is/was soon to..." The exact translation of 快 may be "soon," "almost," or "about to," depending on the context. In this pattern, 快要 is synonymous with 快.

例句： 1) 四人幫快要被粉碎的時候，蕭雲的母親不幸病死了。
2) 他快要病死的時候，醫生找到了一種特效藥，結果把他的病治好了。

造句：

填充： 1) (When he was about to give up all hope), (Public Security Bureau) 來信說那場 (misunderstanding) 已經 (clarified).
2) (When he was about to) 去加拿大 (manage) 他父親的 (business), 他女朋友告訴他她 (pregnant) 了。
3) 人家都已經 (about to go to work), 你還在這兒 (sleep in late).
4) 你應該 (optimistic) 點兒，這件事說不定 (is about to succeed), 你再忍耐一下吧。

3) 不得不… [colloquial]　　　　良心逼使我不得不給你寫這封信。 (p. 140)

SEGMENT XII

1) 再也不/沒 VP 了　　以后就再也沒有音信了吗？ (p. 141)

An emphatic and colloquial way of saying "never VP again/anymore." A more standard way of saying the same thing is "不/沒 再 VP 了." In both these patterns, 不 implies that the act will never be done again from now on, and 沒 implies that the act has never again been done since a certain time in the past.

例句： 1) 我下了决心以后再也不抽烟了。
2) 那年他考大学沒考上，以后再也沒试了。

造句：

填充： 1) 经过那场 (test/trial) 以后，我觉得人生 (never again) 会有什么 (unsolvable problems).
2) 听了你的 (advice) 以后，他 (never again discriminated against orphans and widowed mothers).
3) 自从他和我 (cousin) (divorced) 以后，我 ________________.
4) 噢，原来她是上过男人的当, (no wonder) 从那以后她再也沒 ________________.

2) 快…的时候　　在冬冬快满两周岁的时候，… (p. 141)

"When (subj.) is/was soon to..." The exact translation of 快 may be "soon," "almost," or "about to," depending on the context. In this pattern, 快要 is synonymous with 快.

例句： 1) 四人帮快要被粉碎的时候，肖云的母亲不幸病死了。
2) 他快要病死的时候，医生找到了一种特效药，结果把他的病治好了。

造句：

填充： 1) (When he was about to give up all hope), (Public Security Bureau) 来信说那场 (misunderstanding) 已经 (clarified).
2) (When he was about to) 去加拿大 (manage) 他父亲的 (business), 他女朋友告诉他她 (pregnant) 了。
3) 人家都已经 (about to go to work), 你还在这儿 (sleep in late).
4) 你应该 (optimistic) 点儿，这件事说不定 (is about to succeed), 你再忍耐一下吧。

3) 不得不… [colloquial]　　良心逼使我不得不给你写这封信。 (p. 141)

A slightly more colloquial way of saying "不能不…" (Cf. Grammatical Note VII.3.)

例句： 1) 她沒臉留在工作隊，所以不得不去蘇州她舅舅家了。
2) 他們認爲爲了讓孩子有前途，不得不移民到加拿大去。

造句：

填充： 1) 因爲你那麼 (muddle-headed), 我只好 (remind/alert) 你。
2) 她兒子從鄉下回城沒事干，她就必得 (retire) 讓她兒子 (take over her job).
3) 他那麼 (fierce), 我們沒辦法，只好 (satisfy his demands).
4) 爲了讓自己的 (conscience) 過得去，他必得 (make up for his errors).

改寫 - Reword the completed sentences from the preceding exercise, using pattern 3.

4) 不到 Nu M (N) 我來到加拿大不到兩個月，就… (p. 140)

不到 literally means "not reach," and when followed by a quantity, it means "less than..., within..."

例句： 1) 她表姐結了婚，不到三個月就懷孕了。
2) 這孩子不到三歲就變成了個孤兒，結果是他阿姨把他撫養大的。

造句：

填充： 1) 他 (wholeheartedly) 要作一個好 (husband), 可是結了婚 (less than a year) 就開始 (bully) 他的 (spouse) 了。
2) 冬冬來上海不到兩天 (neighbors) 就開始說他們的 (malicious gossip) 了。
3) 她原來是個很 (reticent/subdued) 的姑娘，可是認識了蕭雲這個 (optimistic) 的朋友 (in less than a month) 她就變成一個 (gregarious and jolly) 的人了。
4) 他 (is both capable and hard-working), 所以把他父親的 (business) 接過來以後, (in less than five years) 就很 (successful) 了。

5) 代-person VP [uncommon] 代我吻吻他吧！ (p. 140/142)

"to VP in...(someone's) stead." The primary meaning of 代 is "substitute, represent." As a coverb, 代 is synonymous with the more commonly used 替.

例句： 1) 我今天不太舒服，你能不能代我去上課？
2) 你放心把這事寄托給我吧，我會好好兒代你辦的。

填充： 1) 你 (don't feel well), 讓我留在 (hospital) (take care of 冬冬 for you) 吧。

A slightly more colloquial way of saying "不能不…" (Cf. Grammatical Note VII.3.)

例句： 1) 她沒脸留在工作队，所以不得不去苏州她舅舅家了。
2) 他们认为为了让孩子有前途，不得不移民到加拿大去。

造句：

填充： 1) 因为你那么 (muddle-headed), 我只好 (remind/alert) 你。
2) 她儿子从乡下回城沒事干，她就必得 (retire) 让她儿子 (take over her job).
3) 他那么 (fierce), 我们沒办法，只好 (satisfy his demands).
4) 为了让自己的 (conscience) 过得去，他必得 (make up for his errors).

改写 - Reword the completed sentences from the preceding exercise, using pattern 3.

4) 不到 Nu M (N) 我来到加拿大不到两个月，就… (p. 141)

不到 literally means "not reach," and when followed by a quantity, it means "less than..., within..."

例句： 1) 她表姐结了婚，不到三个月就怀孕了。
2) 这孩子不到三岁就变成了个孤儿，结果是他阿姨把他抚养大的。

造句：

填充： 1) 他 (wholeheartedly) 要作一个好 (husband), 可是结了婚 (less than a year) 就开始 (bully) 他的 (spouse) 了。
2) 冬冬来上海不到两天 (neighbors) 就开始说他们的 (malicious gossip) 了。
3) 她原来是个很 (reticent/subdued) 的姑娘，可是认识了肖云这个 (optimistic) 的朋友 (in less than a month) 她就变成一个 (gregarious and jolly) 的人了。
4) 他 (is both capable and hard-working), 所以把他父亲的 (business) 接过来以后, (in less than five years) 就很 (successful) 了。

5) 代-person VP [uncommon] 代我吻吻他吧！ (p. 141/143)

"to VP in...(someone's) stead." The primary meaning of 代 is "substitute, represent." As a coverb, 代 is synonymous with the more commonly used 替.

例句： 1) 我今天不太舒服，你能不能代我去上课？
2) 你放心把这事寄托给我吧，我会好好儿代你办的。

填充： 1) 你 (don't feel well), 让我留在 (hospital) (take care of 冬冬 for you) 吧。

2) 我有事要去蘇州幾天，請 (for me) 把做好的 (shirts and pants) 交給 (customers).
3) 冬冬是我的孩子，我要 (love and protect) 他, 怎麼也不能再讓 (uncle take care of him for me anymore).
4) 你告訴蕭雲說是我讓你 (go often to care for her in my stead), 這使我非常 (feel moved/touched).

6) 將/將要 VP [將… is formal] 我將盡力地滿足你的要求。 (p. 142)

As an auxiliary verb, 將 means "will, in the near future, about to." It indicates that the action or event is imminent. 將 is quite formal, and appears only in writing, whereas its more commonly-used synonym 將要 can be used in both speech and writing.

例句： 1) 他們全家將移民到美國去了。
2) 我們將要考試了，你怎麼還不好好兒地念書？

填充, incorporate 將要 into each of the following sentences:

1) (Just as he was about to give up all hope), 他的 (cousin) 來了一封信。
2) 秦楠的信上說她 (is about to) 把冬冬帶回上海，好好兒地盡她當母親的 (responsibility).
3) (Bitter cold) 的冬天 (is about to) 過去，我們 (painful) 的日子也 (about to) 過去了。
4) (Vacation is about to begin), 所有的 ("educated youths") 都預備回家，只 (remains) 他一個 (orphan). 誰來 (take care of) 他呢？

7) 原來 clause 原來他還活着。 (p. 142)

原來 is a movable adverb (i.e., it can occur before or after the subject) which literally means "originally." But aside from this literal meaning, 原來 is often used in its derived meaning "as it turns out," implying that one has just discovered something that has been true all along, but is contrary to one's prior understanding. While the meaning of 原來 can be ambiguous, context will usually make it clear. E.g.:

原來他是中國人。
He was originally Chinese. As it turns out, he's Chinese. (both meanings possible)
原來他是中國人，可是後來變成了美國公民。
He was originally Chinese, but later on he became an American citizen.
原來他是中國人，我還以為他是日本人呢。
As it turns out, he is Chinese. And here I thought he was Japanese.

例句： 1) 噢，原來她是個沒有丈夫而有孩子的母親。

2) 我有事要去苏州几天，请 (for me) 把做好的 (shirts and pants) 交给 (customers).
3) 冬冬是我的孩子，我要 (love and protect) 他, 怎么也不能再让 (uncle take care of him for me anymore).
4) 你告诉肖云说是我让你 (go often to care for her in my stead), 这使我非常 (feel moved/touched).

6) 将/将要 VP [将… is formal] 我将尽力地满足你的要求。 (p. 143)

As an auxiliary verb, 将 means "will, in the near future, about to." It indicates that the action or event is imminent. 将 is quite formal, and appears only in writing, whereas its more commonly-used synonym 将要 can be used in both speech and writing.

例句： 1) 他们全家将移民到美国去了。
2) 我们将要考试了，你怎么还不好好儿地念书？

填充, incorporate 将要 into each of the following sentences:

1) (Just as he was about to give up all hope), 他的 (cousin) 来了一封信。
2) 秦楠的信上说她 (is about to) 把冬冬带回上海，好好儿地尽她当母亲的 (responsibility).
3) (Bitter cold) 的冬天 (is about to) 过去，我们 (painful) 的日子也 (about to) 过去了。
4) (Vacation is about to begin), 所有的 ("educated youths") 都预备回家，只 (remains) 他一个 (orphan). 谁来 (take care of) 他呢？

7) 原来 clause 原来他还活着。 (p. 143)

原来 is a movable adverb (i.e., it can occur before or after the subject) which literally means "originally." But aside from this literal meaning, 原来 is often used in its derived meaning "as it turns out," implying that one has just discovered something that has been true all along, but is contrary to one's prior understanding. While the meaning of 原来 can be ambiguous, context will usually make it clear. E.g.:

原来他是中国人。
He was originally Chinese. As it turns out, he's Chinese. (both meanings possible)
原来他是中国人，可是后来变成了美国公民。
He was originally Chinese, but later on he became an American citizen.
原来他是中国人，我还以为他是日本人呢。
As it turns out, he is Chinese. And here I thought he was Japanese.

例句： 1) 噢，原来她是个沒有丈夫而有孩子的母亲。

2) 他一直沒給我來信，原來早就在加拿大和他表姐結婚了！

造句：

填充： 1) (Public Security Bureau) (investigated) 了三年以後才知道他 (turned out to be innocent).
2) 真 (surprising/unexpected), (as it turns out) 志華不是冬冬的父親 (and) 只是冬冬母親的男朋友。
3) 我從前以爲他很 (kind-hearted), 後來我才發現 (as it turned out) 他是個那麼 (selfish) 的人。
4) 上個月我在那個 (self-employed entrepreneur) 那兒買了一輛 (name brand bike), 後來我才知道它原來 ______________.

8) 當時 當時我看了他這封信，一心就想去死。 (p. 142)

"At that time." By analogy, we also have 當地 "at that place," 當天 "on that day," etc.

例句： 1) 高母當時很贊成志華和秦楠好。
2) 她當時沒有勇氣面對這個問題，所以老瞞着她的父親。

造句：

填充： 1) 孟彬那時候 (must be) 沒有別的辦法留在加拿大，所以就答應了 (that marriage).
2) 我們那時候都很 (respect) 那位 (coach), 可是他的 (errors) 被 (exposed) 以後，我們就 (didn't respect him anymore).
3) (During the Cultural Revolution), 所有留過學的人都被打成 (rightists), 那時候他也被 (isolated and investigated).
4) 在那個 (bitter cold) 的冬天，那位 ("educated youth") 病了，那時候又找不到 (doctor), 又沒有人敢 (get close to her), 結果就病死了。

改寫 - Reword the completed sentences from the preceding exercise, using pattern 8.

9) 曾/曾經…(過) [literary/formal] 以前我也曾相信過他說過的所謂命運。 (p. 144)

The adverb 曾, as well as its synonym 曾經, indicate that the act or event has occurred at some previous time. They convey the same idea as the "experiential marker" 過 which follows the verb. 曾/曾經 and 過 can occur alone or in conjunction with each other. 曾/曾經 has a literary flavor and is used primarily in formal writing.

2) 他一直沒给我来信，原来早就在加拿大和他表姐结婚了！

造句：

填充： 1) (Public Security Bureau) (investigated) 了三年以后才知道他 (turned out to be innocent).
2) 真 (surprising/unexpected), (as it turns out) 志华不是冬冬的父亲 (and) 只是冬冬母亲的男朋友。
3) 我从前以为他很 (kind-hearted), 后来我才发现 (as it turned out) 他是个那么 (selfish) 的人。
4) 上个月我在那个 (self-employed entrepreneur) 那儿买了一辆 (name brand bike), 后来我才知道它原来 ______________.

8) 当时 当时我看了他这封信，一心就想去死。 (p. 143)

"At that time." By analogy, we also have 当地 "at that place," 当天 "on that day," etc.

例句： 1) 高母当时很赞成志华和秦楠好。
2) 她当时沒有勇气面对这个问题，所以老瞒着她的父亲。

造句：

填充： 1) 孟彬那时候 (must be) 沒有别的办法留在加拿大，所以就答应了 (that marriage).
2) 我们那时候都很 (respect) 那位 (coach), 可是他的 (errors) 被 (exposed) 以后，我们就 (didn't respect him anymore).
3) (During the Cultural Revolution), 所有留过学的人都被打成 (rightists), 那时候他也被 (isolated and investigated).
4) 在那个 (bitter cold) 的冬天，那位 ("educated youth") 病了，那时候又找不到 (doctor), 又沒有人敢 (get close to her), 结果就病死了。

改写 - Reword the completed sentences from the preceding exercise, using pattern 8.

9) 曾/曾经…(过) [literary/formal] 以前我也曾相信过他说过的所谓命运。 (p. 145)

The adverb 曾, as well as its synonym 曾经, indicate that the act or event has occurred at some previous time. They convey the same idea as the "experiential marker" 过 which follows the verb. 曾/曾经 and 过 can occur alone or in conjunction with each other. 曾/曾经 has a literary flavor and is used primarily in formal writing.

例句： 1) 我曾勸過他，可他一點兒也不聽。

2) 我在大學的時候曾經學過中文，但是因爲多年沒用而全忘了。

填充： 1) 我 (young) 的時候也 (have had such dreams).

2) 我們一塊兒在鄉下的時候我 (had loved him), 可是那時候我實在是太 (naive) 了。

3) 她未曾 (married to) 過什麼人，哪兒 (suddenly) 冒出個這麼大的孩子？

4) 我幾年前 (have seen the movie "Under the Bridge"), 可是現在一點兒 (impression) 都沒有了。

INCLUSIVE 翻譯 EXERCISE FOR SEGMENT XII:

1) Rest assured, I will do my very best to manage my father's business well (use 把 construction).
2) He considered only his own future, (and) essentially did not consider me and Dongdong at all.
3) I have, in the past, loved him. But that was something from a long time ago.
4) When Zhihua was about (soon) to finish reading Qin Nan's notebook, Qin Nan came to his home.
5) In less than two days after Dongdong arrived in Shanghai, all the neighbors came to know why Qin Nan frequently went to Suzhou.
6) If you want her to forgive you, then you have no choice but to make up for your errors (and) do your best to fulfill her demands.
7) Ever since Qin Nan found out (knew) that Meng Bin married his cousin, she has never written (letters) to him again.
8) In that cold winter, when we were about to give up all hope, the commune suddenly notified us that we could return to Shanghai.
9) At that time, I considered him to be an honest, kind-hearted man; as it turned out, he's the world's most selfish and unconscionable man.
10) After Dongdong took ill, Qin Nan decided that she could not ask her uncle and aunt to take care of him for her (in her stead) anymore.

例句： 1) 我曾劝过他，可他一点儿也不听。
2) 我在大学的时候曾经学过中文，但是因为多年没用而全忘了。

填充： 1) 我 (young) 的时候也 (have had such dreams).
2) 我们一块儿在乡下的时候我 (had loved him), 可是那时候我实在是太 (naive) 了。
3) 她未曾 (married to) 过什么人，哪儿 (suddenly) 冒出个这么大的孩子？
4) 我几年前 (have seen the movie "Under the Bridge"), 可是现在一点儿 (impression) 都没有了。

INCLUSIVE 翻译 EXERCISE FOR SEGMENT XII: See facing page.